THE
PSYCHOLOGY
OF THE
EMERGING SELF

THE PSYCHOLOGY OF THE EMERGING SELF

An Integrated Interpretation of Goal-Directed Behavior

EVERETT D. ERB, Ed.D.

Director of the Counseling Center and
Professor of Counseling Psychology
East Texas State University
Commerce, Texas

DOUGLAS HOOKER, Ph.D.

Chairman, Department of Psychology
Southwestern University
Georgetown, Texas

Edition 2

F. A. DAVIS COMPANY
PHILADELPHIA, PA.

To Shirley

Preface

One of the important, if lesser noted, side effects of the phenomenal growth of sensitivity training, T-group, confrontation groups, and the like, has been renewed interest in the question of how people learn. Briefly, the model these group activities have built upon begins with an involved activity (do), is followed by reflection about, and clarification of possible ways for thinking about the experience (look), followed, in turn, by additional and related activity (do). In the last stage, general principles derived through looking can be tested in behavior.

The thirteen exercises that have been added to this second edition are an experiment in application of this method to the traditional reading format. An exercise (doing) following each chapter (except Chapter 1) is followed by reading (looking), followed by another exercise (doing). Each of the exercises is designed to involve the person in self, other, or interactional analysis of his day to day life as experienced. The chapters meanwhile describe possible hypotheses or general principles or both for thinking about human experience. The reader is thus involved in a do-look-do experience.

As a result of experiencing "The Psychology of the Emerging Self," it is hoped that you, the reader, will be able to:

(1) Increase your understanding of yourself, of the persons with whom you interact, and of the social situations in which you participate.

(2) Increase your skills for creating more intimate, meaningful and rewarding human relationships.

(3) Increase your ability to achieve your present goals more effectively, even as you broaden the scope of future goals.

(4) Develop and continue to refine a value system concerning yourself, other people, and the institutions of society.

In the United States, where it is estimated that one out of every ten school children is destined to spend part of his life in a mental institution, where one marriage in four ends in divorce, where labor-management conflicts cause untold economic loss, where race relations deteriorate into violence, where the aggressively dangerous behavior of juveniles terrifies thousands of people living in large cities, where the population explosion has added to man's difficulty in living closely together in the urban areas, where automation threatens large numbers of workers with wholesale readjustment problems, where the increasing life span has raised a whole new series of social questions, and, finally, where international tensions jeopardize the very survival of mankind, greater sensitivity to personal relationships and increased understanding of human behavior have become not only pertinent but absolutely necessary.

One of the tragedies of the present time, however, is the discrepancy between the knowledge that is contained in the field of psychology and the premises about human behavior upon which the vast majority of people in American society conduct their lives. This book has been written with the expectation that it will be relevant to the day-by-day experiences of its readers and with the hope that it will make a contribution toward closing the gap between the way people live and the present level of professional understanding concerning effective interpersonal relationships.

One of the great dividing lines of human knowledge and experience is crossed when the relative precision of natural science is left behind and the person comes upon the more uncertain intellectual atmosphere of the social sciences and the humanities. With these areas of study, tentative hypotheses are the rule, not the exception. The authors are fully aware of the limitations of such an approach to knowledge and, while it is realized, consequently, that this book may fall far short of providing exact solutions to many of your difficulties in understanding human behavior, it is hoped that in some way it will help you along the unendingly challenging, magnificent, and sometimes painful adventure of becoming a unique self.

According to the 1947 President's Commission on Higher Education, the purposes of general education are to redefine liberal education in terms of life's problems as men face them, to give it human orientation and social direction, and to invest it with content that is directly relevant to the demands of contemporary society. The Harvard Committee on the objectives of a general education in a free society emphasized, moreover, that general education must aim constantly at effective thinking, improved communication, the making of relevant judgments, and discrimination concerning different values.

It is felt that this book will be suitable for use as the main reference work for beginning and non-professional classes in general education, undergraduate courses in the psychology of adjustment and mental health, counselor education, and in the area of personal guidance and effective living. It is hoped that it will prove to be valuable to persons engaged in informal study and discussion groups.

We would like to express appreciation to our friends, William E. Truax, Jr., John P. McQuary, Harold D. Murphy, and R. Paul Johnson, who have offered criticism of parts of the manuscript and provided support and encouragement during the writing of this book. We also wish to thank Carol Dill, Colleen Conoley, and Esther Weir, who offered various suggestions, and Gerry Titus who typed the manuscript.

EVERETT D. ERB

DOUGLAS HOOKER

Acknowledgments

Grateful acknowledgment is made to the following for permission to quote material from the works listed:

Basic Books, Inc., Publishers, New York: "Contributions of existential psychotherapy," Chapter II in *Existence* by Rollo May et al., 1958.

The Clarendon Press, Oxford: *The Study of Instinct* by Nikolaas Tinbergen, 1951.

The Hogg Foundation for Mental Health, The University of Texas, Austin: *A Letter to a Freshman Daughter* by Fillmore H. Sanford, 1964; "Student Mental Health" by Robert F. Peck in *Personality Factors on the College Campus,* 1962.

Longmans, Green and Co., New York: "The Saving Remnant" by David Riesman in *Years of the Modern; An American Appraisal* by Henry Commager et al., edited by John Chase, 1949.

The New Republic, Harrison-Blaine of New Jersey, Inc., 1965.

Scott, Foresman and Company, Chicago: *Abnormal Psychology and Modern Life* by James C. Coleman, 1964.

The University of Chicago Press: "Culture, personality and society" by Irving A. Hallowell in *Anthropology Today,* edited by A. L. Kroeber, 1953; "The Unvoiced Message" by Andrew W. Halpin in *Midway,* No. 3, 1960.

Table of Contents

CHAPTER 1

Introduction

The Study of Human Behavior

In thinking about human beings and why they act as they do, everyone tends to have a built-in do-it-yourself kit for explaining behavior. From the historical and cultural influences of the past and from his own unique mosaic of experiences, each person develops perception of customs, of social institutions, of skills, of duties, of what is meaningful and important in life, and of what is natural, right, and proper in the behavior of man. According to Muller (1958, p. 133), Herodotus stated that "if one were to offer men to choose out of all the customs in the world such as seemed to them the best, they would examine the whole number, and end by preferring their own." The same preferences are likely to be true for explanations of human behavior, and everyone, from the highly trained psychologist to the beginning student, is faced with the difficulty of handling this problem.

You would be quite correct in resenting any implication that the ideas presented in the following chapters are automatically correct and will necessarily have to replace your personal concepts. Instead, the ideas that follow, although considered to be important by some of the people who have made a profession of studying human behavior, are written with the assumption that you will examine and assess them carefully, put them to use in life situations on a tentative and experimental basis, and perhaps augment them with your present views whenever and wherever experience would justify doing so.

In order to be able to incorporate into your value system the concepts that will be presented, it will be necessary to approach your reading with a relatively open mind. You need to be willing to review what you know, consider carefully how you came to believe it, and examine what evidence exists for supporting your present position. Where differences occur between your ideas and those in the book, you must be willing also to decide for or against either position on the basis of the available evidence.

Disagreement may confuse and even distress at first, but the awareness of diversity, complexity, and fluidity, and the ability to accept uncertainty, are among the basic marks of the serious student and the scholar. Unanimity is comforting but it is also often spurious and misleading.

Strangely enough, children, who from two to five years of age approach life with an exhaustible curiosity, often grow up to be adults who never ask the question, "why?" In fact, sometimes even college students seem to regard everything they are asked to think about as an imposition. What has happened to their enthusiasm for learning? It may well be that on the road to adulthood they were offered too many pat answers which they were required to accept and not challenge, and they soon learned that life was simpler when they did not raise embarrassing questions. The students' spirit of inquiry may have been damaged also more or less permanently by a thinly disguised fear of questions on the part of their parents and teachers. As Friedenberg (1960, p. 8) has stated, "Adults who do not basically like and respect adolescents—and this includes a large proportion of those who make a career of working with them—are badly frightened by the increasingly democratic relationships between adolescents and adults that are coming to prevail in our society." Moreover, perhaps both parents and teachers have talked down to young people and to newcomers in a particular area of study on the pretense that they could not understand true complexity and, consequently, must be fed a kind of intellectual pabulum. Is it so strange, then, that some students react passively to such a diet? Probably most people would assume that very young children would not be able to learn several languages simultaneously because the demand on the children's intellect would be too great. It may be, however, that what children can comprehend and learn has been seriously underestimated. One of the authors lived in Port-au-Prince, Haiti, for a number of years and was amazed at the number of pre-school age children he encountered who spoke English, Creole, French, and sometimes Spanish or German. It would seem to be a reasonable hypothesis, then, that children or adults can learn much more than they actually learn or are allowed to learn. The crucial difference seems to be a matter of motivation. The children in Haiti learned the languages because they wanted to in order to communicate with members of their families, friends, neighbors, and servants, and not to satisfy the expectations of parents and teachers or to reach some vague and far-off future goal.

Methods of Evaluating Knowledge

THE USE OF COMMON SENSE

For many people, common sense appears to be one of the great arbitrators concerning the correctness of ideas about human beings and how they function. The concept needs to be carefully re-examined, however, before being too readily accepted as the ultimate criterion for behavior. The first word, *common*, implies that the knowledge is shared by all. Everyone, it is assumed, partakes in the common belief. The second word, *sense*, is related to the way in which people are presumed to have come to share in this commonalty, i.e., through seeing, hearing, tasting, smelling, touching, and so forth. In actuality, however, this shared sensory experience known as common sense has frequently been proved to be incorrect. At one time, for example, common sense assured man that the world was flat. As he looked across a stretch of level ground it was difficult for him not to have the experience of flatness. Despite this obvious reaction, some individuals of uncommon sense kept insisting the world was round. Further evidence, above and beyond the first and more obvious sensory impressions, substantiated the latter hypothesis. The exploits of John H. Glenn, Jr., and the other astronauts confirm what today is accepted by all people, and what was once considered to be a matter of common sense concerning the shape of the world has now been changed.

Another example of the fallibility of common sense may be seen by asking you to guess at the answer to the following problem. Imagine you know a person of well-above average intelligence who has been blind since birth. He is twenty-one years of age and has completed the undergraduate work in college. Among the many things he has learned is the ability to discriminate between a triangle and a square by using his sense of touch. Through tracing the outline of these figures he can discriminate one from the other effortlessly and without error so that the concepts of squareness and triangularity are thoroughly familiar to him. Suppose, furthermore, that he undergoes an operation which results in vision being given to him for the first time in his life. His visual ability in the physical sense is suddenly normal. How long do you expect it would take this individual to *visually* discriminate between a triangle and a square? Fifteen minutes? Two hours? Two days? Common sense suggests that for most people the correct answer would be found within these limits; but how long does it actually take? According to Hebb (1949, pp. 32-33), Senden's evidence indicated that the shortest time in which normal discrimination can occur is about one month

It is quite possible that many of the ideas that you are sure you know about human behavior may be nothing more than a tenuous expression of common sense, but if you are to seek the truth, then the tendency toward relying on the irrational certainty of common sense needs to be replaced with a healthy doubt and too easy and pat answers by a questioning spirit. As Ciardi (1962) stated, "May it not be the greater merit of questions that they lead not to answers but to new questions, and the new questions to others, and they to others yet?" Not having the answers may seem to be fatal, but failure to search for meaningful questions will almost certainly prove to be disastrous.

THE USE OF AUTHORITY

A second method for evaluating knowledge is through the use of authority. Frequently, an idea is considered to be true or not true on the basis of the position taken by a famous man or authority. Because a person is an expert in one specialized field of study, however, it does not mean that he is qualified to make recommendations in all other areas of knowledge. Moreover, further understanding and information may cause the initial position of an authority to become inappropriate and out of date. For example, a few years ago medical experts considered it to be good practice to bleed patients in order to cure a variety of ailments, and even barbers industriously implemented this knowledge. Today obviously such methods would be considered incorrect and the practice of medicine is never entrusted to people without the necessary qualifications. You are cautioned, therefore, against too quickly and blindly accepting ideas, purely because they are presented by recognized authorities.

THE USE OF EMPIRICAL EVIDENCE

Still another, and more reliable, method for ascertaining truth is that of obtaining empirical or observable evidence. The story is told of Aristotle, sometimes credited with the first use of the empirical method, that he settled the argument over how many teeth a woman has by the simple experiment of asking his wife to open her mouth while he counted bicuspids and molars. There were pitfalls on this road to truth, for as the story goes, Aristotle's wife was the exception to the rule and possessed either more or less teeth than the average woman. Whether true or false the story illustrates the point that truth is never easy to discover. Sometimes it depends on the point of view of the person seeking it, sometimes on the method used to obtain it.

Russell pointed out that "every advance in civilization has been denounced as unnatural" (Egner and Denonn, 1961, p. 92) and he offered the following guidelines to the searcher after truth. First, he felt that if a matter can be settled by observation, it is important that the observation be made and the situation not be assumed to be true. Second, he warned against passionate convictions. If another person's position causes anger, the excessive emotional expression is probably an indication of bias and uncertainty. In fact, the greater the anger, the more likely that there is some unconscious doubt about the validity of the person's position. Third, Russell stressed the importance of becoming acquainted with the opinions and ideas that are held in social and intellectual circles outside the ones in which a person lives, and fourth, he cautioned against opinions that flatter one's self-esteem (Egner and Denonn, 1961, pp. 94-96). It may be concluded that intellectual integrity consists of deciding difficult questions on the basis of as much evidence as can be found and on leaving the question open-ended and undecided when the evidence is not conclusive.

In an attempt to gain a broad and inclusive perspective and to reach into areas of study outside the fields of psychology and sociology, illustrations will be drawn from the ideas of historians, philosophers, artists, social critics, and literary figures. Thomas Mann (1958, p. 3), for example, opened his novel *Joseph and His Brothers* with the words "very deep is the well of the past." In a very real way, an awareness of the past enables a person to remove himself from the immediacy of his own concerns and to see his hopes and beliefs in the light of all men's hopes and beliefs. Consideration of Mann's words brings to mind the possibility that what each person thinks he knows is just as fragile and fleeting as what men, five hundred years ago, were sure they knew. The words "Orville, that thing will never fly" linger hauntingly as a reminder of the danger of premature certainty. On many occasions in the past, people have been wrong about man and his potential capabilities, but nevertheless, he still must be seen in a broader perspective than his immediate life situation.

The passage which follows, taken from an adaptation by Karl Menninger (1959) of a series of articles written by Russell Lord and published in the 1941 issues of *The Land,* invites us to view an imaginary movie describing the historical and geological developments on earth for the past 750,000,000 years. Starting at midnight of New Year's Eve and running continuously, the film will last for exactly one year. Thus every second of the movie represents 24 historical years and the average person's life will flash by in three seconds.

For the first few months of the film, the viewer sees only a series of rather monotonous changes and transformations in the land masses. During April, however, single-celled organisms begin to appear and, by the latter part of the month, some of them become multicellular. In May the appearance of the first vertebrates, although still in the form of aquatic life, is observed. By June the large resources of limestone, gas, and oil available today are in the process of being formed under the shallow seas that cover over half the land area that presently constitutes North America. There is still no sign of vegetation however, and it is not until the middle of July that the first land plants become noticeable.

In August the most obvious feature of the film is the presence of an abundance of fish in the seas and waters. During the latter part of September the dinosaurs, which will become dominant for the next couple of months, begin to appear. One of the highlights of the film occurs in October when the mammals start to arrive on the scene. In November the dinosaurs disappear, and by December the mammals have replaced them as the dominant influence on animal life. The land is covered now with trees, plants, and grasses and erosion is limited to specific areas. Most of the rivers are crystal clear and on Christmas Day a stream flowing to the southwest begins the erosion of what is known today as the Grand Canyon of the Colorado.

Man has still not made his appearance as the picture moves into the remaining few days in December. The spectators become somewhat concerned over the possibility that for some reason he may have been forgotten. Finally, around noon of the last day in December, a large, awkward creature—Pithecanthropus, the Java ape man—makes his appearance. He lives in a hazardous manner, menaced both by excessive changes in weather conditions and the wild animals that surround him. Until eleven o'clock in the evening, he remains the only type of human being. Then he is succeeded by the Neanderthal man who is followed shortly afterward by the Cro-Magnon man and then by the Neolithic man.

Only five or six minutes before the end of the film, civilization makes its belated appearance. The Egyptians, Babylonians, Hebrews, Chinese, Greeks, and Romans follow each other in rapid succession. At one minute and seventeen seconds before midnight, Jesus is born. He encourages men to love one another, and for the next minute his followers increase in large numbers. There is much bloodshed among these people, however, concerning matters of belief and doctrine.

With less than thirty seconds to go, Columbus discovers the new world while the Declaration of Independence is signed only a few seconds before the conclusion of the film. The scene is changing rapidly. The virgin forests are destroyed by man and by fire, and the soil, man's most valuable possession, is being washed away to the oceans. At the same time, man is seen accumulating wealth in the form of pieces of printed paper that represent a relatively useless metal that he keeps hidden away in vaults and other safe places.

During the last seven seconds, the number of human beings increases at an amazing speed. Their food supply decreases: more than half of them are hungry and some are starving. They are involved in a continuous series of crippling wars which causes them to annihilate one another. Some of the people are hostile, destructive, and criminal. Others are sick and dying. Nevertheless there are other persons who have healthy and constructive effect upon human existence. During the final few seconds of the picture, they are seen to be engaged in a vital struggle against the destructive influences that gradually are gaining control. Until man came on the scene, the constructive aspects of nature were beginning to win out over the destructive forces. The deleterious behavior of man, however, turned the tide and caused the destructive powers to gain ground again. As the picture reaches its last three seconds, the outcome is still uncertain. It is during these three seconds that you and I were born.

Against such a background of geological time, man seems insignificant. As Russell states, he "is a brief episode in the life of a small planet in a little corner of the universe, and that, for aught we know, other parts of the cosmos may contain beings as superior to ourselves as we are to jellyfish" (Egner and Denonn, 1961, p. 96). Perhaps in the light of such a perspective, it becomes easier to accept man's knowledge as still evolving and tenuous and to appreciate the opportunities which exist for further development and understanding.

Presentation of Goal-Directed Behavior

The remainder of the chapter contains an introduction to the topics that will be encountered later in the book and provides an opportunity for gaining a general understanding of the main ideas before a more comprehensive study of the individual parts is undertaken.

One of the assumptions that is made about behavior is that it may be understood most effectively when one knows the goals a person sets for his life. Figure 1, although a rather complex schematization, attempts to give some tentative order to the various factors which influence the selection of goals.

At the left side of the figure is the human being with his inherited characteristics and individual potentialities. Each person is seen as a self-activating entity, responsible for creating a part of his own environment and capable of becoming not merely a passive recipient of external stimuli, but an individual who is able to express himself uniquely and differently from other people. This ability to create a part of one's environment may be seen even in the behavior of newborn babies in a maternity ward, for it is possible to distinguish differences in the quality, the intensity, and the duration of their rage, in the strength of their suck-

THE PERSON
Individual differences
Internal and external determinants

INTERACTING WITH HIS
PERCEIVED ENVIRONMENT

ATTEMPTS TO
ACHIEVE A

HIERARCHY OF GOALS

I. Orientational Goals

II. Physiological Goals

III. Love, Belongingness, and
Psychological Safety Goals

IV. Achievement Goals
Respect
Wealth
Power
Skill
Enlightenment

V. Subjective Satisfaction in Living
Well-Being — Level I
Psychotic, neurotic, and
over-conformity
Well-Being — Level II
Integration and Actualization

WITH VARYING DEGREES OF
ENERGY MOBILIZATION

LEARNING POTENTIAL
Differential reinforcement
Generalization
Discrimination

EMOTIONS
Positive, ambivalent, and
negative feelings

ADJUSTMENT MECHANISMS
Goal Substitution
Reality distortion
Goal withdrawal
Self-punishment

THROUGH
AVAILABLE

INSTITUTIONS
Man seeking values through
institutions using resources

AND INTERPERSONAL
RELATIONSHIPS

Expressive
Manipulative
coercion
coaxing
evaluating
masking
postponing
Altruistic

FIGURE 1. A schematic presentation of goal-directed behavior.

ing response, and, in short, in a bewildering array of behavior patterns which exist long before substantial learning from the environment has had an opportunity to take place. At such an early age, the infant is already beginning to act in a way which is characteristically his own and, consequently, he is creating, at least partially, the particular environment from which he will learn and to which he will be expected to react.

The environment surrounding a person is represented by the external determinants or the powerful cultural and social forces to which the individual will be exposed during the course of his existence. He grows up learning to speak a particular language or languages as opposed to others and he experiences the company of certain individuals and groups instead of others. For example, a father obviously influences greatly his child's learning experiences inasmuch as the father's income, vocation, religion, politics, and so forth, all have impact upon the child. In the early and formative years, at least, these factors are beyond the infant's control and he may experience them only passively. Such influences are so numerous and so strong that there is a tendency sometimes to ignore the other factors which accompany them and contribute to the shaping of behavior. For instance, the father reacts emotionally also to the child and his behavior is influenced in part by what the child does or does not do. If the infant cries continuously and keeps the family awake at night, he may bring out feelings of hostility in the father, whereas another child, who cries less, is more likely to enjoy a warmer relationship with his parent. The quality of the relationship, in turn, affects what is learned and valued by the child so that his attitudes become interrelated with the type of experience he knows with his father. Where the relationship is warm and loving, the child will not need to react strongly against the values of the parent. Where the relationship is characterized by coldness and friction, there is a much greater chance that the child will want to express some dissatisfaction and disapproval.

Similarly, in every human relationship there is an intermingling of the influence of the environment with the behavior patterns which the person himself is responsible for developing. As the experience of the person increases and he gains a deeper understanding of his particular needs, he begins to make choices for himself and to determine different goals for his life which will be important to him with varying degrees of intensity. To the extent that he is successful, he is able partly to establish his own environment and to reduce the danger of his becoming a slave or victim of the particular setting in which he finds himself.

The specific goals which a person chooses may be seen as being arranged in a hierarchy in which the basic and more primary ones must be achieved successfully before new and higher goals may be realized.

Thus, in a growing and developing person, continuous new goal emergence becomes essential while, in contrast, excessive concentration upon any one goal may be seen as an indication of at least partial failure on the part of the person to cope with his environmental experiences.

The classification of the goals which are important to human beings may begin with the most basic one of orientation. Most Americans, for instance, are oriented toward the responsibilities of good citizenship and, consequently, they were appalled by the behavior that took place in the Los Angeles riots of 1965. No matter how much they might desire to accumulate material possessions, it would be impossible for them to do so by stealing and looting. The people involved in the riot, however, did not share in this orientation, as evidenced by the remarks of one woman in response to having her picture taken in the process of looting, "It ain't your store. What do you care?" Perhaps it is possible to understand, therefore, that depending upon their orientations, people will behave differently in the same situations and also the same way in different situations. A classic example of the influence of differences in orientation has been provided by Snygg and Combs (1949, p. 14):

> Several years ago one of the authors was driving a car at dusk along a western road. A globular mass about two feet in diameter suddenly appeared directly in the path of the car. A passenger in the front seat screamed and grasped the wheel, attempting to steer the car around the object. The driver tightened his grip and drove directly into it.
> In each case the behavior of the individual was determined by his own phenomenal field. The passenger, an Easterner, saw the object in the highway as a boulder and fought desperately to steer the car around it. The driver, a native of the vicinity, saw it as a tumbleweed and devoted his efforts to keeping his passenger from overturning the car.

Since all behavior is determined at least in part by the person's perception of the stimuli around him, and not wholly by a simple automatic response to such stimuli, the orientational goals are considered to be the most important and basic ones in the hierarchy.

The next goals are related to the visceral, sexual, cognitive, sensory, and motor processes, all of which are included under the category of physiological goals. For the most part, these goals are characterized by an urgency that demands gratification before the person is able to move toward the achievement of other goals.

Following the physiological goals is the need for love, belongingness, and psychological safety. Love is expressed most effectively through behavior which allows the individuals involved in a relationship to achieve the particular goals that are important to each of them. Feelings of being psychologically safe are developed when love in this sense is supported by an orientation which is congruent with the objective reality of the outside world.

Once the person's more basic needs have been satisfied, he is able to turn, in his own unique fashion, toward attaining the goals of respect, wealth, power, skill, and enlightenment. Provided his behavior is oriented intrinsically or, in other words, is seen as having merit in itself, the person may be expected to enjoy a sense of fulfillment over his accomplishments. On the other hand, if the attainment of these goals is seen only as being valuable because it makes further achievement possible, then the person experiences little satisfaction and his behavior becomes just another incident in an endless series of failures to accomplish something that is personally meaningful and significant.

Finally, there is the general goal of well-being which may be seen at two different levels. The first level includes a range of people with mental health varying from the seriously disturbed person or psychotic at the lower end of the scale to people who are reasonably happy, content, and successful at the upper level. As measured by most personality tests and as seen by the man in the street, the people in the latter group seem to enjoy a fair amount of good mental health, and frequently they make important contributions to society.

There are also some people, however, who seem to enjoy a more creative approach to life and a second level of well-being is postulated to account for the behavior of those persons who possess a degree of maturity which is achieved by only a few members of society. The behavior of such people is characterized by the knowledge that what they can be, they must be.

Furthermore, a person approaches his goals with varying degrees of intensity. A simple and perhaps not too accurate analogy may be made with an automobile which requires a steering wheel, equivalent to direction or goals, and also gasoline, which is seen as intensity or emotion. If high octane aviation fuel is used in the automobile, the engine will quickly burn up and cease to operate effectively. On the other hand, if a cheap or inferior brand of gasoline is used, the motor will knock and also perform inefficiently. In one case, the gasoline is too strong and consequently disruptive to the reaching of a destination or goal, while in the other case, the gasoline is too weak for effective movement to take place. What is needed, of course, is a brand of gasoline which is neither too strong nor too weak, but one of a more optimum strength that will permit the automobile to operate effectively. Similarly, a person needs an intensity of emotion which is also neither too strong nor too weak but, instead, is adequate enough to make it possible for him to learn and to utilize his potentiality in a way which will allow him to reach his particular goal or destination.

When behavior does not lead to the achievement of goals, certain devices, usually referred to as adjustment or defense mechanisms, are used to offset the feeling of failure. Sometimes the adjustment mechanisms are both healthy and realistic in that they bring about the formation and subsequent achievement of new and more appropriate goals. On other occasions, however, they have the opposite effect of causing the person to ignore or misinterpret the reality of his own experience, thus providing support for the negative connotation that is frequently associated with the term defense mechanism. In an ideal world in which all people are capable of achieving their goals and therefore do not encounter failure, a negative view of adjustment mechanisms would be appropriate. In the world as it actually exists, however, in which the conditions of life almost guarantee some degree of failure in goal achievement, the use of adjustment mechanisms in helping a person overcome his feeling of disappointment after failure may be of considerable value. While excessive dependence on adjustment mechanisms may inhibit goal achievement, not utilizing them at all may lead also to disappointment and frustration. What is needed, again, of course, is a moderate or optimum use that will help the person in eventually obtaining the goals that are important to him.

The goals that a person seeks, the intensity with which he desires them, and the various adjustment mechanisms he uses while pursuing them may be seen as existing at different levels on a scale of awareness or consciousness. Some of the goals a person desires to achieve, for example, are very clearly known to him and may be considered as being at the upper level of the scale. Other goals, which are much more vague and difficult to recognize, may be placed at the lower end of the scale, for they are below the level of consciousness in what is generally referred to as the unconscious. Sometimes the goals are at a higher level than the intensity and adjustment mechanisms while at other times the opposite is the case. In fact, any conceivable combination or arrangement may be realized. However, the more a person is consciously aware of his goals, knows clearly how important they are to him, and understands the adjustment mechanisms he uses, the more he is able to make his own decisions, hold particular beliefs, and behave in a rational manner. Conversely, the more these factors are at the lower and unconscious level of the scale, so that the person is vague and uncertain of them, the more he will have difficulty making his own decisions and formulating consistent attitudes and the more he will be prone to function irrationally instead of rationally.

In order to achieve the goals that are seen as being important, a person must relate to other people through the various institutions that are available in society. Some relationships are primarily manipulative in that other people are coerced or encouraged into behaving in ways that will lead to desired goals. On other occasions, when a person's actions are not specifically directed toward the attainment of a goal, the behavior is seen as being predominantly expressive in nature. For still other people, needs are satisfied mainly through helping other people reach the goals which are important to them. Such behavior is altruistic and is frequently found, for example, in counselors and psychotherapists. It is very closely related also to the goals that emerge in Well-Being Level II.

The study of human behavior would be easy if it could be classified precisely in terms of the foregoing discussion and the outline in Figure 1. Unfortunately, this situation is not the case. Instead, Figure 1 is included with the hope that it will become a tool or guide by which you may examine your own behavior and that of the people around you.

There may be a feeling, at this point, that human behavior is much too dreadfully complicated. Consequently, perhaps it is advisable to offer some words of reassurance. Many of the terms which seem vague will be defined in the later chapters. Furthermore, if you have learned that there is no one simple approach or answer, then undoubtedly you have taken the first step along the road toward sophistication in the study of human behavior.

CHAPTER 2

The Person

Since the introduction of Darwin's theories of evolution, man has been seen as a special kind of animal who is located at the apex of the phylogenetic scale. He is distinguishable from other animals primarily on the basis of the fact that he possesses an intellect which allows him to influence and control his environment. According to Hawkes, (Hawkes and Woolley, 1963, p. 106) man's emerging powers of consciousness and awareness caused him to move in two opposing directions. First, beginning with the making of tools and culminating in modern scientific and technological advancements, he began to control his existing physical environment. Second, he animated the universe with his dreams and images, thus leading to the simultaneous and intermingled growth of ritual, religion, mysticism, mythology, and aesthetics. While man's attempts to control his environment affected his imagery, his dreams influenced, in turn, the way he was able to cope with the environment.

One of the characteristics that sets man apart from all other animals is the possession of language. In commenting on this point, Hallowell (1953, p. 603) noted that:

> Since even a most highly evolved primate, like the chimpanzee, cannot master a human language and there is no evidence that at any subhuman level the graphic and plastic arts exist, extrinsic symbolic systems as media of communication are an exclusively human creation.

It is by virtue of the use of language, moreover, that man uniquely is able to anticipate future events, determine his behavior in a way that is not possible for other creatures, and communicate a wide variety of complex social interrelationships to each succeeding generation.

The way that a human being develops and behaves, however, is determined by influences which may be classified under the following two categories: (1) the internal determinants, consisting of the person's physiological characteristics and the influences of heredity and; (2) the external determinants, stemming from both the general impact of the culture upon all people's lives and from the unique situational experiences that every individual encounters as a result of his own particular relationship to the environment.

Internal Determinants

Each person's life begins when a sperm cell from the male parent fertilizes the ovum or egg from the female. Recent estimates indicate that the zygote or cell which is formed from the union contains forty-six chromosomes which may be thought of as the "carriers of heredity." Within these chromosomes there are believed to be some ten to fifteen thousand genes, all of which are influential in determining some specific characteristic of the body. The number of possible combinations and unique differences is infinite, particularly when one considers the millions of people who potentially could become mates. This uniqueness is one of the cardinal principles of nature for, with the exception of identical twins who develop from a single zygote, no two people are alike. Thus, from the moment of conception, each person is uniquely himself and like no one else.

Differences in sex, weight, height, facial features, bodily conformation, and countless other physical characteristics are readily apparent. Less obvious, however, are the hidden differences in internal organs and bodily functions. For example, no two hearts beat exactly alike and individuals differ as well in their vitamin requirements, the amounts of food and water they consume, their reactions to drugs, and in their needs for a variety of chemical substances. Moreover, the various glands of the body affect energy levels and there is considerable evidence to indicate that the pattern of growth and development varies with the individual person so that everyone deviates to some extent from a hypothetical and non-existent norm or average.

The total living organism is composed of millions of cells which may be considered to be the basic building blocks of the body. The cells have three important functions: (1) irritability, the power to react to outside stimuli; (2) conductivity, the power for change to take place within the cell; and (3) contractibility, the power of the cell to expand or contract through relaxation or tension within the cell itself. These functions make it possible for cells singly or in combination to respond in a meaningful or directional way, even at a simple level, to outside stimuli, irrespective of whether they are caused by another cell or a foreign body.

Cells may be grouped together to form tissues which, in turn, may be combined into larger structures known as organs. It is through the use of the organs related to sight, hearing, taste, smell, touch, pain, temperature, and kinesthesis that man maintains contact and relationship with both his internal and external environment.

Although a person comes to know the world through his sense organs or receptors, he is sensitive to only a small number of the stimuli which actually exist. Some sounds are too soft for him to hear, some touches too light to feel, some lights too dim to see. Thus, the whistle which is unnoticed by a human being may be heard clearly by a dog. The blind man, who has developed his hearing to a greater degree than the ordinary person, may walk right up to a wall and know exactly when to stop short of it. It is interesting to note, however, that if his hearing is shut off, he is liable to walk into the wall in the same way as the person with normal sight who is blindfolded.

It is possible, moreover, for changes in the levels of sound, touch, taste, and smell to be too minute for the difference to be registered. The term *threshold* has been introduced to designate the points or levels at which stimuli move from having no effect to having partial effect to having full effect. Thresholds vary from individual to individual so that a sound may be heard by some people but yet remain completely unnoticed by other persons. Furthermore, the same individual may experience different thresholds from time to time. On one occasion he may react to a sound to which he remains oblivious when it occurs the next time.

These differences in sensitivity are influenced by the person's physical endowment, capacities, interests, emotions, and feelings. The individual who is badly frightened, for example, is seldom sensitive to the pleasant aroma of a nearby rosebush. While cells, organs, and thresholds all are referred to separately, it should be remembered, however, that the human being functions not as a series of isolated parts but as an integrated whole. Thus, what happens to one part of the body is related intimately to what occurs elsewhere, and everything that a person experiences is at least partially determined by the state of his physical being.

External Determinants

The sociologist Coutu (1949, pp. 3-42) has coined the phrase, "tendencies-in-situations," to accentuate the fact that a person's behavior is not only a product of his internal organization and physiological processes but is influenced as well by the external situations in which the individual finds himself. The following example used by Coutu may help to clarify the effect that "tendencies-in-situations" have upon human behavior.

At several periods during the most horrible war in history our American society was torn and battered by problems of production. The nation experienced strikes, work stoppages, absenteeism on an appalling scale. . . .

The press . . . finally put the blame on something stereotyped 'labor.' . . . People . . . were quick to follow the press in naming 'labor' as the scapegoat for all their ills. They argued that if the boys on Guadalcanal could be brought home, while the factory workers at home were sent to the jungles, we should accomplish full production and our fears and frustrations would vanish. The 'boys over there,' they pointed out, did not enjoy an eight-hour day, nor did they receive high wages with time-and-a-half for overtime.

Now what was the structure of reasoning here? Highly characteristic of popular dichotomous thinking was the assumption that we have two kinds of people in our beloved country: one kind is loyal, patient, devoted, sacrificing, and selfless; the other kind, selfish, greedy, pampered, lazy, and disloyal. Presumably Selective Service managed to get all of the first kind into the armed forces, and all of the other kind somehow went into industrial production. Obviously, so the reasoning went, if we could bring the first group home, they could and would produce relentlessly and with joy and singing. . . . This reasoning was enunciated by public speakers: factory workers were to be sent to the battlefields where they would fight because they would have to fight, a condition, presumably, that did not apply to the first group. . . .

The workers at home were blamed as men; *the conditions under which* they worked were assumed to be of no significance. . . . Presumably if there was any situation, there was only one — war; and war was assumed to be war whether one was at the front or in an emergency industrial plant . . . (actually) . . . the situations of these two groups hardly resembled each other in any respect. . . .

If social psychology is to follow the outmoded Aristotelian line that everything is in the man, that the situations in which he behaves are irrelevant, then nothing is left but the medieval concept of free will, unitary causes, blame, scapegoats, brickbats, and continued social frustrations. . . .

Even in normal times our population is broken into large numbers of segments each of which at times throws at the other segments every conceivable form of invective. . . . Capitalists and employers are called economic royalists, greedy and selfish exploiters, and corrupters of the body politic; workers are called 'reds,' 'radicals,' 'socialists,' 'lazy feather-bedders,' and 'irresponsibles;' New Dealers are called 'reds,' 'bureaucrats,' 'tax-eaters,' and 'crackpots;' while other groups are called 'niggers,' 'sharecroppers,' 'dagoes,' 'wops,' 'kikes,' 'hunkies,' and 'okies' and are constantly blamed for one social event or another.

Actually, in the circumstances described by Coutu, it is reasonable to assume that had the soldiers been working in the war production plants, the majority of them would have joined in the strikes and other techniques employed for the advancement of their own interests. Similarly, most of the production workers, on finding themselves at the battlefront, would have performed like soldiers. The same hypothesis holds true for a variety of conflicting groups. If the situations were reversed, for instance, most of the members of labor unions would follow the course of management personnel and other persons advocating opposing points of view.

The fact that a person acts differently from situation to situation attests to the influence of external determinants. At the same time, however, there is also a stability from one experience to another which indicates that the person's internal organization and orientation also have effect upon his behavior. Generally, the less a person understands about himself, the more he is likely to do what other people in the same situation are doing. Conversely, the less specific the type of behavior expected of him, the more the internal factors contribute toward influencing the person's behavior.

The Complementary Nature of the Determinants

The early theories of the physical sciences concerning man's place in the universe were dominated by the concepts of force and pressure, and it was believed that a person could not initiate any act without the application of some external force upon him. In physics, however, upon which, strangely enough, the idea of dominance through external force originally was based, the concept of inner passivity is no longer tenable. Other views are also being explored in psychology, and the interpretation of human behavior that is based primarily on the importance attached to external stimulation and an unwillingness to recognize the place of individual initiative and responsibility is being questioned seriously.

To a large extent the environment does stamp out its human products, for every person is born into a social setting that provides only a limited opportunity for unique and individual expression. It is from these available alternatives that the person has to forge his particular patterns of behavior. The environment, for example, may provide only experiences A, B, and C, and the person, consequently, can respond only in terms of A, B, and C. One person may react to A, another individual may prefer B, and still another person may choose C, for each individual possesses sensitivities and potentials which cause him to select some aspects of the environment to become his own. Moreover, every person is potentially capable of losing his choice, thereby becoming what some outside source decides he should be. The presence of one potential does not negate the other. In some circumstances the capacity for choice or freedom is crushed; in others, it flowers. The question as to why freedom should exist only as an absolute has seldom been raised. It would seem to be equally possible, and even probable, that man is both determined and irresponsible and determining and responsible. If he is but a creature of his past, it is difficult to understand how he ever managed to move beyond living in a cave. On the other hand, by looking at the world of today, as contrasted with the world of the past, it becomes easy to entertain the idea that man is capable of creating far beyond his natural environment.

In attempting to clarify the comparable situation in physics, Neil Bohr (1961) developed the principle of complementarity in which he stated that there are two major theories about the ultimate nature of matter: the "particle" and the "wave." The older particle theory explained many phenomena but failed to clarify others and, similarly, the wave theory explained facts which could not be accounted for by the particle theory. Thus, the two theories were equally valid, but alternatively instead of simultaneously. Each theory explained some phenomena but failed in areas where the other one was successful.

The relationship between the internal and external determinants is also complementary in that these factors are inadequate and incomplete in themselves, for none of them can be omitted without doing violence to an understanding of the total reality of the person's behavior.

Perhaps the intimate intertwining of the internal and the external determinants may be illustrated effectively by making reference to the concept of intelligence. Generally, it is accepted that intelligence is a result of the inherited capacities of the person, but this statement in itself is not sufficient. If, for example, you were to ask either one of the authors to perform in some academic capacity and observe his behavior, you would be likely to conclude that he possesses a reasonably high degree of intelligence. On the other hand, if you were standing nearby when his car broke down and again observed his behavior, by and large limited to lifting the hood and staring blankly at the motor, you would be much more likely to conclude that he is stupid. There are, of course, inherited differences in intelligence among people, but it is a mistake to talk about these differences without considering the social situation in which the person is functioning.

The relationship between a person's internal organization and the social experiences that he encounters becomes very noticeable in his choice of friends and associates. In every situation a person is drawn to some people more than others. At times, he is attracted to, or repelled by, people whose personal attributes resemble such important figures in his life as parents, brothers, sisters, etc. Generally, however, the person has the strongest feelings for or against the people who are in closest contact with him. When he approves of himself, he is drawn to people who are like himself; when he disapproves of himself, he is more likely to be attracted to people who are very different.

The ability and willingness to provide gratification and satiation for other people is at the heart of interpersonal attractiveness. Whereas the sharing of common interests increases the likelihood of two people finding each other's company mutually satisfying, the presence of diverse interests lessens the possibility of a meaningful relationship being formulated. As a result, with the possible exception of people who possess a high degree of well-being, most stable marriages and friendships occur between people of similar backgrounds and value systems.

The concept of friendship and marriage gratification potential may be extended even further to include the degree to which the emotional needs of the persons in the relationship complement each other. Thus, the person who wishes to dominate other people chooses the company of persons who are not likely to offer any resistance and, correspondingly, timid and passive people find authoritarian persons attractive. Similarly, for more democratic reasons, people who value both giving and receiving in personal relationships prefer the companionship of individuals who also hold such an orientation.

Emphasis on Internal Determinants

Probably it is true that the relative degree of emphasis that a person gives to either the internal or the external determinants depends to a large extent upon his orientation. Two factors, however, have influenced the authors' decision to place the greater emphasis on the internal determinants. In the first place, the external influences have been examined so thoroughly by psychologists, sociologists, and anthropologists that, at the present time, there is a greater need for recognition of the internal factors. Secondly, one of the purposes of this book is to help you gain a greater appreciation and sensitivity to human behavior. It is felt that this objective has a better chance of being realized by helping to modify your perceptions, instead of undertaking the almost impossible task of trying to change the social situation in which you live. In commenting about human behavior, Matson (1964, p. 164) noted that:

> Life is not process merely but *tendency;* not a settling but a striving; not permanence but change. Its normal direction is toward ever-increasing levels of complexity and heterogeneity, with accompanying tension and effort rather than toward homogeneity, the reduction of tension and the restoration of equilibrium at a lower level. The struggle of life is not for survival but for growth; its goal is not being but becoming.

The fact that many persons fail to grow and that they allow their lives to be governed by outside events does not mean that the continual struggle to go beyond the self is not true of some people. Exercising of choice is not absent, only, perhaps, infrequent. What actually exists, if only in a few people, is potentially at the command of many persons.

The people who make the choice to grow far beyond the cradle, far beyond childhood, discover what Peckham (1962, p. 350) referred to as the profoundest satisfaction of being human, namely the ability to create the world, to destructure and to restructure it, to disorient and to reorient themselves. Rank (1956, p. 72) noted, moreover, that the whole emphasis of man's "experience is changed from the battle against a real fate which has created him, to the acceptance of his own willing individuality which not only creates its own reality but also affirms that which is given, in terms of self-determination."

Thus, much of man's behavior may be interpreted as an attempt to find or create an environment that allows him to be whatever he is and become whatever he must become. Whether the behavior is inherited, caused by some experience in the social situation, or by a combination of these influences, is not really the vital question. What is more important is the recognition or denial of man's ability to perceive the appropriateness of his actions in terms of the achievement of the unique goals and purposes of his life. The view of man which sees him only as a respondent to external stimuli is one in which, as Allport (1961, p. 90) stated, "What is conspicuously missing is the forward or future thrust that seems always to mark mature motivation."

The further possibility of the existence of innate differences between human beings is supported by a recent discovery in which variations in the electrical rhythms of the brain cells were found to divide individuals into two principal types: those persons who tended to think in visual images and those persons whose thought was largely verbal (Hawkes and Woolley, 1963, p. 112). Moreover, infants all over the world, irrespective of the culture in which they were raised, learn first of all to distinguish the vowels *a* and *i* and the consonants *m* and *p*. Such sounds as the sibilants *s* and *i* and the fricatives *f* and *th* are the last ones to be mastered, despite the children's varying differences in experience. Aphasics, who are suffering from progressive lesions of the brain, lose control of sounds in exactly the reverse order (Hawkes and Woolley, 1963, p. 110). Thus, it would seem that symbolic sound emergence is ordered internally and does not result from the influence of external stimuli.

The behavior of weaverbirds would appear to indicate also that the organism cannot inevitably be molded by external events. After six generations of having been reared among other birds and being deprived of their own proper nesting material, the seventh generation of these weaverbirds were still able to weave their ingenious nests when they were provided with the appropriate opportunity (Hawkes and Woolley, 1963, p. 107).

The Milner-Olds (1954) experiments at McGill University offer a hypothetical explanation of innate differences. Fine wire electrodes were inserted through the skulls of fifteen rats into various areas of the brain and connected to an electrical stimulator. When the current was turned on, it was found that the rats would continually press a lever in order to receive a weak electric shock. When the electricity was turned off, however, and they no longer received any satisfaction, they would stop pressing the lever after about seven attempts and go to sleep. The tentative hypothesis may be drawn that certain parts of the brain may be connected quite specifically with emotional and motivational influences or behavior and this understanding, when applied to human beings, may be the source of innate preferences, of individual differences, and of the emerging self.

Campbell (1959, p. 30) has pointed out the presence of what have been called innate releasing mechanisms to designate the inherited structure in the nervous system that enables an animal to respond familiarly to a circumstance never before experienced, and at the same time ignore other stimuli which should have apparently equal potentiality for arousing the animal. For example, he described how:

> Chicks with their eggshells still adhering to their tails dart for cover when a hawk flies overhead, but not when the bird is a gull or duck, heron or pigeon. Furthermore, if the wooden model of a hawk is drawn over their coop on a wire, they react as though it were alive—unless it be drawn backward, when there is no response.
> Here we have an extremely precise image—never seen before, yet recognized with reference not merely to its form but to its form in motion, and linked, furthermore, to an immediate, unplanned, unlearned, and even unintended system of appropriate action: flight, to cover. The image of the inherited enemy is already sleeping in the nervous system, and along with it the well proven reaction. Furthermore, even if all the hawks in the world were to vanish, their image would still sleep in the soul of the chick—never to be roused, however, unless by some accident of art; for example, a repetition of the clever experiment of the wooden hawk on a wire. . . . Living gulls and ducks, herons and pigeons leave it cold, but the work of art strikes some very deep chord! (Campbell, 1959, p. 31).

Campbell (1959, p. 34) noted further that the human nervous system was the governor, guide, and controller of a nomadic hunter for man's first 600,000 years, whereas it has been serving the comparatively safe farmer and city dweller for scarcely 8,000 years. It is likely, he concluded, that in the central nervous system, images sleep from man's earlier way of life, the releasing stimuli of which no longer appear in nature but possibly may be found in man's art.

Jung believed, moreover, that the personal experiences of the individual are influenced by archetypes or systems of reactions of the human race which are stored in what he referred to as the collective unconscious. He noted (1956, pp. 24-25):

> This psychic life is the mind of our ancient ancestors, the way in which they thought and felt, the way in which they conceived of life and the world, of gods and human beings. The existence of these historical layers is presumably the source of the belief in reincarnation and in memories of past lives. As the body is a sort of museum of its phylogenetic history, so is the mind. There is no reason for believing that the psyche, with its peculiar structure, is the only thing in the world that has no history beyond its individual manifestation. Even the conscious mind cannot be denied a history extending over at least five thousand years. It is only individual ego-consciousness that has forever a new beginning and an early end. But the unconscious psyche is not only immensely old, it is also able to grow unceasingly into an equally remote future. It forms, and is part of, the human species just as much as the body, which is also individually ephemeral, yet collectively of immeasurable duration.

Human beings experience feelings of being off course when external events push them into a particular direction which, from the external and objective point of view seems to be right, but which internally and subjectively seems all wrong. The ability to attend to internal promptings that "this is right for me" or "wrong for me" in the face of conflicting external urgings is an instance of a person being himself and it may be a part of what it really means to be human.

Individual Differences

Immediately following birth, growth and development of the human being takes place at a rapid rate, particularly around the end of the period of childhood, but soon thereafter it begins to slow down. Generally, after about four weeks, babies may be expected to have developed the ability to follow movements visually. After some 16 weeks they can balance their heads and at around 28 weeks they are able to use their hands to grasp and manipulate objects. At 40 weeks most children can sit and crawl and at around 52 weeks they can stand and move about in an upright position.

These generalizations, however, must be seen in the light of the fact that always there are considerable differences among individuals and, consequently, expected patterns of growth and development cannot be applied accurately to the specific behavior of a particular child. Some children, for example, learn to talk, walk, read, or write earlier than would be expected while others are slow in developing these functions. Puberty occurs early in some instances and late in others. Invariably the rate of growth and development never is found to correspond perfectly with the child's chronological age.

One of the most widely recognized sources of individual differences is intelligence. While no one knows exactly what is meant by intelligence, people who possess it to a high degree are presumed to be better off and more fortunate than the persons who do not. Cyril Burt (1958), the eminent British psychologist, estimated that approximately twenty-three percent of the variation found in intelligence test results appeared to be due to environmental factors, whereas seventy-seven percent was due to genetic or inherited factors. While final answers to questions concerning the origin of intelligence probably will not be found for a long time, the notion that intelligence is at least partially innate appears to be justified. Perhaps it is safest to assume that inheritance decides the level of intelligence that each person possesses, thereby setting a maximum limit on what potentially can be learned from any particular experience. The influence of the environment, on the other hand, determines to what extent the person has the opportunity to utilize his innate ability.

The Nature of the Human Being

The following four assumptions may be made concerning the nature of human beings. Although at the present time it is impossible to prove which, if any, are correct, the one which is selected makes a great deal of difference to what a person observes and concludes about human behavior.

THERE IS NO HUMAN NATURE

With this assumption, it is taken for granted that the human being is like a blank sheet, or the tabula rasa of John Locke, upon which anything may be written by experience. Thus, the environment becomes the only and absolute determinant of human behavior. The person is only re-active. Moreover, he is not even selectively reactive, for all external stimuli have equal potentiality for influencing behavior in a mechanistic or stamped-in manner.

HUMAN NATURE IS EVIL

The view of man as basically sinful and destructive appears to have influenced Western society profoundly. Thomas Hobbes, for example, saw him as selfish and aggressive, and it was generally believed that if man were left to his own devices, he would be naturally evil. Therefore, something, and usually something quite painful, had to be done in order to avoid the actions which would result from his being himself. As a result of such corrective measures, it was expected that he would learn to behave constructively.

HUMAN NATURE IS GOOD

The assumption may be made also that man is naturally good and only when he is thwarted or destroyed by such unfortunate experiences as inadequate relationships with parents or, according to Marx, inequitable income distribution, does he begin to lose this goodness. Thus, evil is not inherent in man but, instead, arises from the way human beings are treated by their fellow men. Such a viewpoint was popular during the last 18th and early 19th centuries and expressed particularly in the Romantic Movement.

HUMAN NATURE IS BOTH EVIL AND GOOD

The assumption may be made also that man has equal potentiality for both constructive and destructive behavior. It is unlikely that he will be totally good, even if he is not corrupted by his experience, for even under the best of circumstances he will fall far short of becoming what he hopes to become. On the other hand, it is also unlikely that he will be totally bad, for even if he is not disciplined or forced to assume certain expected patterns of behavior, in all probability he will engage in some constructive behavior as the result of his inner impulses. Thus, neither an emphasis on the release of constructive feelings nor upon the importance of disciplining destructive impulses will alone provide an answer to the human dilemma. Perhaps man needs both release and discipline, although because of the structure of society, he probably will experience the disciplining of his destructive behavior more than the releasing of his constructive feelings.

A Compromise Point of View of Man

Part of the problem surrounding the controversy over these assumptions is that such terms as good and evil tend to confuse more than clarify the issues that are involved. Nevertheless, it is quite obvious that man behaves both constructively and destructively and thus perhaps it may be assumed correctly that he has potential for both constructive (good) and destructive (evil) behavior toward himself and toward others.

The concept of frustration tolerance may be utilized to explain why destructive behavior occurs without relying on the assumption of the presence of evil forces. From conception to birth, or roughly during the first nine months of existence, the organism experiences almost immediate and perfect gratification of every need. With birth, however, comes a disruption of this ideal state of gratification and the infant is forced to cope with the inevitable delays that occur between the onset of need and its satisfaction. He knows what he desires and he wants to be gratified right away. If he is forced to wait for his bottle, he responds to this failure to minister to his needs with howls of rage. In time, his rather violent and destructive reaction is modified and he learns to accept delay and disappointment.

The question may be asked whether this modification of behavior replaces the former destructive response or is only superimposed upon it. There is considerable evidence that beneath the surface of almost every person lies the former child who still wants his way immediately. When another person disagrees with him and what he desires is not realized, sometimes he responds destructively.

Both the constructive and the destructive tendencies are very much part of human behavior and thus the problem revolves itself around the question about the conditions that encourage these respective tendencies. The tendencies are neither absolute or inevitable, nor avoidable or erad-icable. The world is not composed so much of good guys or bad guys as it is of constructive people who have minimized their destructive behavior and destructive people who have minimized their constructive behavior.

In actuality, what a person is destructive about changes, for he is more destructive under some circumstances and in certain environments than in others. The goal of a sane society, therefore, must be to deal with this potential destructiveness and work realistically toward the eradication of situations which allow it to flourish.

The principle of homeostasis asserts that one of man's goals is the maintenance of a "steady state" outside as well as inside his body. Thus, any threat of change mobilizes and directs his energies toward a return to the original state or level of existence. At the same time, man possesses a drive for change, known as heterostasis, which also mobilizes his energy. Because he is a great deal more than a creature of passive adjustment to threatened change, man possesses a built-in discontent which makes him so dissatisfied, with both the environment and himself, that he seeks also to effect change.

Within the pattern of seeking change, the person utilizes different levels of functional organization. Many of his internal physiological changes are mediated at automatic levels under the control of the lower brain centers. More important, however, for this discussion are the more purposeful, non-automatic patterns of behavior. The term *ego* for ex-ample, has been used often to designate that part of the personality which perceives, attends, experiences, reflects, and chooses. It is the function of the ego to direct energy toward the achievement of all of the person's goals. As Menninger (1963, p. 126) stated:

> He pursues his ends, seeking to express his intentions and fulfill his needs as he perceives them and as he finds opportunity. He tries to survive,

with minimal pain and maximal pleasure, including the pleasures of achievement, of pride, and of loyalty to principle. All this requires an infinitude of doing, of trying and failing, of trying and succeeding, of trying and partially succeeding and having to compromise. It involves going ahead, stepping aside, stepping back, perhaps even running away. It involves fights and embraces, bargains and donations, gestures and conversations, working and playing, reproaches, rewards and retrenchments.

Thus, the ego or, as used in the context of this book, the person's orientation, organizes and directs behavior. If man does not merely respond to stimuli but, instead, actively pursues the achievement of certain purposes, then an awareness of these goals becomes an important key to the understanding of human behavior. Consequently, the next seven chapters are presented in an attempt to provide a more detailed description of the goals that human beings generally and probably you, the reader, particularly seek to achieve.

SUMMARY

1. Man may be distinguished from other animals on the basis of intellect and his ability to communicate through the use of language.
2. The complementary nature of the relationship between internal and external determinants becomes very apparent when one considers the manner in which the effectiveness of a person's behavior changes from one social situation to another.
3. Recognition of the primary influence of the internal determinants supports the premise that man has the ability to create an environment that will permit him to develop to the full extent of his potentiality.
4. A person is more likely to be influenced by the external determinants, however, when he has only a vague understanding of himself and the goals for his life.
5. General statements concerning human development are best considered in the light of a wide variety of differences among people.
6. Because man is capable of living both positively and negatively, it becomes increasingly necessary for society to find ways of eliminating the conditions that encourage the release of destructive behavior.

EXERCISE 1

Knowing the Self – Part A

Many of us seek information about the kind of person we are. The answer is never easy to discover, however. The following exercise will not provide any final answer but may offer valuable cues for thinking about the kind of person you are. Begin by checking the following statements according to how you think you actually feel and act. Use an X in the appropriate column. Since no one but yourself will see this, be as honest as you possibly can.

GENERALLY TRUE	GENERALLY FALSE	
_____	_____	1. I am very sensitive to criticism.
_____	_____	2. I have a tendency to be critical of others.
_____	_____	3. I react very positively to praise.
_____	_____	4. I am too aggressive.
_____	_____	5. I am too passive.
_____	_____	6. I tend to label persons as members of a group rather than accepting their individuality.
_____	_____	7. To be controversial makes me anxious.
_____	_____	8. I am accepting of others.
_____	_____	9. I often behave spontaneously.
_____	_____	10. I resist over-conformity.
_____	_____	11. I trust my impulses.
_____	_____	12. I trust my thinking.
_____	_____	13. I can easily express anger when I feel it.
_____	_____	14. I can easily express affection when I feel it.
_____	_____	15. I sometimes rebel against even reasonable authority.
_____	_____	16. After reaching a decision I often keep wondering if I have done the right thing.

_____   _____   17. I am easily discouraged when things go wrong.

_____   _____   18. I am often bored and apathetic.

_____   _____   19. When I am right I can really produce.

_____   _____   20. My memory is very unreliable.

_____   _____   21. Usually my actions are appropriate for the situation I am in.

_____   _____   22. In general, my actions are efficient for meeting my needs.

_____   _____   23. I usually have to drive myself to get things done.

_____   _____   24. Often I am irritable and distractable for no apparent reason.

_____   _____   25. I like people who are different.

_____   _____   26. I am open to new experience.

_____   _____   27. I accept the consequences of my actions.

_____   _____   28. In most situations I feel I belong.

_____   _____   29. Fear of being embarrassed often keeps me from acting.

_____   _____   30. If someone were to ask, "What are your greatest faults?" whether I chose to answer or not, I would pretty well know what they are.

_____   _____   31. If someone were to ask, "What are your greatest strengths?" whether I chose to answer or not, I would pretty well know what they are.

As a second step, go back over the preceding statements, but this time check them not according to how you really are but how you would like to be. Use an 0 in the proper blank.

One source of much personal difficulty is the amount of discrepancy, or lack of congruence, between how you are and how you would like to be. To check this, go back over the 31 items and color in the proper space on the Self-Satisfaction Scale below.

If you checked your actual behavior (the first time through) and your ideal behavior (the second time through) the same on an item, color out that number on the left-hand side of the scale. Treat each item separately. You are satisfied with yourself on that item. If, on the other hand, you checked the item differently the second time from the way you checked it the first time, color in that item number on the right-hand side of the scale.

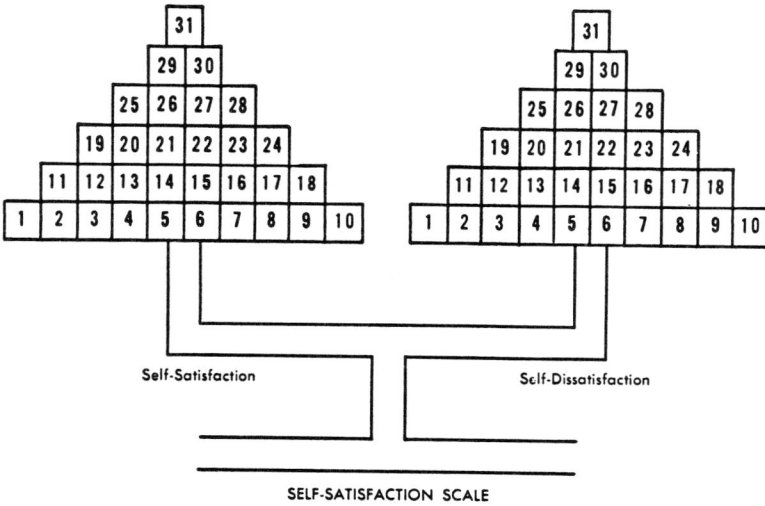

SELF-SATISFACTION SCALE

Which way does your satisfaction scale tip? Do the results bear out your prior thoughts about your satisfaction with yourself? Some experts maintain that no one can be sure just how you should be or just how you should want to be, but it is pretty important that the two not be too far apart. Do you agree? You might wish to relate the results of this exercise to your motivation for self-change.

If you wish, reproduce the items and have others check them as they think you would check them according to their knowledge of you. Do they tend to see you similarly or differently from the way you see yourself?

Finally, give some thought as to how you would prefer to decrease discrepancies between the self you are and the self you would like to be. Would you prefer to change the behavior to fit the ideal or to change the ideal to fit the behavior?

CHAPTER 3

The Hierarchical Nature of Goals

As discussed in Chapter 1, the various goals of human behavior may be arranged in a hierarchy. The orientational, physiological, and love, belongingness, and psychological safety goals, which all people need to have satisfied, are located at the lower end of the scale. Next in order, as indicated in Figure 2, are the five achievement goals. They are also important to everyone but are expressed uniquely by each person through the particular combination and degree of emphasis that he gives to the specific areas of respect, wealth, power, skill, and enlightenment. Finally at the upper end of the hierarchy are the two different levels of well-being. Although on occasion the hierarchy may need to be supplemented, it is believed to be workable and comprehensive enough for most human behavior to be related to one or more of the categories.

It is difficult to give the appropriate amount of recognition to the various theorists whose ideas have influenced, at least in part, the discussion of human goals. The particular way their views have been incorporated does not justify ascribing credit directly but, at the same time, there is too much similarity to ignore the debt that is owed to these writers. As a result, the system of goal classification that is presented is more of a synthesis of the ideas of other people than it is an original approach with the authors. Specific recognition will be made as the discussion proceeds, but it should be noted that ideas have been borrowed particularly from the works of Maslow (1954), Lasswell (1951), and Peckham (1962).

While there are important psychological and philosophical differences in the meanings of the terms need, drive, and goal, in the context of this book they are treated as being roughly equivalent to one another. Need is a broad and all inclusive term that is used in connection with both physiological and social desires. A person may say, for instance, that he needs to eat, that he needs a new car, that he needs a vacation, etc. In every case, there is the implication that something unpleasant will happen if his need is not satisfied.

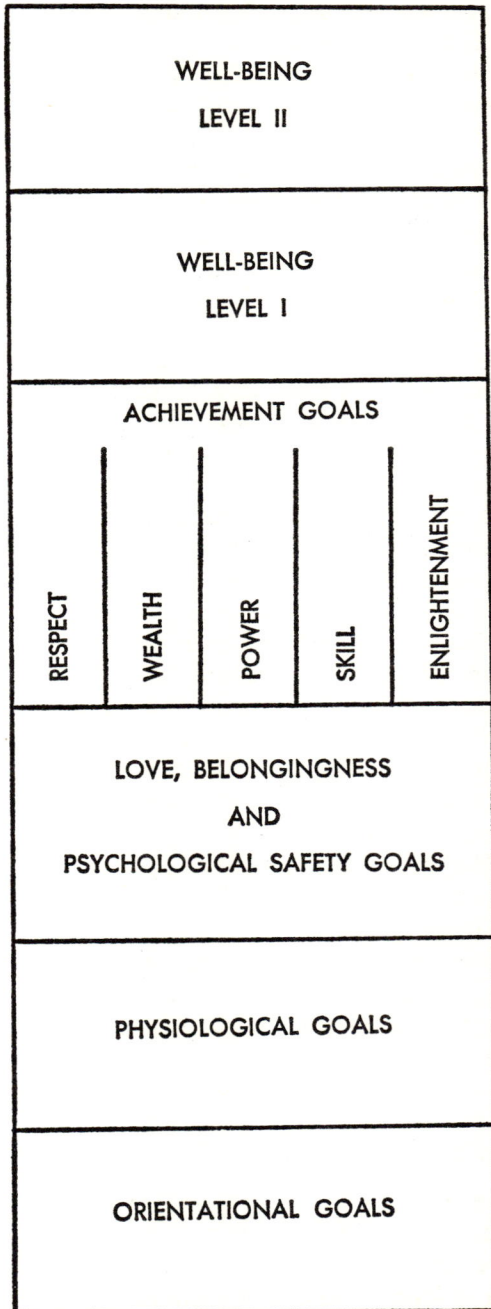

Figure 2. The hierarchy of goals.

The concept of drive refers primarily to arousal states in the organism which may be anticipated on the basis of knowing the conditions to which the organism has been exposed. An animal which has not been fed for some time, for instance, may be assumed to have a hunger drive and, similarly, one which has not had any water may be expected to be thirsty. Evidence of drive may be found also in an organism's physiological condition in that stomach contractions, for example, have been correlated positively with behavior which is oriented toward finding food. Drive may be inferred as well by observing restless activity in the organism and noting its increased sensitivity and attention to specific aspects of the environment.

The difficulty involved in influencing a person's life situation and physiological functioning makes it preferable to observe human behavior in terms of the goals that people strive to attain. Generally, these goals are the objects, feeling experiences, or situations that end or change behavior. They may be either positive or negative but, for the authors' purposes, the negative goals are considered in terms of being equivalent to their positive counterparts. As a result, a person whose behavior is directed toward avoiding punishment is seen as seeking physiological and psychological safety.

McDougall (1931, p. 411) stated that among the objective indices of goal behavior are (1) persistence of activity, (2) variation of activity, and (3) termination of activity. Persistence of activity is expressed through the frequency with which behavior is directed toward a particular goal, the length of time goal direction is maintained, and the resistance to distraction from other goals. Thus, the strength of a student's motivation toward achieving the goal of enlightenment may be judged by the frequency with which he studies and reads, the amount of time he gives to these activities, and the degree of difficulty involved in causing him to engage in some other type of endeavor. Variation of activity, according to Bindra (1959, p. 56), is related to the presence of several patterns of behavior which lead to the same goal and the adaptation of a person's behavior to changes in the position or state of the goal. Termination of activity occurs, in turn, when the person attains the goal or is diverted to other behavior by the introduction of a more attractive goal.

Relationship of Behavior Patterns to Goals

Human behavior may be understood most effectively when the goal that a person is striving to achieve is known by the person observing the behavior. Perhaps, for instance, you would picture a woman standing in a kitchen with a frying pan and a cake tin before her. Which one should she use? The answer, of course, will depend on whether she wishes to fry eggs or bake a cake and one would need to know whether she is preparing breakfast or dinner before drawing any conclusions concerning the appropriateness of her behavior.

In this simple example, the relationship between the observed behavior and the goal may be determined easily. In actual life experiences, however, it is frequently not that clear and sometimes people make the mistake of assuming that their own particular goals are the ones that the other person has in mind. The behavior they observe seems inappropriate and often they condemn it as being odd, confused, stupid, or even immoral. Unfortunately, it is much easier to depend upon this approach than to go to the trouble of finding out the goals that the other person is attempting to achieve.

Imagine, for example, that you know a freshman girl in college who is failing Professor Dogmatic's course in spectacular style. She rarely goes to class, has fallen behind in her daily assignments, and has been totally unprepared for his tests. Since, as far as the professor is concerned, her goal should be that of gaining an education, he dismisses her as stupid, lazy, and rebellious. Conversation with the girl reveals, however, that her primary goal in life has nothing to do with obtaining an education. Quite simply, she is in college to find a husband. Once this goal is understood, her behavior pattern of constantly dating and meeting every available man makes very good sense. In actuality, it makes a lot more sense than if she were to spend her time studying in the library and staying in her room in order to prepare assignments. Professor Dogmatic's accusation of stupidity is invalid for, in terms of her particular goal, the girl's behavior is highly intelligent. The mistake Professor Dogmatic made, of course, resulted from his inability to realize the goal toward which she was moving.

The importance of understanding and identifying goals has been stressed by many people. According to Mumford (1961, p. 184), Aristotle was one of the first to emphasize the teleological and goal-seeking nature of all organisms. More recently, Kelly (1958, p. 59) noted that a person's processes are channelized psychologically by the way in which he anticipates events. Allport (1961, p. 224) has theorized, moreover, that while it is useful to know what a person can do, what effect he has on other people, and what his desires are, the picture is always incomplete unless one knows what he is intending and what he is trying to bring about in the future. Finally, Russell (Egner and Denonn, 1961, pp. 468-469) pointed out the importance of realizing that all human activity is prompted by desire and that if one wishes to predict human behavior, it is necessary to know the whole range of man's desires, together with their relative strengths.

This dynamic quality of goal-seeking behavior is one of its most outstanding features. Goals are in a constant state of flux, for they vary from time to time and from situation to situation. Some goals may be attained quickly while others take years and sometimes a lifetime to achieve. As Allport (1961, p. 221) has stated, motives or goals may be transient, recurring, momentary, persistent, unconscious, conscious, opportunistic, tension reducing, tension maintaining, or tension seeking. The relationship among these various goals is never fixed rigidly but is evolving continuously as a result of the experiences of the person. The nature of this process may be understood more easily by reference to Mumford's statement (1961, p. 302):

> Organic planning does not begin with a preconceived goal: it moves from need to need, from opportunity to opportunity, in a series of adaptations that themselves become increasingly coherent and purposeful, so that they generate a complex, final design, hardly less unified than a pre-formed geometric pattern.

The orderly nature of goal oriented behavior has been emphasized by Lasswell (1951) and by Adler (Ansbacher and Ansbacher, 1956, p. 173). Lasswell has postulated a stable overriding objective which is the most preferred of all goals and gives direction to the entire life. He sees the achievement of the worth and dignity of man as being of primary importance. Unfortunately, this goal tends to be abstract and it loses touch with the experience of living as it is known by most people. Similarly, Adler has pointed to the development of a rather consistent and monolithic dominating goal, called the life style, which is evolved during the early years and subsequently dominates the direction of the person's behavior.

Although it is true that life styles and plans do exist in terms of an orientation toward life, and frequently an over-all consistent direction in a person's behavior may be observed, goal oriented behavior is not necessarily limited rigidly to a single dominant and permanent goal. Instead, it is seen in terms of a sequential series of changing objectives, each of which directs behavior for a period of time in a particular circumstance or situation and then recedes, perhaps to reappear, perhaps to remain in oblivion.

Most physiological goals, for example, are capable of being satisfied temporarily. As a person eats, he begins to reach a condition in which food holds little attraction and motivating power; it may even become repugnant to him. With many other goals, however, it is more difficult to find satisfaction. As Russell has stated, "man has some desires which are, so to speak, infinite, which can never be fully gratified, and which would keep him restless even in Paradise." (Egner and Denonn, 1961, p. 469) Goal directed behavior, therefore, involves something more than relieving a state of unrest or incompleteness which when removed allows the organism to return to a state of acquiescent bliss.

According to Mumford (1961, p. 5), human life swings between two poles: movement and settlement. At every point, one trades mobility for security and immobility for adventure. A person seeks peace and cessation of activity and, at the same time, he realizes that the solution of a problem and the attainment of a goal only lead to the formulation of another problem and a further goal. The easing of a difficult situation or the achievement of a goal may bring a sense of satisfaction, together with moments of peace and comfort, but inexorably the period of satisfaction and relaxation gives way to the tension created by the demands of a different social setting and the person's need for new goal achievement.

The child, for instance, masters drinking from a glass and so gives up his bottle or the breast. Later he is expected to change his habits of elimination and to exchange the security of the home for the adventure of the school. Old friends and acquaintances are augmented with new ones and so life becomes a series of peaceful interludes that follow successful adjustment to the expectancies of growth and development.

Frequently the attainment of a goal is emphasized at the expense of the experiences that potentially may occur during the course of reaching that goal. Students, for example, become so wrapped up in the importance of obtaining a degree that they value little else. Invariably the day of graduation is greeted with an exorbitant amount of joy and celebration. They have "arrived" finally only to find that in their concern to reach their goal as expediently as possible, they have missed many opportunities for growing, developing, and learning which would cause future problems to loom less threateningly on the horizon. In fact, difficulties seem to occur most frequently when settlement and rest are preferred to mobility and activity. The main negative criticism of such ideal societies as the one envisioned by Bellamy (1917) is that they emphasize only the static element of perfection. In actuality, no man can ever achieve happiness or emotional maturity in a permanent or complete sense, for they have to be won anew every day.

This viewpoint may be illustrated by asking you to picture a man who is successful in his work, respected in the community, happily married, and who is known to enjoy a varied number of activities of life among which is the drinking of an occasional cocktail. It may be said that such a man has a high well-being status. As time passes, automation causes his job to be less significant, his wife dies, his children marry and leave home, and his proclivity for cocktails turns into a series of alcoholic sprees. For a period of time, his life sinks to a low ebb and his well-being status declines. Later he meets a woman who, through caring for him, succeeds in encouraging him to control the use of alcohol and make another start. As he finds rewards through achieving new goals, his well-being status rises and he becomes increasingly able to handle whatever new problems he encounters.

The need for continuous adjustment and growth as an ideal condition of the emerging self makes it necessary for adults as well as children to exchange whatever they see as familiar, comfortable, and tried and true for the nebulous uncertainty of the future. As a result, the demands of adjustment placed upon the sixty-five-year-old man at retirement may not be so very different as at first they would seem from those expected of the eighteen-month-old child who is involved in the rigors of toilet training.

Thomas and Znaniecki (1960, pp. 407-409) have described the wide range of reactions to the demands of growth and development. At one extreme is the philistine who tends to achieve the same goals over and over again in the same manner and rejects in so far as it is possible the emergence of new goals. Such a person feels that growth is for children and he usually manages to hate or at least oppose anyone who is concerned with change and improvement. At the other extreme is the changeling or weather vane person who is at the mercy of every influence so that he is constantly attempting to achieve new goals and who because of the bewildering rapidity with which he changes them is inevitably doomed to failure. In the more desirable middle range is the person whose personality may be described as settled and organized but who accepts the possibility and necessity of change. His orientation includes growth and development as a part of life and a necessary condition for positive mental health. In such a person the introduction of a new goal does not just add to the existing ones but, instead, produces an overall change and a new configuration which alter the characteristics and approach to life of the person.

The Balancing of Goals

Many different goals are sought by human beings and some degree of balance in terms of their relative importance is desirable. Figure 3 contains a schematic representation of three persons who differ in the amount of

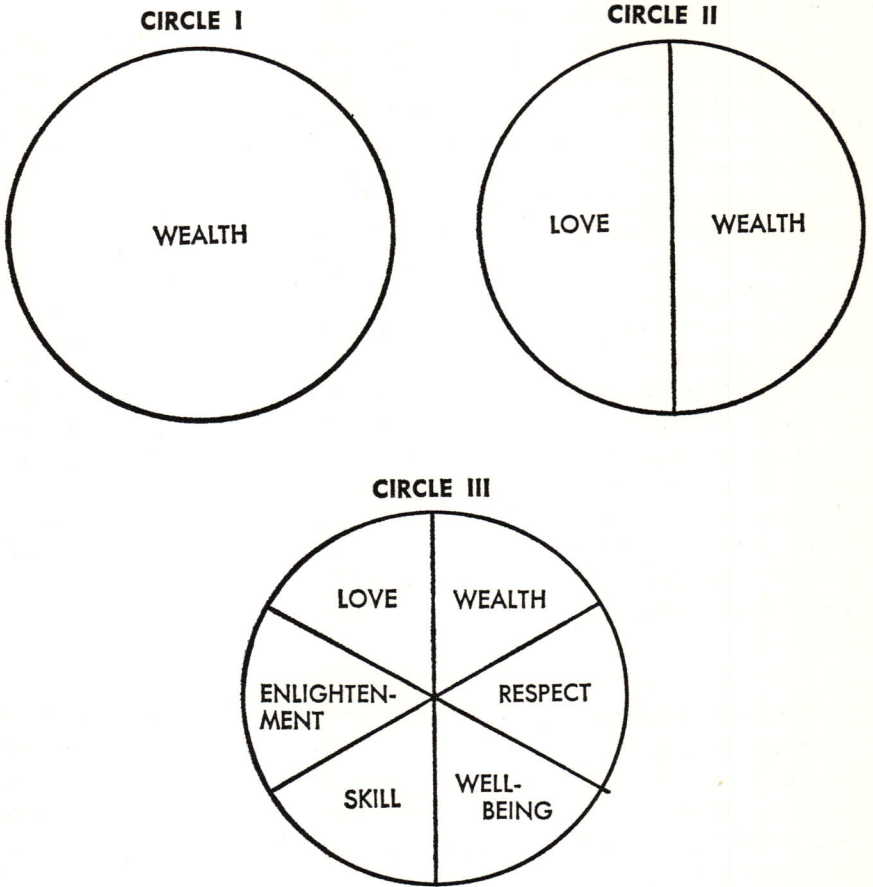

FIGURE 3. Schematic representation of the goals valued by three different persons.

emphasis given to the various goals of their lives. The circle labeled I represents a person for whom wealth has become his sole objective almost to the point that he sees other goals as relatively unimportant. Circle II denotes a person who has stressed wealth also but, at the same time, because his family is equally important to him, he has devoted time and energy to the giving and receiving of love and affection. The third person, depicted by Circle III, has balanced proportionately the attention given to attaining a number of different goals. Suppose, now, that all three of these men lose their money. Obviously, the man whose goal has been primarily that of accumulating wealth will be affected most adversely, for there is little of importance in life left for him. He may turn even to such an extreme measure as committing suicide. Probably this situation occurred when men were jumping out of the windows of high buildings after losing their fortunes in the financial crash of 1929. Imagine, in addition, that the other two men lose their families in automobile accidents. The one who now has the least reason to live of course, is the person who has confined himself to making money and relating to his family. The remaining man, who is still able to turn toward attaining the other goals of his life, is much more likely to make whatever adjustments are necessary to continue living.

This analysis, of course, is hypothetical and should not be taken too literally because there is also some danger in having too much balance. If there were not overly committed individuals who pursue one goal primarily at the expense of all others, there might not be any Einsteins or Pasteurs, or for that matter, Sam Sneads or Mickey Mantles. Despite this reservation, however, too many people tend to neglect breadth of experience in order to pursue assiduously a few specific goals. In the opinion of the authors, most persons would lead much richer lives and would be far better off if they would increase the number of goals that are important to them.

Deprivation Versus Gratification

One of the most noticeable characteristics of American society has been the emphasis given to the Protestant Ethic and the American Dream, both of which have stressed hard work, persistence, and even deprivation and personal suffering as being necessary for the development of character and integrity. The extreme emphasis on deprivation may be seen very clearly also in the mendicant Dominican and Franciscan orders where the practice of poverty and the denial of a variety of goal satisfactions are the most important patterns of behavior. Although the intentions of the members of these groups were most honorable, the negative influence of the deprivation resulted probably in the torturing and killing of countless people by the Dominicans in the Inquisition and the eventual degeneration of the Franciscans (Dunham, 1964, p. 201).

At the same time that deprivation and doing without have been stressed, gratification of a child's needs and other practices that would make it easier for him to obtain his goals have been rejected on the basis that they would spoil him and, consequently, be harmful to his development. In actuality, however, gratification of a person's needs is considerably more beneficial to personal development than deprivation, for as Durkheim (1960, p. 449) noted, "no living thing can be contented, or even go on living, unless its wants are sufficiently harmonized with the means at its disposal."

Gratification makes it possible, therefore, for a person to move toward new goals and live in a healthy, growing, and emerging way. Although it does not follow necessarily that because a person is allowed to attain his goals his behavior will be ideal, it is reasonable to expect that he will behave in a little or even a considerably better manner than if he has been stopped from reaching his goals. Before a person is able to give gratification to other people, however, he must be reasonably concerned with satisfying his own needs and goals. In distinguishing between self-love and selfishness, Fromm (1956, p. 60) stated that the "affirmation of one's own life, happiness, growth, and freedom is rooted in one's capacity to love, i.e., in care, respect, responsibility, and knowledge. If an individual is able to love productively, he loves himself too; if he can love only others, he cannot love at all."

The selfish person, in contrast, "is interested only in himself, wants everything for himself, feels no pleasure in giving, but only in taking." When a person has enough self-love or respect for himself to want to attain some of his own goals, he will have also enough genuine respect for other people to want them to gratify their needs and reach their particular goals. If he attempts to love other people before he has learned to love himself, simply because he feels that he is expected to be unselfish, then he will be unhappy and most likely find some subtle and destructive way of releasing his feelings.

Imagine, for example, that you know a young couple who after being married for about a year or so have just had their first child. Because the husband is beginning his career, the economic situation is precarious and they live in a small relatively uncomfortable apartment. Despite a rather drab and restrictive life, they are reasonably happy and their hopes for the future sustain and encourage them. The wife's father dies and her mother is left with a small income which is adequate enough for her to live alone quite comfortably. She prefers living with the young couple, however, and because they have been taught always that their first duty is to their parents, they agree for her to live with them. The mother has always felt unsafe and unsure of herself and very quickly her need to dominate is expressed in telling the couple how to raise their child, what to buy, where to go, etc. These remarks are expressed in a very subtle and tricky way so that outright hostility seldom occurs. The mother's advice is offered always with the couple's "welfare at heart" so that if they resist her ideas, they somehow end up feeling guilty for having mistreated her.

Time passes and the couple argues over minor matters with increasing rancor. Home is not so much fun and the husband begins working late. An understanding secretary lets him cry on her shoulder and very quickly a liaison is formed. Because of the various strains that occur within the family, the child's pleasant disposition begins to deteriorate. He learns to play the grandmother against the parents and the parents against each other, and generally the relationships in the family become increasingly unpleasant and destructive.

If the couple had possessed more self-love and respect for themselves, however, they would have been able to discourage the mother from joining them or else would have welcomed her into their home and loved her despite the faults and domineering ways. Because of this more self-respecting attitude, letting her live with them would not have been such a sacrifice on their part and her presence well might have served to help integrate the family unit.

It has been suggested that goal gratification is the ideal condition for growing children and that self-respect and self-love are necessary if parents are to be effective. Obviously the child's need for gratification is going to collide with the parents' need to maintain respect for themselves. Sometimes children are wonderful company but at other times they are little monsters. It becomes necessary, therefore, for parents to take care of their own needs in order that they may truly and unselfishly love their children most of the time. The wise and realistic father denies his child on occasion and indulges himself. He may join a country club and take his wife out to dinner once a week even though it may mean that his children will do without certain things and perhaps not have as many toys as their playmates down the block. In this way, the parent preserves his own integrity and takes care of his personal needs to the point where he is free to give his children affection and love that is real and genuine. He may even be capable of offering them a reasonable amount of independence and increasing opportunities for determining the goals for their own lives. Thus, as they approach adulthood, they will be free to move in directions which are important to them without feeling that they have failed in their responsibilities to their parents.

SUMMARY

1. The various goals of human behavior may be arranged in a hierarchy, starting with the orientational and physiological goals and ending at the top of the scale with the two levels of well-being.

2. People understand the behavior that is expressed in a social situation more fully when they are familiar with the goals that each person is striving to achieve.

3. Goals vary in their relative importance to a person's life, depending upon his experiences and social situation.

4. A person's attitude toward life moves from one extreme of seeking comfort and the cessation of activity to the opposite desire for the emergence and successful achievement of more stimulating and challenging goals.

5. Behavior is likely to be effective when the person enjoys a wide variety of goals that tend to be balanced in terms of their importance to his life.

6. Contrary to popular opinion, deprivation and personal suffering do not contribute significantly to the development of character and integrity.

7. Human development tends to move along a lot more easily and smoothly when a person's needs are recognized and gratified.

8. A person must love and respect himself before he is in a position of being able to take care of other people's needs with any degree of adequacy or sensitivity.

EXERCISE 2

Knowing the Self – Part B

Both cooperative and competitive behaviors are constantly demanded of all of us. In our society "beating the other guy" is often highly rewarded in school, in industry, and even in social situations. At the same time, cooperative behavior is also desired and desirable. At times, in certain situations, withdrawal behavior (neither competing nor cooperating) is the best solution. The following exercise is designed to help you think about the balance in your own personality between these various strategies.

Check each of the following statements to best describe yourself.

GENERALLY   GENERALLY
   YES   No

_____   _____   1. Do you tend to pursue personal, private goals (as opposed to group, institution, and community goals)?

_____	_____	2. Are you relatively unpredictable?
_____	_____	3. Do you tend to keep your plans to yourself—operate on the theory that things go best if you alone know exactly what you are up to?
_____	_____	4. Do you seldom make your needs known to others—prefer to keep them guessing?
_____	_____	5. Do you frequently use bluffs and threats to influence others?
_____	_____	6. Do you frequently stereotype others?
_____	_____	7. Do you frequently block others from reaching their goals (get there first with the most)?
_____	_____	8. Do you pay little attention to the needs of others (nice guys finish last)?
_____	_____	9. Are you out to win at all costs (I cry all the way to the bank)?
_____	_____	10. Are you on the lookout for the "main chance" (kid me not, the end does justify the means)?
_____	_____	11. Do you isolate yourself as much as possible?
_____	_____	12. Do you daydream frequently?
_____	_____	13. Are you relatively quiet in groups?
_____	_____	14. Do you consider yourself to be non-assertive?
_____	_____	15. Do you often dwell on problems (worrier)?
_____	_____	16. Do you make many more changes, of all kinds, (jobs, homes, schools, etc.) than ordinary?

Some people might say that if your answers to items 1 through 10 were "yes" you are highly competitive. If your answers to items 11 through 16 were "yes" you withdraw frequently and neither compete nor cooperate.

Do you agree? To further sharpen the discrimination for yourself try to rephrase statements 1 through 10 into their opposites so that they now describe cooperative behaviors.

1. EXAMPLE: Do you tend to pursue team, institutional, or community goals (as opposed to personal private goals)?

2. _____

_____

3. _____

_____

4. _____

_____

5. _____

_____

6. _____

_____

7. _____

_____

8. _____

_____

9. _____

_____

10. _____

_____

If you generally agree with these ten statements you have created, you are probably a cooperative person.

As a further step, try to add to the lists of competitive, cooperative, and withdrawal behaviors. Watch persons who typically use each of the strategies as guides.

Additional Competitive Behaviors.

1. _____
2. _____
3. _____

4. _____
5. _____

Additional Cooperative Behaviors.

1. _____
2. _____
3. _____
4. _____
5. _____

Additional Withdrawal Behaviors.

1. _____
2. _____
3. _____
4. _____
5. _____

In a general way, after completing the foregoing exercises, do you estimate yourself as being:

_____ more competitive

_____ more cooperative

_____ more withdrawing

Are you satisfied with being this way? _____   _____
                                         Yes   No

If not, which strategy would you like to use more in your day-to-day behavior?

_____ competitive   _____ cooperative   _____ withdrawal

If you do wish to change, in the following space list some of the things you feel you could rather easily accomplish that would make you more competitive or cooperative.

1. _____
2. _____
3. _____
4. _____
5. _____

CHAPTER 4

The Orientational Goals

An orientation represents a picture or image of reality, consisting of the ideas, feelings, attitudes, and values which form a person's cognitive representation of the world or, in other words, the way the world looks to him. Sometimes an orientation is simple and primitive, as when it belongs to a very young child; on other occasions, with mature and enlightened adults, it may be complex and sophisticated. In fact, orientations of every conceivable type influence the way people react to their environment.

Suppose, for example, that due to the influence of his orientation, a person perceives a fungus as a non-poisonous mushroom. If his viewpoint is in agreement with objective reality and the fungus is in actuality a mushroom, then eating it is quite harmless. On the other hand, if his orientation differs from objective reality, and what he believes quite firmly to be a mushroom is really a toadstool, then by going ahead and following his erroneous perception, he is in danger of becoming sick and even dying. Similarly, all orientations vary in the degree of their usefulness for guiding behavior, from those which correspond with objective reality to the ones which cause the person to view his environment in terms of his own distorted and subjective version of reality and thereby prevent his seeing and experiencing what, in actuality, is out there.

From a somewhat pessimistic viewpoint, these ideas would seem to suggest that man cannot be sure of anything whatsoever, for the world to which he responds may be only a product of his own orientation or imagination. From a more optimistic outlook, however, such uncertainty would imply that man is not merely a stamped-out product of his environment, but, instead, is an activated entity who is responsible continuously for the reality in which he exists. Of all the numerous orientations which man creates, some become recognized and accepted generally and constitute what is conceived as objective reality; others are considered to be personal and subjective. The fact, for example, that as you read there is a book in front of you is a part of objective reality which can be confirmed by any observer of your behavior. Your reaction to what you read, however, which probably constitutes a much more vital part of your experience, makes up what is known as subjective reality.

Szczesny (1961, p. 79) noted that as soon as man began to live consciously, he conceived of the desire to strive and wish in terms of his own insight and he found intolerable any difference between his motives and his behavior. Lecky (1951), in turn, developed his study of personality around the individual's need to be consistent while Rogers (1951, p. 487) saw the actualization, maintenance, and enhancement of the perceived self as the basic striving of man. The implication that may be drawn from these theories is that holding to an orientation that has helped a person adjust to his environment is an important goal of mankind. Such an attitude has been observed specifically by psychotherapists of different schools of thought, who are almost unanimous in their agreement over the neurotic person's difficulty in changing his orientation toward himself. He may feel so inferior, for example, that no matter what degree of success or superior achievement he may experience, he is unable to see himself as being anything but inadequate and incompetent. Thus, even an unpleasant fact which fits into the existing pattern is preferred quite often to another more attractive one which does not belong.

Any discussion of orientations is in a way a paradox for, as Peckham (1962, p. 260) pointed out, the existence of order is an illusion, but, nevertheless, the experiencing of order is still essential to maintaining life. The difficulty lies in avoiding the tendency to allow the temporary order, which is necessary for existence, to harden like cement so that new orientations and concepts of reality are denied the opportunity of being created.

When the desire for order becomes excessive, the person attempts to bring every aspect of life under control, causing individual autonomy and the right to choose new orientations to be lost. Throughout history, reformers who have presented new ideas have deplored the strong resistance to change of the privileged classes and their tenacity in clinging on to old perceptions and prerogatives, even when these ideas were no longer in their best interests. Inevitably, it seems, special privilege makes it hard to see the value of new orientations and perhaps Jesus was commenting on this phenomenon when he stated that it was easier for a camel to pass through the eye of a needle than for a rich man to enter the Kingdom of God.

An experiment by the physiologists Hernandez-Peon, Sherrer, and Jouvet (1956), which demonstrated the existence of a neurological mechanism that can stop sensory signals from reaching the cerebral cortex of the brain, may help to clarify the discussion of orientations. Stainless steel electrodes were implanted into a cat's cochlear nucleus at the first relay station of the ear. Clicks were sounded in the cat's presence and the changes in a recording apparatus that was connected with the electrodes indicated that it was able to hear the clicks. Some mice in a small closed glass jar were then placed in front of the cat. The clicks were repeated, but the cat's earlier responses disappeared almost entirely. Evidently, the neural impulses to the clicks had been stopped at or before the cochlear nucleus and the cat's preoccupation with the mice had caused the auditory stimulus to be relatively ineffective or non-existent. Thus, the experiment had produced a different orientation in the cat inasmuch as it did not respond to the clicks of which it had been aware when the mice were not present. In a similar manner, people go through life with their perceptions being influenced by orientations. The student in the classroom, for example, who is oriented toward thoughts of his girl friend and the development of his social life is no more capable of responding to the lecture going on before him than the mice-oriented cat was able to hear the clicks which were sounded in its presence.

Some years ago, a friend of one of the authors became an important executive in a dynamic and growing business. As his responsibilities increased, he found himself working longer and longer hours, spending less time with his wife and children, and giving up, one by one, the wide variety of activities that previously he had enjoyed. One day he discovered a small lump on his abdomen which later was diagnosed as being malignant. After an operation and during the subsequent period of treatment, there was no way of telling whether the growth would continue or whether it had been arrested and for months he did not know how much longer he had to live.

As a result of these uncertain conditions, the man's life changed completely. He curtailed severely his business activities so that he worked only four days a week and no more. He began to spend time playing with his children, and courting his wife, and enjoying what he described as "the things he had always wanted to do." He took long solitary walks, skied, went to concerts and plays, and even tried his hand at painting. The cancerous growth did not reappear and the man's health remained good. As time passed, the old habits began to replace the new ones and within three years he was again working day and night.

The point to bear in mind, of course, is that the man's behavior was dependent upon his orientation. Before the diagnosis of cancer, he believed that he had all the time in the world for doing what he wanted. Once he became ill, however, and was in danger of dying, a new orientation was forced upon him. He could not escape from the fact that there was a strong likelihood that his days were numbered and that, in a short period of time, death would become a reality.

The Origin of Orientations

While it is true that a person's orientation depends primarily upon the unique interaction he chooses to have with his environment, a number of different factors, which are described below, influence in part the specific form that the orientation will take.

Orientations Are Innately and Constitutionally Determined

Tinbergen (1951) observed that some instinctive acts in animals are innately connected with specific environmental stimulus patterns so that certain external circumstances or events bear a dynamic relationship to behavior within the organism. The shape of a hawk produces fear in fowl, for example, while that of a goose evokes interest. As a result of these and related observations of animal behavior, Bindra (1959, p. 83) concluded that, "there are marked species differences in the 'sensitivity' to various types of stimulus patterns."

From differences among animals, it is a short but logical step to the hypothesis that there are also innate differences in sensitivity to different aspects of the environment among human beings. Whereas one person may be constitutionally more sensitive to auditory stimulation, another person may be more aware of visual images and patterns. Although the case for innate differences in human sensitivy cannot be proved in any final sense, it also cannot be disproved. Thus, it would seem safer to retain the possibility that some of the differences in orientation are to some extent innate and constitutional.

Orientations Are Created as Well as Given to Man by Nature

Campbell (1959, p. 40) pointed out that within the essential functions of man is the urge to fashion images, to organize external events, and to create new stimuli to which he can respond. Frequently, he creates artificial stimulus situations that are more effective in determining behavior than anything to be found originally in nature. Cosmetics and articles like those vulgarly known as "falsies" offer presumably an improvement over what nature has provided. Under certain conditions, even the butterfly will pursue a man-made model with amorous intent in preference to the natural female of the species. All in all, man's cultural development may be described as a story of release from experience in a world that nature provided and evolution into the world of his own creation and ingenuity.

Orientations Are Determined by Familiarity

A person tends to see whatever is familiar to him as the true, the beautiful, and the good. The Communist may feel that Marx is the true prophet and that capitalists are monsters. The American, needless to say, does not share these views. To many Cubans, Castro is a hero; to Americans he is a dictator. The American says of something he cannot understand, "It might as well have been written in Greek." The Greek, in the same situation, is likely to say, "It might as well have been written in English."

A study by Howes and Solomon (1951) demonstrated that the speed with which a word is recognized when focused upon a screen for varying brief intervals depends upon the frequency with which the word appears in standard printed English. Familiar words are recognized more easily, which apparently indicates that out of all the potential stimulation from the environment, there is a distinct readiness to recognize and respond to that which is familiar. The old saying, "you can take the boy out of the country but you cannot take the country out of the boy," illustrates perhaps to some extent that all people are limited in their responses to a new situation by the familiar aspects of their earlier environment.

Even reaction to pain is at least partially a matter of familiarity growing out of experiences in the past. Melzack and Scott (1957) reared ten dogs under conditions which protected them from all harmful stimuli so that the animals had no opportunity to learn to withdraw from unpleasant experiences. Their behavior was compared at maturity with that of their twelve litter mates who were reared normally. The dogs in the restricted group walked into lighted matches repeatedly and one dog actually struck his head against some hot water pipes more than thirty times in a single hour. Having a paw or tail stepped on elicited no sign of pain although the same experience brought forth howls from the dogs raised under normal conditions. Similar differences may be seen in the behavior of ice hockey and football players who often sustain serious injuries without experiencing the pain that most people would find excruciating.

Reaction to basic perceptual experiences may be modified also by familiarity. Stratton (1897), for instance, wore inverted lenses which turned his world upside down as well as reversing it from left to right. The immediate effect was an extreme upset in the orientation of vision. He found, however, that after only eight days the new visual motor coordination became quite good and with the further passage of time and, consequently, greater familiarity, he suffered little discomfort. In fact, when the upside down lenses were removed, brief difficulty in orientation to the "right side up" world was experienced.

One of the problems surrounding familiarity as a determiner of orientations is the almost inescapable human tendency to see experiences which are slightly familiar as very familiar and other experiences that are somewhat strange as sharply alien. To the extent that this reaction occurs, the person's potential for living is inhibited, for he spends his time concentrating on whatever is familiar and, subsequently, avoiding any experience that is liable to prove to be new, different, and potentially threatening.

Orientations Are Determined by Interests, Values, and Desires

The importance of interests, values, and desires in determining a person's orientation may be seen in a study by Postman, Bruner, and McGinnies (1948) who administered a test of values to a group of people and then exposed them for brief intervals to words representing the various areas of the test. The subjects recognized words from their dominant value system with greater speed than words associated with beliefs that were not important to them.

In another study, Allport (1954, pp. 180-181) asked a group of men to rank a series of pictures of girls, which were without any captions, in terms of the relative beauty of the girls. The procedure was repeated, but the second time the picture of each girl was given a name associated frequently with a different national or religious group. It was found that the rankings changed greatly in that girls with Jewish sounding names were placed lower than when they had been unnamed; girls with Anglo-Saxon names were ranked higher, and generally the order of preference followed the social status ascribed to the particular group. In both studies apparently, the values and desires of the subjects decided the particular orientations with which they approached the experiments and their responses were influenced accordingly.

Orientations Are Determined by the Influence of Other People

A number of different studies may be used to support the premise that orientations are determined by the influence of other people. Siipola (1935), for example, informed half of her subjects before an experiment began that the words they would see flashed upon a screen would have to do with animals or birds; the remaining subjects were told that the words would be related to travel or transportation. The "animal" group responded to six nonsense words with 63 percent animal or bird responses and 11 percent travel responses. In contrast the "travel" group responded to the same meaningless words with 14 percent animal words and 74 percent travel and transportation words.

In an experiment by Sherif (1935), the subjects were placed in a very dark room and shown a small stationary spot of light which due to optical illusion appeared to move. The estimates of this illusionary movement varied widely from individual to individual, but in groups of people where the responses of other people were known, the estimates tended to approach the average for the group.

Orientations Are Determined by the Person's Conscience

Orientations are modified always by the extent to which the person's conscience has been developed. As a result of the reactions of parents and the other important people in his life, the person learns what is the right and proper way for him to behave. Generally, such responses tend to be negative in nature and, by and large, they are related to the ideas and actions which other people would prefer to have prohibited. To the extent that the person is stopped from engaging in activities which are truly harmful, the influence of the conscience upon his orientation is beneficial. To the extent, however, that the expectations of other people are a denial and rejection of the attempts of the person to achieve his own goals, they represent a needless restriction of the person's experience. In point of fact, in many cases what is told the child is seldom a description of what the parent has actually experienced in life but, instead, is a reaction to what he was told during childhood he should experience. Perhaps this statement may be understood more easily by considering whether you would want to pass along to your own children your ideals about appropriate behavior for dating or your actual dating experience.

Allport (1961, p. 135) noted that from about age six, children learn a more or less blind obedience to adult standards. In fact, the habit of expecting and obeying external rules is so prevalent that even at play they are outraged if their games are not played according to precise and rigid rules. In a similar manner, an adult may follow the intense and tyrannical values of a dictatorial conscience to the point that he is restricted during his entire life to the limited world of childhood experience.

In a way, this type of distortion may be looked upon as the corruption of the conscience by the id, seen by Freud (1920) as representing unconscious motivational tendencies which are totally amoral. Thus, man, while acting in the name of virtue, is able to express destructive impulses. According to Brophy (1962, p. 170):

> The religious fanatic who believes that he is fulfilling the Christian moral precepts when he burns heretics is not making a moral mistake but an intellectual one. Moral argument will get nowhere with him, because he is convinced he is morally right; our only hope is to point out to him his unacknowledged destructive wish, which has blinded him to the logical necessity whereby loving one's neighbor is incompatible with burning him.

She added (1962, p. 171):

> Our concern today is with bigger bonfires than we burned the heretics in, but our fear is precisely the same: namely that in despite of our conscious wish to preserve life something will persuade us that destroying it is somehow compatible with saving it.

Orientations Are Determined by Unconscious as Well as Conscious Experiences

Many orientations may be traced to conscious influences in the life of the person, but others are the result of experiences which are difficult to recall and are seen as remaining below the surface of conscious awareness at what is referred to as the preconscious level. Still other orientations, stemming from experiences of which the person is completely unaware, are considered to be at the even deeper, unconscious level.

In thinking about unconscious processes it is helpful to remove them from the realm of the mysterious, mystic, or supernatural. No doubt sometime or other, you have known the experience of driving along a highway having absolutely no awareness of the details of the journey. Turns were made, the road followed, speed adjusted, other cars passed, etc., all without any conscious awareness of what was happening. Such behavior, however, together with purposeful forgetting, slips of the tongue, slips of the pen, and a variety of similar errors which have been emphasized by Freud (1920), may be seen as evidence of some very real unconscious influences at work. For one person, a slip of the tongue may be purely an accident, but for another person it may be a meaningful clue to some unconscious intention. As mentioned in Chapter 1, most people live, at least in part, according to their conscious interests, plans, and intentions, but, at the same time, much of their behavior is influenced by experiences which are below the level of conscious awareness.

In an experiment by Smith, Spence, and Klein (1959), an unchanging picture of a man with an expressionless face was flashed on a screen and the subjects of the experiment were asked to report changes in man's expression. Simultaneously the word "angry" was flashed on the screen at exposures that were so rapid that the subjects were unaware of having seen the word. Under such conditions, the subjects tended to see the man's expression as becoming angry. When the word "happy" was flashed on the screen in the same manner, they tended to see the face as becoming happy, thereby indicating that they were being influenced by stimuli of which they were completely unaware.

Orientations Are Determined by Deprivation and Gratification

Levine, Chein, and Murphy (1942) showed some black and white ambiguous drawings to students after they had been deprived of food for various periods of time. It was found that the persons who had been without food for three and six hours perceived considerably more food objects in the drawings than the students who had experienced only one hour of food deprivation. Although still remaining higher than the one hour group, the frequency of food responses fell off for the group of students who had been without food for nine hours.

Another study by Bruner and Goodman (1947) involved a group of children from rich families and another group from poor families who were asked to estimate the size of some coins. The children from the poor families saw the coins as being larger than the children from the rich families, supporting the idea that often a person will overestimate the importance of the very thing of which he has been deprived.

Orientations Are Affected by Alcohol, Drugs, and Chemicals

The effects of alcohol and drugs of many kinds upon orientations are well known. Reality for the person who drinks five martinis at a party obviously changes during the course of the evening. Similarly the student who takes No-Doze tablets to keep him awake during the early hours of the morning in order to cram for an examination undoubtedly develops an orientation that makes it possible for him to remain awake and continue studying.

Orientational Congruence

The degree of congruence of a person's orientation with objective reality and the orientations of other people may be considered in terms of the following four categories:

1. Irrational unshared orientations which do not correspond with either objective reality or the views of other persons. Such orientations are not only inadequate in helping people achieve goals but, in addition, the people relying upon them fail to gain the support of other members of society.

2. Irrational shared orientations that are also not congruent with objective reality but which correspond closely with the beliefs of other people. Such viewpoints are based on objectively inaccurate observations and, as a result, they do not lead to successful goal achievement. Nevertheless, the people advocating them are supported by their friends and associates and are encouraged to persist in their endeavors.

3. Rational unshared orientations which correspond to objective reality but not to the views of other members of society. In such cases, the person's behavior is realistic, but he is unable to communicate his ideas to other people and, consequently, he rarely experiences interpersonal relationships that are rewarding and satisfying.

4. Rational shared orientations which correspond closely with objective reality and the beliefs of other people. Not only does the person's

behavior lead to the achievement of his goals, but it is approved as well by the other members of society.

It should be noted, however, that no orientation ever fits completely and permanently into any one of the four categories in that, of course, the degree of congruence is liable to vary from time to time and from one situation to another.

Irrational Unshared Orientations

At best, the orientations of the psychotic, the seriously disturbed alcoholic, and the neurotic correspond only to a limited degree to objective reality and the orientations of other persons. The psychotic, for instance, who thinks he is Napoleon, and the alcoholic, who has deteriorated to the point that he sees snakes on the wall, are both acting from what are for them very real perceptions. Their experiences, however, cannot be affirmed by other people because there is nothing in the environment that corresponds to what is described.

The neurotic's perceptions are relatively less idiosyncratic and come somewhat closer to corresponding with external events. He may suffer, for example, from an unreasonable fear of snakes which causes considerable discomfort and imposes a limitation upon his behavior. Although the snakes that he perceives may also be seen by other people, he cannot assess realistically the danger to which he is exposed. Thus, being told that injuries from snakes are rare, compared to those occurring during automobile travel or from slips in the bath tub, helps very little in reducing fear and changing the neurotic's attitude.

Because snakes do exist and on occasion they bite people with untoward results, many people in America share the neurotic's fear of snakes. In this sense, the neurotic experiences both a partial correspondence with objective reality and a degree of commonalty with the views of other people that are impossible for the psychotic.

Irrational Shared Orientations

While most people in America do not see snakes where snakes do not exist or suffer from extreme fear of them, often they are looked upon erroneously as undesirable slimy creatures which are best destroyed whenever possible. Because this perception is assumed generally to be true and to some extent may be supported by objective reality, many people believe it to be more correct than the scientific view which is closer to the truth.

The same type of mistake may be observed in the behavior of people who believe that a rain dance brings rain. When no rain falls, they may choose to assume that it was an error in the dance that caused the failure and not the utilization of a faulty system. As a result, they are likely to turn to the dance time and time again, thereby causing their mistaken orientation to be maintained indefinitely.

Rational Unshared Orientations

Although some orientations correspond very closely with the external and observable events of objective reality, they are not necessarily shared by the other members of society. Thus, a person may take a position that places him in close touch with reality but which, at the same time, causes him to have little in common with other people's expectations as to what is right and proper in behavior.

Distinguishing between the orientation of the individual whose behavior fits into this category and the non-conforming person with the irrational approach to life has always been one of the major problems of society. Both persons hold to positions which seem strange and foreign to people whose value systems are based exclusively upon familiar and known experiences. The creativity of a Leonardo da Vinci, for example, may be perceived very easily as the bizarre raving of a madman. Unfortunately, there is always the danger under such circumstances that a person's potential for making a unique contribution may be lost in satisfying the particular orientational reality of the majority of the members of a social group.

Rational Shared Orientations

It is a fortunate occasion when the orientations that correspond to objective reality are shared widely among the members of a social group. Agricultural production, for instance, and basic practices in hygiene and sanitation leading to healthful living are valued by most people. To the extent that society encourages the development of such orientations, it is able to provide an environment that is conducive to the successful attainment of the goals of its members.

Rationality Versus Irrationality

Generally man is considered to be a rational creature who places emphasis primarily on reason as being the basis for his behavior and beliefs. Brinton (1961, pp. 304-313), however, described the following three levels of thinking which indicated that this conclusion may itself be irrational or the result of wishful thinking: (1) undisguised irrationality, (2) irrationality that is expressed through personal feelings, and (3) realistic rationalism.

Frequently the first level of thinking, commonly known as anti-intellectualism, is expressed through opposition to liberally educated groups.

McCarthyism as it developed in the United States, fascism as it flowered in Italy and Germany, and communism as it seems to be evolving in the Soviet Union and Red China, are all social movements that have resulted from the adoption of anti-intellectualism as a way of life. Typical of this type of thinking is Mannheim's (1936, p. 130) description of fascism, as occurring when history is made neither by ideas, nor by the masses or silently working forces, but by elite groups of people who exert themselves at appropriate moments from time to time.

In American society, a great amount of undisguised irrationality is offered in advertising with the expectation that it will increase sales. It has led to what Henry (1963, p. 50) has referred to as the pecuniary pseudo-truth, defined as a false statement made as if it were true, but not intended to be believed. No proof is offered and no one finds it necessary to look for it because the proof is assumed to lie in the fact that it sells merchandise.

Part of the difficulty stems from the fact that it is very easy to accept blindly and go along with whatever information is supplied. There is the additional danger that the person may be taken in by ingenious promises of immediate relief and help with his problems. Frequently, for example, the irrationality of a quack's breezy assurance that all will be well is preferred to the professional person's description of the long uphill battle toward physical and mental health. Quick and easy solutions to the lovelorn at the price of a five cent stamp are much more attractive than the painful experience of self-examination under the guidance of a professional therapist. Similarly, a message which stresses that a person must study and think and discipline himself if he is to achieve rationality and know something of the truth is less appealing than one which declares that all that is necessary is to think positively.

At the second level of thinking, irrationality is expressed through personal feelings, hunches, intuition, etc., all of which are considered to be superior to rational thought. According to Mumford (1961, p. 489), the Romantic Movement was a revolt against rationality because it acknowledged the varieties of human temperament and aspiration; the need for change, contrast, and adventure; and, most important of all, the necessity of an environment that was visibly responsive to the individual's personal efforts.

The highest level of thought, however, is realistic rationalism in which reason, although held to be man's best hope for the future, is admitted freely to have no great strength. In fact, realistic rationalism is likened to a small flickering candle which must be shielded carefully in order to avoid having it blown out by man's passions, masquerading as reason. It is both easier and more flattering to believe that man is sweetly reasonable most of the time and only occasionally unreasonable than it is for him to admit that he is usually irrational and only truly rational in a limited number of situations.

Mumford (1961, p. 51) has pointed out that as the activities of modern man seemingly have become more rational and benign, in actuality they are more irrational and malevolent. Nothing is more rational, for example, than the use of the automobile for transportation; yet, at the same time, nothing is more irrational than the stoic acceptance of the slaughter on the highways of hundreds of thousands of people. As Hebb (1958, p. 16) has pointed out, the capacity for rational thought and behavior may be paralleled by a capacity for living irrationally.

Again according to Mumford (1961, p. 158), this process of contradiction began with the Greeks who overemphasized inner order and abstract perfectionism to the point that the violent, tormented side of life tended to be forgotten. The concept of the baroque, as it shaped itself in the seventeenth century, showed the continuation of the trend. Abstract, mathematical, and methodical characteristics were expressed in rigorous street plans, formal city layouts, and geometrically ordered gardens, but, at the same time, the painting and sculpture of the period embraced the sensuous, rebellious, and anti-classical aspects of life, while people's clothes, sexual life, religious fanaticism, and statecraft, all expressed the irrational elements hidden below the surface.

During such periods as the Enlightenment it was felt that substantial rationality could be nurtured easily and quickly by means of education. Subsequent events in the form of man's inhumanity to man have indicated that the process is not that simple. As Brophy (1962, p. 172) has stated, the educational horses have been taken to the school waters for some time now, but it seems most of them drink very little and some of them will not drink at all. The problem has turned out to be not such a matter of education but of motivating people to really value the torturous search for knowledge.

At the heart of truly rational thought is the ability to detach oneself from the situation so that the person is able to recognize what Whitehead (1929, p. 552) refers to as the real good, instead of the apparent good or the object of appetite. Perhaps an experience of one of the authors while he was living in Haiti may be used to clarify this point. In this generally poverty stricken country, he found himself living in a house and being served by five Haitians whose combined salary was $22.00 per month. From a personal point of view, this situation provided a most satisfying state of affairs. It was not difficult to accept the opportunity of being waited upon by five fellow human beings who responded unquestionably to any expressed wish, at a cost to the author that caused almost no sacrifice of other goods and services. By looking at the situation, however, from a detached point of view, it was possible to see the fallacy in defending the totally unfair social conditions as being abstractly good, simply because they were enjoyable and served to enhance the author's personal welfare.

Scientific Thought as Substantial Reality

At some point in history man began to think for himself instead of conforming to the wishes of people in positions of authority. The right to question was no longer considered heresy but the duty of the educated person. As reasoning became increasingly important, existing orientations were challenged repeatedly. Man's behavior was freed from being governed by subjective wishes and he began to judge customs, habits, laws, and social institutions on the basis of substantial reality or, in other words, in terms of the actual and objective nature of his experience. The motto of the Royal Society of London, for instance, became, "We accept nothing on authority." Subsequently, most men of science have learned to disagree purposefully and to tolerate uncertainty while awaiting further evidence and developments. The emphasis on the scientific method has brought about the realization that truth and objective reality may be found, not through emotional self assertion, but through diverse, careful, and cumulative observations.

Artistic Creation as Substantial Reality

One of the age old functions of art is the creation and communication of a sense of order and meaning. According to Peckham (1962, p. 259) art claims no illusionary authority, "art is 'true' because it is a lie and doesn't pretend to be anything else. Art cannot redeem the world, but it can give the man who looks at the world the experience of value." Not only does the artist pass along possible orientations about experience, but he presents the person viewing his work with the additional opportunity of restructuring old orientations and attending to wider aspects of experience with a fresh approach.

The Differing Realities of Divergent Orientations

Perhaps you will imagine that three men have their own unique way of perceiving life. One of them chooses to look at his environment through a telescope, the second one relies only upon the naked eye, and the third prefers using a microscope. Each man gains sensory impressions that are quite different from those experienced by the others and, consequently, he tends to feel that the world he knows is actually the world of reality and the experiences of the other two men are mistaken and erroneous. If a fourth person, however, is given the opportunity of viewing life, in turn, through a telescope, with the naked eye, and then by means of using a microscope, he would realize quickly that although each picture of the world was very real, it was primarily a function of the method of observation.

Perhaps the analogy may be extended even further by adding the concept of a searchlight which illuminates and brightens some aspect of experience while, at the same time, leaving other events in darkness to remain unnoticed. Thus, for example, due to his medical orientation, a physician may observe certain characteristics in a person's appearance and behavior which would be unrecognized by a sociologist. Similarly, the social scientist would be cognizant of behavior patterns that would never come to the attention of the medical practitioner.

In actuality, people approach life with orientations which are similar to the analogy of the telescope, naked eye, microscope, and searchlight. Each orientation obscures what it does not illuminate and, consequently, restricts a person to dealing with only the limited segment of reality that it brings into focus. Without such orientations, however, people would know absolutely nothing of the world about them and, probably, they could not even manage to stay alive.

Competition Between Orientations

If a person with a telescopic orientation examines the same aspect of the environment as a person with a microscopic viewpoint, the experiences of the two men are obviously going to be very different. They may even become quite upset over discovering that their particular interpretations of reality are not the only ones that exist and that other people are not necessarily willing to agree with them and go along with their positions.

Perhaps a vastly oversimplified illustration may help to clarify the difficulties that are involved. Imagine, for example, that you are watching a football game and on a crucial third-down play, a forward pass falls incomplete as the intended receiver is challenged for the ball by the defensive halfback. In all likelihood, there will be a number of different accounts of what took place. The supporter of the defensive team may feel, for example, that the incompletion was due to the strong but perfectly fair play of the halfback. From the other side of the field, the fan of the offensive team may disagree strongly, claiming that pass interference occurred and the officials were mistaken in not assessing the appropriate penalty. A less biased and more sophisticated spectator may have watched the linemen closely, noting that their performance was actually of primary importance in deciding the outcome of the play. In contrast, a visitor from Europe, accustomed to the spontaneous and almost continuous action of the soccer field, may completely fail to comprehend and appreciate what was taking place before him. In fact, it is quite likely that he would view his first American football game with amazement and bewilderment, wondering perhaps why a game in which kicking a football is so obviously a minor part ever came to be called "football."

As may be seen, observations of what happens at a football game are dependent upon the person's orientation. They vary substantially from one individual to another and, consequently, it is often extremely difficult for people to come to any agreement during the course of a single incident. One possible solution to this problem would be to allow the players, officials, and spectators to vote according to what they have seen. In such a case, of course, the decision of the majority would be considered to be the most accurate description. Another possibility might involve, insofar as possible, the critical and impartial examination of the different versions and the selection of the one which would, overall, be the most beneficial. Other alternatives might include the acceptance of the official's decision as being correct or the recognition of the ability of certain football experts and a willingness to allow them to decide what took place. An even more decisive way of reaching a conclusion would be to permit selected people in the crowd to carry firearms. Very likely, their version would quickly prevail, for when a person looks down the barrel of a gun, he tends to have little difficulty seeing what the person holding the gun has noticed.

It would appear true that throughout history, man has solved the problem of who is right far more frequently with clubs and guns than he has by relying upon the tabulation of votes or the rational comparison of the relative usefulness of the different orientations of mankind. The atomic bomb is perhaps the ultimate weapon for the technique of persuading other people to see reality the same way as the person who threatens to wield the weapon. Unfortunately, by this means, there is always the danger that the struggle over whose reality shall prevail may end in the complete absence of any reality at all.

When a man doubts the validity of his orientation either consciously or unconsciously, he tends not only to defend it strenuously but also if necessary to attack rival and opposing positions. He may become so emotionally involved that the desire to be right takes precedence over the recognition of objective evidence. When a man is in too much of a hurry to make his orientation prevail, the goal of power probably has replaced his search for truth and enlightenment. The divine right of kings, dictatorships, and aristocracies, for example, have all evolved through man's attempts to solve, by means of the expression of power, the problem of whose value system will be followed. On the other hand, when only a few alternatives are available, the violence of one orientation being pitted against another becomes a lot less frequent. Thus, wars are not fought over such questions as "do cows lay eggs," but over issues in which there are several possible directions to move, each possessing some evidence of being the best. If a person has real confidence in his position, however, he will be relatively unconcerned about the existence of an opposing point of view, feeling probably that sooner or later it is destined to fall.

To have it suggested that much of what a person believes may be only an orientation toward reality and not reality itself may be a disturbing experience. To make the mistake, however, of believing that all of one's values are an accurate reflection of reality is to succumb to error throughout life. Perhaps, as a consequence, you may wish to examine critically the nature of your own orientational system and face the question of how much of what you believe is really true and how much of it is an expression of a desire for your ideas to be accepted as being part of the world of objective reality.

SUMMARY

1. An orientation is a picture of the way a person looks at the world.
2. Because of the close relationship between orientations and human behavior, many people find it desirable to hold on tightly to the orientations that have enabled them in the past to adjust to their particular social situations.
3. Orientations are modified by a number of different factors, among which are the person's innate characteristics, his interests and desires, the influence of other people upon his life, the conditions of gratification and deprivation that he has encountered, and his overall experiences and feelings of comfort and familiarity with his surroundings.
4. Orientations vary in terms of their relative congruence with objective reality and the viewpoints of other people.
5. While on the surface it may seem that man has become more rational, in actuality, much of his behavior is an expression of an orientation that is primarily irrational and, consequently, potentially very dangerous.
6. The mark of a rational man is the ability to detach himself from his personal and social experiences and decide upon the behavior that will lead to what is referred to as the "real" good.

7. The differing realities of divergent orientations are somewhat analo-
gous to the sensory impressions that would be gained if a person
were to use his normal vision to look at some segment of life and
then turn to examining it through a microscope and a telescope.

8. If a person is to emerge into his full potentiality as a person, he needs
to be re-evaluating his orientation and searching continuously for
more constructive ways of relating to the contrasting and opposing
viewpoints in the world.

EXERCISE 3

Knowing the Self — Part C

In understanding yourself better, it may help to take a second look from
a somewhat different point of view at the amount of satisfaction or dissatisfaction you have with yourself.

Go through the following statements and check the item or items that
complete the sentence to best describe how you feel, act, or think of yourself. Then in the space to the left of the item, in the column headed "Satisfaction Index," put in the percentage of 0, 25, 50, 75, or 100 that best
expresses your satisfaction with your answer. If you would not change
your answer for anything, give that answer a 100 percent satisfaction rating.
If you would give a great deal if your answer could honestly be different,
give that item a 0 percent satisfaction rating. The remaining percentages
express relatively greater or lesser satisfaction. Since no one will see your
answers but yourself, be as honest as you possibly can.

SATISFACTION
INDEX

_____　　1. I am predominantly

　　　　　　　　　　　_____ past oriented (always looking back).

　　　　　　　　　　　_____ present oriented (always looking at right
　　　　　　　　　　　now).

　　　　　　　　　　　_____ future oriented (always looking ahead).

　　　　　　　　　　　_____ equally past, present, and future oriented.

_____　　2. I am satisfied with

　　　　　　　　　　　_____ my physical competencies.

　　　　　　　　　　　_____ my emotional competencies.

_____ my social competencies.

_____ my intellectual competencies.

_____ all of these.

_____ none of these.

_____ 3. Generally, I am a (an)

_____ open person.

_____ closed person.

_____ 4. Generally, I am a

_____ trusting person.

_____ suspicious person.

_____ 5. Generally, I am a

_____ tense person.

_____ relaxed person.

_____ 6. Generally, I am a (an)

_____ self-directed person.

_____ other-directed person.

_____ 7. Generally, I am a (an)

_____ consistent person.

_____ inconsistent person.

_____ 8. Generally, I am a

_____ joiner.

_____ loner.

_____ 9. Generally, I am a

_____ directive person.

_____ submissive person.

_____ 10. Generally, I make decisions with

_____ certainty.

_____ uncertainty.

_____ 11. Generally, I consider myself to have

_____ little harmony with life.

_____ inner harmony.

_____ harmony with my environment.

_____ 12. Overall, I evaluate myself as

_____ superior.

_____ average.

_____ inferior.

_____ 13. Generally, I tend to think I have a conscience that is

_____ too strong.

_____ too weak.

_____ about right.

_____ 14. Generally, I think of myself as

_____ possessive.

_____ non-possessive.

_____ 15. My interests tend to be

_____ very broad.

_____ typical of others my age.

_____ limited to a few areas.

_____ 16. My moods tend to be

_____ variable.

_____ constant.

_____ 17. In general, in thinking of my physical appearance I am

_____ proud.

_____ content.

_____ ashamed.

_____ 18. In general, I am pretty

_____ integrated within myself.

_____ divided within myself.

_____ 19. In general, failures make me

_____ try harder.

_____ tend to give up.

_____ 20. In general, I find it

_____ easy to make decisions.

_____ neither easy nor hard to make decisions.

_____ hard to make decisions.

_____ 21. In general, I

_____ lack self-control.

_____ have realistic self-control.

_____ have rigid self-control.

——————————— 22. In general, I feel my estimates of other people are

—————— highly accurate.

—————— reasonably accurate.

—————— unreliable.

——————————— 23. When faced with open conflict, I usually

—————— make a direct attack.

—————— withdraw.

Now add all the figures in the Satisfaction Index column and enter the total below.

÷ 23 items =

———————————————   ———————————————

Total of Satisfaction   Your Personal Satisfaction
Index Column   Index

Several general statements can be made concerning possible relationships between this score and motivation for change.

Persons with low satisfaction scores are likely to feel so much dissatisfaction that the prospect for change is overwhelming. If your score is in this range, you might want to work on a single change at a time, avoiding attempts at broad changes.

Persons with fairly high satisfaction scores are likely to be able to handle well planned changes pretty effectively. While sufficiently dissatisfied to want to change some things, they may have sufficient satisfaction to move in the desired direction with a minimum of personal disruption.

Persons with very high satisfaction scores are unlikely to be motivated toward change.

As a second step, go back over your answers to the 23 items, but this time try to imagine that some other person has given these answers. When you have finished, check the statement below that best describes your feeling about this person.

Would you like to —————— meet him?

—————— work with him?

—————— have him for a friend?

—————— have him as a family member?

—————— have only a limited relationship with him?

—————— have nothing to do with him?

How does this way of looking at yourself (as you would look at another) fit with the Satisfaction Index score you obtained? Are the results consistent or contradictory?

As a final step, pretend that a good friend or a member of your family is to check those 23 items as he or she thinks you would check them. Pretend that the person you have selected is taking this test not for himself, but for you. Go back through the items a final time and decide how you think the person close to you would select choices for you. When you have finished, check the results below.

The person close to me would have checked them

_____ very much as I did.

_____ somewhat as I did.

_____ very different from what I did.

How do these results coincide with your previous answers and with your Satisfaction Index? How does it feel to think of yourself as you think others see you? Do those close to you really know you or are you privately different from your public self?

CHAPTER 5

The Physiological Goals

The physiological goals, which have been referred to variously as biogenetic, primary, basic, and unlearned, are considered by Maslow (1954, p. 82) to be "the most prepotent of all needs" because they impose a pressing urgency upon man that requires his immediate attention. According to Becker (1964, p. 28), however, unlike other organisms, man is a "time-binding" animal who has a notion of the past, the present, and the future. Because of this awareness, he is capable of consciously delaying his responses and of calling upon past solutions in order to determine his orientation toward physiological experiences. There is always the danger, however, that the person's orientation will cause him to delay or misrepresent these experiences, thereby making him unable to see them realistically. The person who looks upon himself as non-sexual, non-hostile, or non-loving, for instance, is liable to dismiss or distort the physiological aspects of sex, anger, and love. Unfortunately, many people are caught up in such conflicts and, as a result, have difficulty in determining whether their behavior should be based on the "biological morality" of being what they feel physiologically or the "social morality" of living in terms of what others have told them they should be experiencing.

Figure 4 may be used to illustrate the effects of the relative degree of congruence between the person's physiological experience and his perception of this experience. In the first case, there is a close relationship between what the person actually experiences organically and what he perceives he is experiencing. In the other case, however, the person's orientation causes him to mistake the nature of his organic experience, thereby causing internal conflict. Only when the perception of organic experience is accurate will internal experience be consistent.

The physiological goals may be considered in terms of the following three categories: (1) visceral goals, (2) sexual goals, and (3) cognition, sensory, and motor goals.

Considerable Congruence Between
Organic Experience and Perception

Organic
Experience

Perceived
Organic
Experience

Organic
Experience

Perceived
Organic
Experience

Limited Congruence Between
Organic Experience and Perception

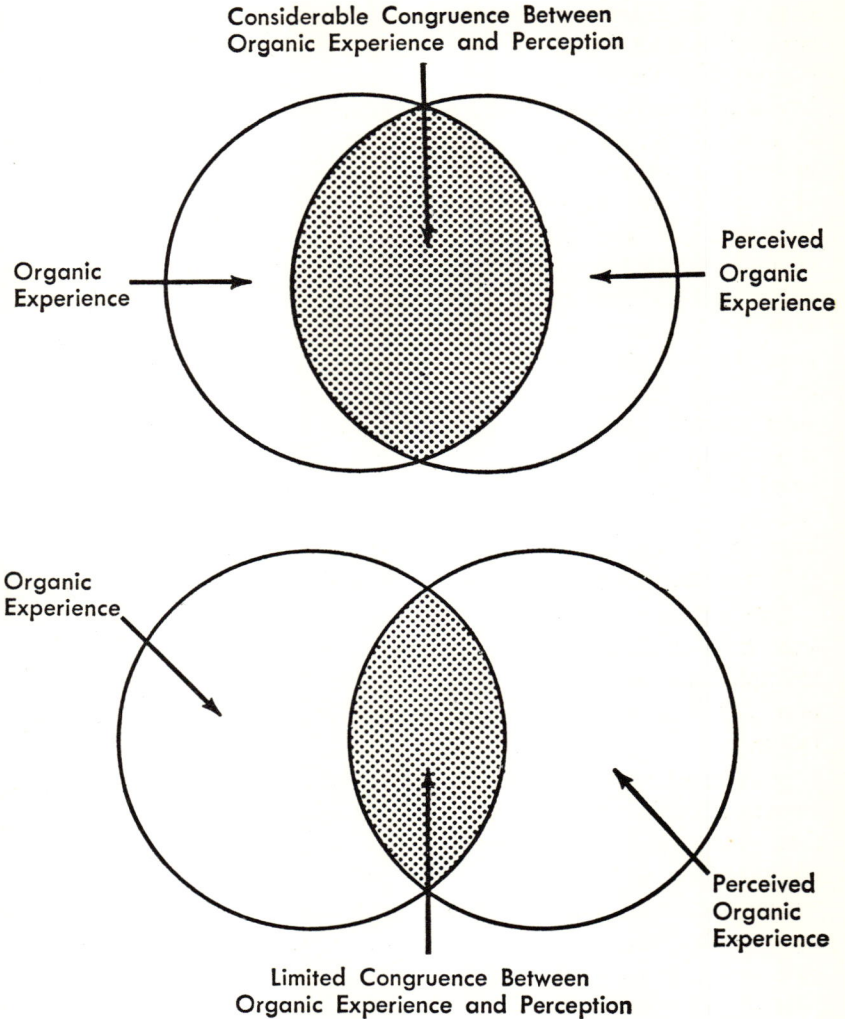

FIGURE 4. Congruence between organic experience and perception.

Visceral Goals

The visceral goals are concerned with the obtaining of food, water, oxygen, and sleep, the elimination of waste matter, the protection of the body, and the avoidance of harm. They are especially important during the early stages of life and in situations where people are living under conditions of severe and prolonged deprivation. In addition, there are also occasions when even the person who is striving to attain the higher goals in the hierarchy finds suddenly that his visceral needs are exerting control over his behavior. As you read this book, for instance, you are interested probably in gaining enlightenment and respect and your behavior is directed toward achieving these goals. If someone were to come up behind you, however, and place a hand over your mouth and nostrils in such a position as to shut off oxygen from your lungs, your main objective of the moment probably would change suddenly and violently. Doubtless you would lose interest in studying, the trappings of civilized behavior would begin to disappear, and you would fight and if necessary kill in order to gain oxygen and stay alive. It would take just a few seconds for the need for air to become absolutely essential. Only after the hand was released, the need for air satisfied, and a recovery made from the shock of the experience would it be possible for you to begin to think once again of studying and allowing the original goals to resume their earlier importance. It is quite possible, moreover, that another person, faced with the same circumstances, would prefer to die without offering resistance and, consequently, would refuse to struggle. In fact, if death were inevitable and if it were important for the person to "die bravely," his orientation could easily cause him to cooperate with his murderer.

The influence of the physiological goals upon human behavior varies from time to time and from situation to situation. Perhaps the following example may help to illustrate how under the appropriate conditions, the need for food may replace the desire for sex as a primary motivating factor.

Soldiers who are stationed at isolated army posts where the company of women is denied them are notorious for the collection of pin-ups of girls that adorn the walls of their dwellings. Conversations about women are often endless and both the soldiers' dreams and their waking moments appear to be dominated by the thoughts of wives, girl friends, and women in general. A group of conscientious objectors during World War II, however, displayed different behavior patterns (Keys et al., 1950). As part of a research project in which they were participating, these men endured severe limitations in the amount of food that they were allowed to consume. In a short time, pictures of food began to appear on the walls of their huts, replacing the shapely girls. Presumably chocolate cake and fried chicken became more exciting than Betty Grable and Linda Darnell. Conversations about food occurred regularly, and both day and night were spent dreaming about different meals that would satisfy their hunger needs.

The interests of the men in the first group understandably revolved around the awareness of the absence of the company of women and the desire for sex. The men in the second group, in contrast, were concerned primarily with the even more pressing problem of easing their hunger pains. Apparently the importance of sex and food in the goal hierarchies of the two groups of men depended upon the nature of their deprivation so that their choices of pictures represented the most vital physiological need that was not being met. It is quite probable, however, that after a few solid meals conscientious objectors would replace the cake pictures with the more customary pin-ups of girls, and that the soldiers, upon returning to a happy marriage in which their sexual goals were met, would choose to place pictures on the walls of their homes that were more closely related to their new interests.

Today in the United States most people rarely encounter any difficulty in satisfying their basic visceral goals. Thus, they are able to turn their attentions toward the achievement of other somewhat higher goals. As a result of these fortunate circumstances, they are able to appreciate a beautiful sunset or find the grandeur of a view from the top of a mountain to be a rich and rewarding experience. For others, visiting an art gallery or listening to the music of Brahms and Beethoven is both intellectually and emotionally satisfying. None of these experiences, however, means much to the starving man who would prefer not to go hungry, or to anyone who is deprived of the opportunity of obtaining the goals that he strives to achieve.

The following analogy is a case in point. The mathematician, J. D. Williams, has likened the earth to a partly flooded cellar, 25 feet by 25 feet, of which only about one fourth of the floor is dry. The American enjoys the use of a 6-foot by 2-foot dry spot. There are 15 other inhabitants of the cellar, all of whom are armed. Two thirds of them are incredibly poor and hungry, but the American has about half of the food and other supplies in the cellar (Wrenn 1962, p. 18).

Unfortunately, people who have been lucky enough not to be restricted in the achievement of their basic goals and in the realization of their potentiality sometimes make the mistake of confusing the abundance of their social situation with their own natural superiority. It is quite likely, however, that if the lives of these people were characterized by deprivation instead of gratification, they would be considerably less poised socially and their behavior would be a great deal more provincial and unsophisticated. Similarly, if the social situations of the deprived persons were changed so that they experienced gratification, it is equally possible that they, in turn, would be highly accomplished and sophisticated.

Very often it is easier to assume that another person's relatively limited accomplishments are caused by his inferior ability or the absence of moral fiber and integrity than to take the trouble to focus attention on the social conditions that have deprived him of the opportunity of attaining the higher goals in the hierarchy. If the man who is hungry is to be helped, he needs to be given food instead of being told that his condition is a result of his own fault. Even more realistically beneficial is the assistance that makes it possible for him to find a way of feeding himself effectively, thus providing him with an opportunity not only to satisfy his hunger but also to gain ir respect for himself.

Sexual Goals

Although people cannot exist very long without air, water, food, sleep, and elimination, it is possible to live without ever knowing sexual fulfillment and gratification. While the potential for sex is present in everyone, sexual desires are subject to individual differences. Thus, in one person the drive may be very strong and in another person it may be relatively weak.

During the early stages of life, the sexual drive is believed to be diffuse and generalized. A study by Spitz and Wolfe (1955, pp. 144-155) of three different groups of infants from one to two years of age indicated the importance of parents accepting the generalized sexual behavior of children. The infants in the first group were raised in an institution for motherless children in which they received adequate physical care but almost no mothering. The ones in the second group were raised also in an institution, but in their cases the parents lived with them. Some of these children received a considerable amount of fondling and attention but the others were ignored by their mothers. The third group was composed of children from homes where the parents showered a great deal of love and affection upon their offspring.

The behavior of all the children was observed at different times over a period of several days. It was found that genital play was almost entirely absent among the unloved group, occurred to some degree in the moderately loved group, and took place frequently among the greatly loved group. Thus, it would seem that the children who were living in a loving interpersonal relationship sought diffuse bodily stimulation at a very early age and that such responses, which presumably are necessary for healthy sexual development, tend to be inhibited when the child is not loved or accepted.

If the child is made fearful of generalized sexual behavior during the early years, there is strong likelihood that sexual development may be arrested. The girl, for instance, who has been told repeatedly that "nice girls do not have sexual desires" may suffer from conflict over the difference between the bodily experience she feels and what she has learned to believe from her parents. Even after marriage, when such feelings become acceptable, it is quite possible that she will still have difficulty in expressing her sexual desires. There is always the possibility, moreover, that inhibiting sexual behavior by means of edicts from parents may make the forbidden fruit more attractive. Frequently, in fact, promiscuous behavior becomes a way of punishing and embarrassing the parent against whom the son or daughter is rebelling.

In more serious cases, the sexual activity may become fixated with immature objects or non-genital organs so that the impulses are expressed toward persons of the same sex, children, animals, articles of clothing, or through such patterns of behavior as stealing, exhibitionism, and inflicting or receiving pain. While at first glance these adjustments may seem to provide at least a partially adequate compromise solution, the energy which is invested in activity that is not a full expression of the heterosexual relationship is usually wasted in terms of its contributing appreciably to the person's further growth and development.

Apparently, socially disapproved forms of sexuality are far more common than generally is supposed. Although reticence about communicating highly personal information obviously causes severe limitations to any study of sexual behavior, the Kinsey Reports (1948 and 1953), which are the most ambitious studies that have yet been undertaken, indicate clearly that there is considerable discrepancy in American society between sexual behavior and sexual ideals.

Psychiatrists and psychologists have devoted attention to the sexual factor in human behavior to the point that sometimes they have been accused of possessing a morbid curiosity over these matters. In America, as is the case with a number of other societies, the sexual need is considered to be one which requires special control, and it is, therefore, much more subject to being thwarted and frustrated than, for example, the desire for food which can be satisfied relatively easily. Problems undoubtedly are created by the postponement of marriage and the necessity of young people, who are physically and emotionally ready to express their sexual desires, doing without the accepted institutional outlet for sexual gratification. In fact, whenever a physiological need that is experienced by all people is subject to possible curtailment, conflict, and misunderstanding, then inevitably the stage is set for some troubled behavior.

Among the realistically unpleasant consequences of non-approved sexual behavior is the obvious danger of disease and pregnancy. While both can be minimized, the fact remains that they do occur. The lives of thousands of couples have been blighted by the unwanted pregnancy they thought could never happen to them. Probably a great deal more important in the overall sense, however, is the subtle psychological damage that results from the internal conflict and guilt caused by acting in ways which are inconsistent with the ideals a person has been taught to follow. Many young people and so-called moderns still feel that sex is bad, although outwardly they may claim to believe just the opposite. The unconscious conflicts which result are expressed sometimes through the use of language, wherein the worst insult one person can direct toward another has a sexual connotation. In much the same manner, many of the pointless and often ugly "dirty jokes" are also symptomatic of conflict in the acceptance of sexual behavior.

The standards that society imposes, however, cannot be dismissed lightly. Sex before a person is ready for it and without the support of the culture is like any other experience that comes too soon in the developmental sequence. Instead of facilitating continued growth and development, it leads to a fixation and the increased need for defensive behavior. While the complete life includes rich and rewarding sexual experiences, blatant rebellion in which sex is seen as being worth the price of the most severe conflict with society ends inevitably in tragedy.

Probably one of the best safeguards against the distortion of the sexual impulse is the encouragement of a realistic acceptance of sex as a natural part of life. Classes in marriage and family life and in sex education have helped to develop more sensitive attitudes toward sexual activity and have led to a greater awareness of the necessity of making sexual decisions in terms of whether or not the people involved are willing to live with the consequences of their behavior.

In the judgment of the authors, some orientations have included straight-laced views that have been strongly opposed to sexual behavior. Other viewpoints have over-emphasized sex to the point that it seems to be the only thing in life that matters. Both positions, however, are distortions of the more healthy attitude which accepts sex as a joyous part of living, expressed most creatively under conditions that lead to the reduction instead of the increase of conflict with society.

Cognitive, Sensory, and Motor Goals

As in the case of the person who is denied the opportunity for full sexual expression, it is quite possible for an individual to live adequately without ever experiencing complete cognitive, sensory, or motor satisfaction. Because these goals are not readily apparent, there is a tendency to minimize the fact that as a thinking, sensing, and acting creature, it is essential for man to be engaged to some extent in exciting activity.

The necessity for such experiences may be seen even at the animal level. According to Nissen (1931), rats crossed an electrified grid for the sole purpose of exploring a new maze. Harlow and others (1950) found that monkeys needed no reward to induce them to manipulate mechanical puzzles. Schiller (1957) noted, furthermore, that when he allowed adult chimpanzees to play with two sticks, 19 out of 20 of them succeeded in joining the sticks within a period of 15 minutes.

A number of studies have been carried out as well on the stimuli which arouse the curiosity of human beings. Berlyne (1960) seated people in a dark room before a tachistoscope, an apparatus in which visual stimuli are flashed before the subject's eyes. He found that the characteristics of incongruity, complexity, surprise and irregularity in the stimulus figures were the most effective for maintaining the interest and curiosity of the subjects.

Anyone who has reared a child will testify to the existence of a curiosity which causes him to be exploring new situations constantly and asking questions about whatever he does not understand. Children appear to need to know, not necessarily for a purpose, but simply just to know. Cattell (1957, p. 516) found a want he called "exploration" which varied with different individuals. As a result of his tests, he felt that curiosity and the need for exploration were evidenced by the desire to read books, newspapers, and magazines, to see films and plays, to study paintings and sculpture, to listen to music, to know more about science, to learn about mechanical and electrical gadgets, and to satisfy curiosity about neighborhood affairs.

Among his list of basic physiological needs, Murray (1938, pp. 77-78) included sentience which appears to correspond to the motives of curiosity, sensuous stimulation, and gratification. One of the means of satisfying this desire is through seeking excitement and adventure. As Russell pointed out, savages value gifts of intoxicating liquors more than anything else they are offered (Egner and Denonn, 1961, p. 472). Apparently the break from a routine existence is welcomed universally. In many cultures, gambling exists despite attempts to abolish it. Children ride merry-go-rounds and roller coasters while grown men race cars and climb mountains. Talese (1963) described the experiences of five men: Manolete, the matadore; Stirling Moss, the race car driver; George Leigh-Mallory, the mountain climber; Toni Mott, the skier; and Jimmy Doolittle, the flier, all of whom took tremendous chances to "experience the ecstasy of cheating death."

Sometimes the need for excitement has been considered to be of questionable value in that it seems to accomplish little of constructive nature. Perhaps it may be understood more easily, however, if it is seen as motivated by a physiological need for increasing stimulation. The possibility that the desire for dangerous excitement may be quite common is supported by the fact that many men march off to war with greater enthusiasm than might be anticipated. It is interesting, moreover, to note the excitement that is generated when ex-servicemen reminisce about their war-time experiences. More recently, a number of people lived more stimulating lives during the dangerous days when the United States and the Soviet Union confronted each other over the missile crisis in Cuba. Perhaps this need for excitement may be used to explain also why some people prefer to live on the brink of nuclear extinction rather than turn to the international exchange of ideas and the rational compromise of views and policies in an attempt to avoid the possibility of world disaster.

The need to escape from boredom is similarly a physiological goal. A study by Bexton, Huron, and Scott (1954) indicated that college students, who were paid to lie on a bed under conditions of severely reduced environmental stimulation, quickly expressed a strong desire for some relief from the situation. Hebb (1955) stated that they displayed such a strong need for help in combating the boredom that they even asked to read a pamphlet on the dangers of alcohol, written for six-year-old children, from fifteen to twenty times during the course of a 30-hour period. Other students were offered a recording of an old stock market report and repeatedly requested that it be given to them.

Frequently, people go to almost extreme lengths in order to escape the boredom that they feel. A number of husbands and wives, for instance, quarrel for no other reason than to break the dull routine of their invariable and unchanging lives; other people only find themselves becoming vivacious and stimulating when they are faced with the necessity of finding solutions to different and unusual problems that challenge their abilities. As a result it is suggested that you consider very seriously attempting to find the time and the financial resources for taking vacations, holidays, and trips and for participating in other activities that are helpful in counteracting the routine nature of many of the tasks involved in daily living.

SUMMARY

1. Although on occasion the attainment of certain physiological goals may become the most urgent of man's needs, in most situations he is able to decide for himself under what conditions the goals will be achieved.

2. The degree of importance of the various physiological goals changes from time to time, depending upon the person's life experiences.

3. Many people are able to live quite adequate and creative lives without ever experiencing the satisfaction of achieving the full expression of their physiological needs.

4. The circumstances under which many persons are forced to exist make it necessary for them to be concerned primarily with finding ways of satisfying their most basic needs.

5. Sexual activity is expressed most creatively in relationships that do not arouse guilt or embarrassment or create conflict between a person's desires and the expectations of society.

6. The desire to escape boredom and find excitement in extreme form is combated most effectively by making sure that a person's life situation contains some novel elements and a number of stimulating challenges to his abilities.

EXERCISE 4

Building Interpersonal Intimacy

Following is the description of a series of assumptions about the growth and development of intimate versus alienated human relationships. No one can know for certain whether these assumptions are generally true or false. You should, therefore, examine them and decide if they apply to your life. If you decide they would be inappropriate for you, you might want to spell out the assumptions you are making about how these contradictory relationships are created.

Assumption 1—The cycle leading to loving, meaningful relationships begins with *risk*. This means each party in a relationship takes a certain amount of chance by revealing something about himself. Thus each knows something about the other and is known. Each exists for the other in some degree of his personal uniqueness. On the one hand, this does not mean indiscriminately "spilling your guts" and immediate revelation of intimate things about the self. On the other, it does mean going beyond talk about the weather, last night's TV show, or classes you are taking. It is different from small talk.

Some of the flavor of the meaning of interpersonal risk may be brought about if I share with you the fact that my oldest son is a retarded child. Perhaps through possession of this personal information about me I am not just another writer, but a little more human to you. I also run some risk in that some might feel this is inappropriate information to include here. In like manner the professor who allows you to express yourself in class or to select your own reading material is taking a risk. The employer who assigns you a more responsible task than ordinary is also taking a risk. Any person who really listens to another runs the risk of being convinced of some alternative and thereby needing to change himself.

Assumption 2—When we risk, we communicate on a meaningful and accurate level. The risk taker describes something about himself. If the other reciprocates, part of him is described. The two have communicated in terms of "I am like this or that." In contrast to the indisputable fact that it is raining or sunny today, meaning has been given to each. To own shyness, sensitivity, or any personal quality is to communicate about the self in a revealing way. The mask we sometimes wear to hide ourselves has been temporarily discarded.

Assumption 3—When we communicate, we *share*. We have overlapped or interpenetrated. The communication has temporarily brought us a little closer together or, conversely, temporarily driven us a little further apart. We are not blandly neutral to one another. In either direction we are not replaceable by any other. Through risk and communication our uniqueness is known and shared, and the emptiness of polished conformity is avoided.

Assumption 4—As we risk, communicate, and share, mutual *trust* is engendered. I know where you are. You know where I am. Since trust is present, each can now risk a little more self-revelation. The excitement of growing intimacy prevails in the relationship. Each partner experiences the intrinsic joy of knowing, being known, caring and being cared for, of being recognized and responded to for what he really is. Moreover, it is generally true that as you experience more of the other you find it possible to experience more of yourself. The experience of trust replaces the cynicism of interpersonal suspicion.

The total cycle beginning with risk is as follows:

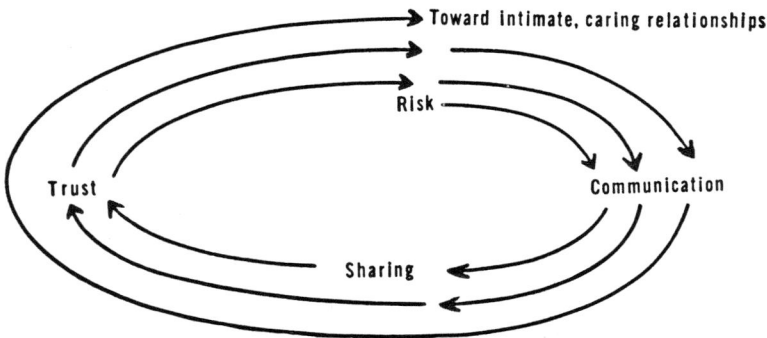

Unfortunately, just as there is a cycle of loving relationships, there is also one of alienation. It moves in the opposite direction as follows:

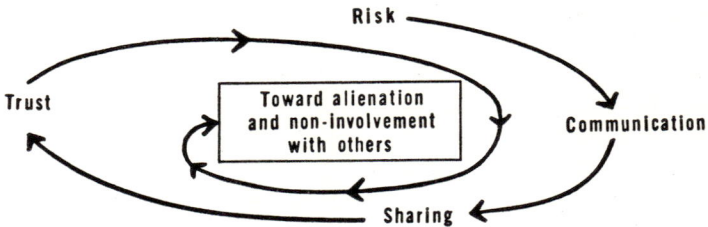

The cycle begins with the existence of another person toward whom it is felt "If this other should know me as I am, he will reject me." It also begins with disinterest in the other. In communication, sharing and trust are impaired. Following this, even less risk can be taken and the relationship becomes shallow and superficial. In my opinion, many marriages founder in just this manner. Each partner assumes he will be rejected if he reveals himself as he really is. The cycle of alienation is launched between them. After several years together, the couple literally has nothing meaningful to say to one another. One mask lives with another on a diet of superficiality. The cycle likewise describes many relationships between parents and young people where neither person dares present himself as he really is. Non-sharing of the essential self leaves him with the weather and other neutral, non-emotional subjects which are insufficient fare to sustain interpersonal involvement. In the attempt to be overly safe he has neutralized himself. Parents try to present themselves as they think a good parent should be. Young people try to present themselves as they think good sons and daughters should be. The result? Nobody knows anyone and alienation from those supposedly closest to you is experienced.

The classroom is often the epitome of such relationships. The teacher functions without risk. The student does likewise. Meaninglessness is interrupted by the bell and all escape happily from their non-involvement.

Taking risk by the expression of affection is one of the hardest things for many of us to do. Telling others that you like the way they look, act, or express themselves makes us too vulnerable. We may be rejected. We may be accused of false flattery. The compliment may not be reciprocated. The other side of this coin is equally difficult. Telling the other of your negative response involves obvious risk. Usually, we avoid the person instead, somehow assuming this will cause less hurt. Avoiding and ignoring are thought to be better than telling. Incidentally, in this way the person gets no information about what has interrupted the relationship. Too often we live in little insulated boxes from which neither positive nor negative responses are forthcoming.

Remember that in the beginning these ideas were presented as guesses which might or might not be accurate. To help assess their validity for you, try to remember the nature of particularly warm and satisfying human relationships you have experienced. Did they grow in the way that has been suggested here or in some other way? Try also to recall other relationships that rather quickly went sour—that ended in mutual alienation. Try to draw accurate generalizations from these experiences. In the light of these thoughts, list in the following space some of the conditions which you believe help foster intimate (as opposed to shallow) relationships.

_____

_____

_____

_____

CHAPTER 6

Love, Belongingness, and Psychological Safety

As long as man's physiological needs are being satisfied, he is in a position of being able to turn toward the achievement of other goals and objectives. The ones which are next in order of importance, according to Maslow (1954, p. 2), are the need for safety and the desire for love and affection. In the context of this book, however, safety is a function of the amount of love that a person has received and his feeling of belongingness, and it is not the physical necessity of protecting the body from injury and harm, which was discussed under the visceral goals in the previous chapter. As a result, love, belongingness, and psychological safety have been combined to form the third level of the hierarchy.

The Meaning of Love

Because it is the main influence in determining a person's feelings of psychological safety, the concept of love needs to be clarified very carefully. There exist many meanings of love but, in the context of this book, love is considered to be expressed through behavior which aids and allows the persons involved in a relationship to achieve the goals that are important to each one of them. Such a pattern of behavior has been described by Sullivan (1947, p. 143) as occurring, "when the satisfactions and security of the loved one are as significant to one as one's own satisfactions and security."

Many people believe that they are expressing love when, in actuality, they are providing just the opposite in the form of a destructive and hating relationship. The parent, for example, who spoils the child, and even makes sacrifices in order to give him everything he wishes, is failing to love in a complete sense because he is unwilling to allow the child to move toward the personal achievement of his own goals. Although the parent unquestionably is meeting the child's physical needs, the fact that he withholds the interest, attention, and companionship that is so important to the child is an indication that there is an absence of real love in the relationship. In a similar manner, the parent who consistently denies his child "for his own good" or, in order to satisfy a personal need for power, insists that his child direct himself toward goals which are not of his own choosing is also failing to provide a relationship that is characterized by love.

Instead of being forced to conform in such a way to another person's expectation, it is much more helpful for the individual to be prized as a total being, irrespective of whether he possesses some specific and distinctive characteristic or is moving toward what is considered by other people to be a particularly desirable goal. Some children, for instance, are loved regardless of whether or not they perform outstandingly well in the classroom. Other students, however, are loved only as long as they are academically successful and are rejected as soon as they fail to maintain the expected high standard of achievement. As a result, to love, and thereby create in the other person a feeling of psychological safety, requires the acceptance of the other person no matter what his behavior may entail, and the minimizing of pressures which force him to conform to the expectations of the people with whom he is interacting.

A person does not acquire this ability to be accepting very easily and probably no one ever achieves it completely. It should not be confused, however, with the more passive attitudes of tolerance and indifference, for even the most accepting person is quite unwilling to allow his child to play baseball in a busy thoroughfare or handle a loaded revolver. On the other hand, the accepting parent does not insist that his child wear black socks when the white ones the child would prefer to have will do equally as well. Whereas stopping the child from playing in the street is an expression of love, inasmuch as it protects his ability to achieve eventually the goals that are important to him, forbidding him from wearing the socks of his choice is not, for it deprives him of the opportunity of assuming responsibility for his behavior on a level at which he is capable of making a sensible decision.

Thus, in the relationship characterized by love, if he so wishes, a person is free to be different from the people around him. The child of the business man may choose to become a poet and the son of a poet is free to follow a career in business. The person who is loved on such a level has no question but that he is seen as a person of importance and worth. As a result, he learns to believe in and trust his own powers of determination and he is able to function in the manner of an autonomous and well-integrated person.

Varieties of Love

MOTHERLY LOVE

Motherly love is the expression of care for the helpless in which the gratification of the child's needs is as important as the personal satisfaction of the mother. Because the child is unable to reciprocate the mother's love fully, it does not always appear as if the relationship provides sufficient gratification for the mother. Children do provide satisfaction for their mothers, however, or otherwise they are unloved. When the mother's goals fit the idealized pattern of care and concern for the child's welfare, and when the behavior of the child is consistent with the mother's picture of what he should be and how he should behave, then the mother's need for belongingness and her desire to achieve skill and respect are met, and all is well.

Many mothers have goals which are in conflict with the taking care of children, and consequently, the unending demands for attention which are placed upon them become a source of frustration and non-gratification. In such cases, the mother may hate the child, consciously or unconsciously, and either reject him directly or express her destructive feelings through over-protection, demands for perfection, or through a variety of approaches designed to cause him to conform to her wishes.

When the mother is more comfortable with her role, however, she feels adequate enough to at least allow the child the opportunity to be partially himself and still enjoy a relationship of love and affection with her. Undoubtedly, the greatest test of the truly loving mother is her ability to let go so that the child can move away from her into an expanding environment, safe in the knowledge that there will be no loss of love as the opportunities for providing the mother with direct and personal gratification become less and less.

SELF-LOVE

Many writers have stressed the fact that a person must love himself before he can love other people. While this statement is unquestionably true, the person must be loved first of all by someone else before he can love himself and, in turn, love other people. The ideal cycle, then, is one of receiving gratification from others, finding gratification through the efforts of the self, and finally experiencing gratification through the ability to satisfy the needs of other people.

It is perhaps only too obvious that many people do not love themselves because frequently they behave in a way which inevitably leads to dissatisfaction and frustration. The student, for example, who does not love or respect himself, may find that, although he realizes the importance of doing well academically, he just cannot seem to settle down to studying. He has difficulty passing his courses and, consequently, he is in danger of "flunking out" of college, and thereby defeating his dearest plans for the future.

BROTHERLY LOVE

Brotherly love is that rare state of constructive behavior that leads ultimately to the emergence of a selfless morality that is found only in people who are living at Well-Being Level II. Menninger (1963, pp. 294-295) stated that to live is to love and persons will strive continuously to find and touch persons and things through work and play. The individual concerned with loving in a truly brotherly sense seeks to embrace strangers, foreigners, and, in fact, all others, none of whom has necessarily gratified him directly in any way. His ability to love has escaped the limitation of being restricted only to those persons who either have already proved to be of value to him or who hold the possibility of being able to help sometime in the future. In fact, he even loves the people who may have frustrated him and reaches out continually with the care, respect, responsibility, and knowledge that Fromm (1956, p. 60) emphasized as being the essential aspects of love. He offers a giving and then a receiving hand, even in casual meetings with strangers, with an air of spontaneity that ensures that his social interactions represent the very essence of living.

MYSTICAL LOVE

The mystical view of love is so removed from the everyday physical world that sometimes it is easier for people to think in terms of such a transcendental view of love instead of expressing their love through behavior which leads to the gratification of a member of a family, a friend, or a neighbor. Such an emphasis on mystical love is unlikely to be satisfying, however, because it is only through the establishment of meaningful relationships with fellow human beings, and the reconciliation of the difficulties which inevitably occur, that the religious person is able to find an expression of love and life that is complete.

The church has a unique opportunity for developing this kind of love for, as Howe (1961, p. 27) pointed out, "the mission of the church is to participate in the reconciling dialogue between God and man." Recently Bishop Robinson (1965) has stressed the necessity for the church to offer man, through the provision of an accepting community, an opportunity for finding a gracious neighbor. Unfortunately, there are many indications that the church is failing in this capacity. The excessive concern with outward appearances, as expressed through the building of impressive edifices and heavy emphasis upon the importance of increasing the sizes of congregations, has caused many deeply committed Christians to be highly critical of what is happening within the framework of the organized church.

LOVE OF AESTHETICS, NATURE, AND OBJECTS

The emotion of love may be generalized and extended to a love of music, art, certain geographical locales, nature, animals, and, in fact, to a whole range of emotional experiences and objects. While not an expression of love in the complete sense, these healthy extensions of human love provide feelings and experiences which enrich life. In extreme form, they make up for the absence of human love and as such provide a trustworthy indication of a person who is not sure of himself in personal relationships. Some persons, for instance, seem to lavish more care and attention on their cars than upon the significant people in their lives. The phenomenon of transferring love to something else is seen even more clearly, however, in the cases of exaggerated love for animals. Frustrated in their attempts to love and be loved by their fellow men, a few people seek to find the satiation of their need for love through relationships with lower and non-human organisms. The undemanding dog, cat, or bird with its uncritical response provides a safe relationship for such emotionally damaged persons. Unfortunately, such attachments are always developed at the expense of the potential for finding a richer and more rewarding form of love. In America, millions of dollars are spent for dog food and yet hungry children are still to be found. Hospitals for animals are maintained in cities where children go without medical attention, and poodles receive haircuts and coats that are more expensive, elaborate, and decorative than those that most persons consider necessary for human beings.

LOVE OF ORGANIZATIONS

Another perversion of human love is found sometimes in an attachment to organizations. Persons come to hold stronger positive emotional feelings for the nation, state, corporation, fraternity, or sorority than they have for the people within these organizations. As Dunham (1964, p. 170) pointed out, "In proportion as the whole body is cherished, the individual member is suspect of fault." Only too often members of fraternities, sororities, and other groups are treated with indifference and even hostility because their behavior does not conform rigidly to the "image" and expectation of a particular organizational group. Even more tragic than the love of organizations is the fact that a large number of business and professional men express greater care and concern for their occupations than they do for the members of their families.

PERSONAL EXPRESSON OF LOVE

If you find that your need for love is not being satisfied, you might consider trying to direct your behavior toward providing more gratification for the persons with whom you come in contact. You could begin, for instance, by attempting to understand the nature of the goals that are important to your friends and associates. By being prepared to help them achieve their goals without necessarily receiving any recognition or affection in return, you will find that you have taken a course in life that is very difficult to follow. You may find also, however, that your need for love is met with a suddenness that is overwhelming and almost miraculous.

Belongingness

A person's sense of belongingness is increased when he is recognized as being a competent and important member of the social groups in which he participates. The positive attitudes, for instance, that the members of a person's family display toward him help to increase the person's feelings of self-esteem. As a result, he has the advantage of knowing that there is a secure home base where he belongs and to which he can turn without hesitation should it ever become necessary. In a similar manner, a teacher may help his students feel that they belong in the classroom by calling them individually by name, encouraging their participation in class activities, and recognizing their ability to make important contributions to the progress of the class.

The Ego

The ego, which is seen as being synonymous with such terms as self, identity, self-esteem, is influenced greatly by the connection between love, belongingness, and psychological safety and the individual's orientational congruence with the objective reality of the outside world. Following birth, a person begins to experience relatively constructive or destructive interpersonal relationships, finding himself to some extent being loved or not loved, and he comes to see himself as belonging in terms of the degree of interest that is shown toward him by other people. At the same time, he is able to examine his orientation in terms of its relative congruence with the viewpoints of the persons with whom he comes in contact in the day-by-day experiences of living.

Psychological Safety and Ego Development

During the early months of life, the newborn infant enjoys ideally a state of effortless pleasure and gratification. Because he is totally dependent upon his parents, both physiologically and emotionally, the slightest suspicion that he may be losing their support is liable to bring out feelings of unsafety and anxiety. In order for these feelings to be held at a minimum, it becomes essential that the child be reassured continuously that his parents love him and are concerned over what happens to him.

Evidence to support the hypothesis of the importance of the relationship of love and belongingness and feelings of psychological safety may be found in some experiments reported by Harlow and Zimmerman (1958) in which rhesus monkeys were removed from their mothers immediately after birth and provided with surrogates or mother substitutes consisting of wooden frames, similar to bird cages in shape, covered with terry cloth and sponge rubber, and wire frames of similar size. Half the monkeys were able to obtain milk from the cloth mothers and half from the wire mothers. After a while, the monkeys preferred having contact with the cloth mother over receiving food from the wire mother and when they were frightened, moreover, they sought the cloth mother constantly, regardless of whether or not they received food from her.

After the monkeys were half grown, they were placed in a room full of a variety of objects. When the cloth mother substitute was present in the room, the monkeys felt free to roam around returning to the mother for love and affection before venturing off to explore some other object. When the mother substitute was not present, however, the monkeys would either freeze in a crouched position or go to the mother's usual place and, upon not finding her, run around the room crying and screaming. It was evidently necessary for the monkeys to receive affection from the substitute mother before they could feel safe enough to explore new objects and situations.

In a study of 600 infants, Ribble (1943) found that when they were loved and mothered they grew in the expected manner. When the children had only their physiological needs met, however, without being fondled and caressed, they developed illnesses and even tended to wither away and become smaller.

Numerous studies were conducted during World War II with children in England. Generally, it was found that the ones who remained with their families in London during the blitz were better adjusted, despite the physical danger of the bombing to which they were exposed, than the children who were evacuated to the quieter and more peaceful areas of the country. Apparently, because the close and affectionate ties with their parents were maintained, the children in the large cities tended to be more sure of themselves than those who were exposed to living in a strange and different environment with people who, in many cases, cared little, if anything at all, for them (Freud and Burlingham, 1943).

Becker (1962, p. 37) pointed out that because of a child's need for love, even under ideal conditions, he must, to some extent, "banish everything from his awareness that does not please the parent." As a consequence, he learns to attend primarily to what the important people in his life expect of him. If these demands and expectations become too severe, however, the child is forced to deny a great deal of his own experience in order to make sure that life proceeds smoothly and that he does not lose the parents' love.

It is important to note that psychological safety is necessary for the adult as well as the child. Kluckhohn and Leighton (1958, pp. 224-227), for example, have described the Navaho Indians' overwhelming preoccupation with the uncertainties of life and their concern with the many threats to their personal safety. The following five formulas for ensuring security have dominated the behavior of the Navaho, and they would seem also to have value in an examination of the concerns for safety of Americans:

1. Maintain orderliness in those sectors of life which are little subject to human control. Perhaps this attitude is not such a far cry from the American way of life. Some teachers make a practice, for example, of never requiring a particular seating arrangement in their classes. Students are free to sit wherever they wish and change seats should the occasion warrant it. Invariably, however, the students prefer to retain the same seats throughout the semester and frequently they react with hostility and annoyance when something occurs which forces them to move from their accustomed location.

2. Be wary of non-relatives. Many people regard strangers, foreigners, and persons who are "different" with a great deal of mistrust. Kluckhohn and Leighton emphasized the differences between legal theory and the actual practices in personal relations of too many American citizens, symbolically expressed through labels like "wops" and "greasers," and by Jim Crow laws and lynchings. They pointed out that the contrast constituted one of the severest strains undermining the equilibrium of the American social system.

3. Avoid excess. For many years, a great deal of emphasis in American society has been placed upon the importance of being average and like everybody else. To do anything to excess has been akin to committing a crime, but the same behavior in moderation was perfectly acceptable. Slichter (1956) noted changes in economic and social conditions which have encouraged the growing demand for moderation. Moreover, the negative attitudes which have been expressed by many people toward the extremely intelligent person, particularly before the Russians sent up the first Sputnik, supported the general belief that to be of average ability was more desirable. In actuality, the stereotyped view of the bright person being a sickly, non-social bookworm is not correct. Terman (1954) has indicated that the gifted are not only brighter, but healthier, more athletic, better adjusted socially, and generally superior in every way.

4. When in a new and dangerous situation, do nothing. The growing tendency for this occurrence to take place in American life may be illustrated by a frightening incident, described in the *New York Times* on March 27, 1964, which took place in Queens, a suburb of New York. For more than half an hour, thirty-eight respectable law-abiding citizens watched a man stalk and stab Catherine Genovese in three separate attacks. Twice the killer was frightened off but when no one telephoned the police, he returned to continue the assault. Finally, after the woman was dead, some one hesitatingly called the police. When asked why they had not done so sooner, most people responded by saying that they "didn't want to get involved."

5. Escape. A number of critics of the American scene have seen Americans as being overly concerned with using entertainment as a means of escape. Barzun (1954, p. 155), for instance, noted that people want recreation, refreshment, and reverberation after they leave work. Generally, the heavy emphasis on athletics, movies, television, and the excessive use of alcohol all may be interpreted as indications of ways of escaping from life situations.

An example of the influence of psychological safety upon behavior which is more closely related to an understanding of American life may be found in the experiences of American soldiers who were subjected during the Korean War to the psychological process that has become known as brainwashing. For instance, a soldier who is a prisoner of war and an inveterate smoker discovers that if he informs on his friends, he will be given the cigarettes he desires so much. At first, the idea is unthinkable and then later he finds out that he can inform his captors of inconsequential matters and still receive cigarettes. Furthermore, nothing will be done to the soldier on whom he informs, except that the offender will be given a ridiculous little talk in which the error of his ways is pointed out. One day the soldier sees a friend throw a piece of paper on the floor and he informs on him. He receives his cigarettes and his friend is given a lecture. Others begin to inform on their friends and very quickly the soldiers become increasingly suspicious of the men around them and rapidly reach the point of not trusting one another at all. The disintegration in the relationships is increased by some of the soldiers confessing publicly to a series of misdemeanors and in that way gaining additional favors and benefits.

A study by Lifton (1960) of the psychiatric aspects of thought reform disclosed that the same techniques are being used upon the Chinese citizenry with similar results. People are isolated from their fellow men and, after living without love, they will seek to belong or to be safe through whatever relationships and behavior are available to them, thus making it possible to shape their behavior in any prescribed direction.

A person's need for love and belongingness is continuous and, consequently, the affection and support that was received in the early years of childhood is not sufficient to sustain the person indefinitely without the continuation of love in the adult years. When the person is given love regularly, however, he is able to move into new and personally satisfying relationships. Because he was treasured as a child, he respects himself and, in turn, values other people for themselves and not merely as a means of satisfying his need for companionship. He feels psychologically safe and, consequently, he is free to both give and receive love and acceptance in his relationships with other persons.

Orientational Congruence and Ego Development

In addition to being influenced by the amount of love that a person receives, ego strength is increased to the extent that the orientation that a person learns from his family corresponds with the experiences he encounters at other times during his life. Even under the most optimum of conditions, however, an orientation can provide only an idiosyncratic and selected view of reality, stemming entirely from a chance occurrence of time and place. To the child, and often to the adult as well, the particular frame of reference that a person possesses is seen as being the only one that could possibly exist. Because his viewpoint serves to make manageable the world in which the person lives, it provides a feeling of comfort and security. The person is able to discriminate about human behavior to the point that he can predict with reasonable accuracy that if he behaves in a certain way, a particular result will follow. As described in Chapter 4, this sense of security is threatened, however, when he is exposed to different and sometimes dangerous and alien orientations which challenge the correctness and appropriateness of his position.

Whenever a person decides to move to another environment, he is forced to rely on his anticipated picture of what the new social situation will be like. While this expectation of reality may eventually prove to be far from accurate, it is at the time the only basis the person has for his behavior. As he relates to the people in the new social group in terms of his own particular orientation, the newcomer may find himself questioning what is indisputable to most of the persons he meets. To a large extent, he finds their behavior as consisting of a series of "typical solutions to typical problems of typical actors." When he challenges or disagrees with their views, he is subjected to reprimand, rejection, and even ridicule and, consequently, it becomes increasingly difficult for him to modify his orientation. Only when the threat to his safety has been removed is he able to make whatever adjustments are necessary for socializing freely with the people in the new environment.

The history of first generation immigrants to America testifies to the severity of such an adjustment. The person learns in the home an orientation which was appropriate in the old country but which is inadequate for living amid the conflicting orientations of modern America. The difficulty he encounters may be seen particularly in the high rate of crime and lack of economic success that is characteristic of the members of each minority group during the early years of their living in the United States.

To modify any kind of "thinking-as-usual" to correspond to another person's "thinking-as-usual" places great demands upon the individual's ego strength. Even the person who is loved despite the fact that he chooses a different orientation from his parents, and who, consequently, probably possesses a great deal of ego strength, is likely to have his confidence dissipated by the struggle to function in an environment in which his actions and consequences of his behavior are not acceptable.

Some people find this struggle too severe and return to their old and familiar environment, thus causing the opportunity for the expansion of their world to be lost. Other people carry the old environment to the new social situation. On a college campus, for instance, a country boy may adjust to his new circumstances by restricting his relationships to a group similar to himself. On a global scale, little bits of England are found to exist even in the most unlikely places in the world. Afternoon tea and formal attire for dinner in the tropics attest to the Englishman's unwillingness to modify his "thinking-as-usual." The more dominant person may even attempt to use whatever power and prestige he possesses to impose his orientation upon the people in the new environment. In such countries as India and South Africa, for example, the influence of the British way of life is readily noticeable even today. Less dramatic than the cases described above, but of far greater importance, are the influences listed below which cause the person to re-evaluate and where necessary modify his orientation:

Mother	Community
Father	State
Immediate Family Members	Nation
Neighborhood	World
Church	Universe
School	

Interrelationship of Psychological Safety and Orientational Congruence Upon Ego Development

As indicated in Figure 5, when a person (A) feels psychologically safe because he knows that he is loved and that he belongs and there is a high degree of congruence between his orientation and the reality that he encounters in living, he is able to move freely toward the achievement of a wide variety of goals. He learns to cope relatively easily and comfortably with a changing, expanding, and increasingly demanding world and, although he may not agree with or like all that he encounters, he becomes increasingly confident of his ability to respond effectively in many different social situations. His self concept becomes more positive and altogether he enjoys the high level of well-being that is characteristic of the emerging self.

When a person (B) feels psychologically safe, however, but lacks orientational congruence with objective reality and the beliefs of other people, he is liable to experience severe conflicts and some painful disappointments. Due to his feelings of psychological safety, his capacity for change and new learning is unusually high, but, at the same time, because his orientation fails to correspond with external reality, he experiences little success in goal achievement. Such a pattern of behavior is found frequently in the person who shows a great deal of promise, but for some reason or other always manages to fail to attain any significant degree of accomplishment. As a result, often he experiences a great deal of conflict over his concept of himself as a person which, because of the conflicting influences of his feelings of psychological safety and his inability to find congruence with the reality of the external world, is difficult for him to resolve.

PERSON A	PERSON B	PERSON C	PERSON D
Loved—safe plus Correspondence of Orientation and Encountered Reality	Loved—safe plus Lack of Correspondence between Orientation and Encountered Reality	Unloved— nonsafe plus Correspondence of Orientation and Encountered Reality	Unloved—nonsafe plus Lack of Correspondence between Orientation and Encountered Reality
↓	↓	↓	↓
Ability to Achieve Goals and Learn New Behavior in Expanding Reality	Little Ability to Achieve Goals but High Ability to Learn New More Efficient Behavior	Ability to Achieve Goals but Little Ability to Learn New Behavior	Little Ability to Achieve Goals or to Learn New Behavior
↓	↓	↓	↓
High Level of Well-Being— the Emerging Self	Struggle and Conflict Outcome Unknown	Over-conformity Lack of Personal Satisfaction	Psychotic, Neurotic, Anti-social Adjustment

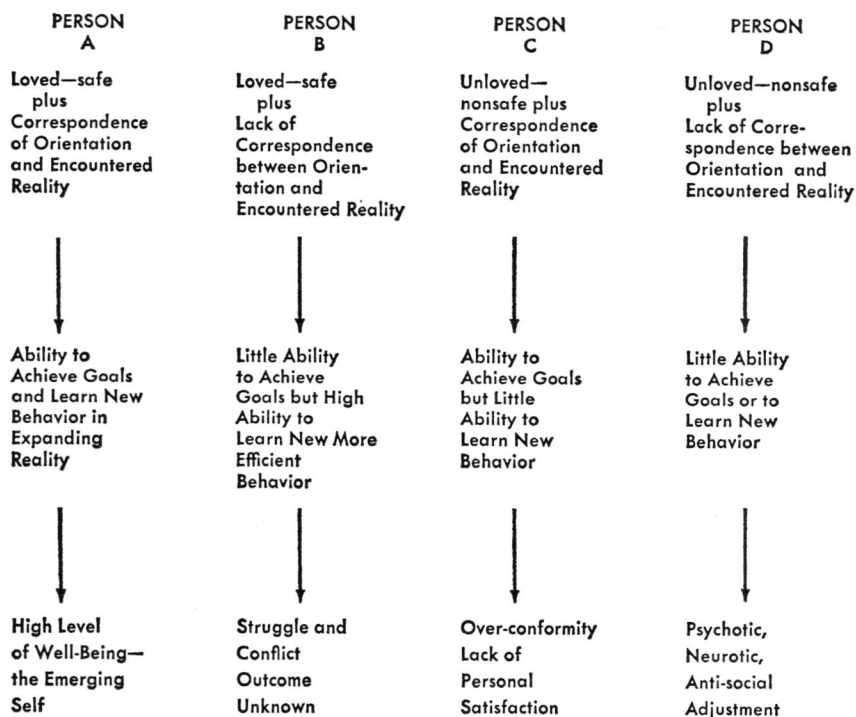

FIGURE 5. Relationship of psychological safety and orientational congruence on behavior.

In the third example in Figure 5, the person (C) is unloved and un-recognized and, consequently, does not feel psychologically safe enough to move freely into new and challenging aspects of life. Because his orientation corresponds with the viewpoints of the people around him, he is more likely, instead, to conform to the pattern of behavior that generally is expected in his particular social group. Invariably his experiences fail to really satisfy him and because his effectiveness is liable to be limited to only a few specific areas of endeavor, his potentiality to some extent always remains unrealized. The "mamma's boy," for instance, who has been victimized by a destructive mother who speaks of love but acts with hate, can only find belongingness through relating to her orientation, inappropriate as it is for functioning outside the immediate environment of his home. The price of survival for such a boy is loyalty to the mother and he may continue to pay for it for the rest of his life. Because few people with different value systems are able to love and accept the boy, the mother has succeeded in binding him irrevocably to herself and her way of life.

When the failure to receive love, however, is combined with an absence of orientational congruence, the person (D) is in danger of becoming psychotic or neurotic or of suffering from some other pattern of disturbed and anti-social behavior. His orientation is unsuitable for him to function adequately and, because he does not possess sufficient feelings of psychological safety to permit him to seek out a new environment, all he can hope for at the best is to withdraw from or distort reality or perhaps find some small minority group which shares his defiant outlook on life.

The rich complexity of the possible interactions of psychological safety and orientational correspondence may explain why the studies which have been conducted on the different ways of socializing children have proved to be so contradictory. Child's (1954) summary indicated that although there may be a general theme underlying the results of a specific practice, there is a distinct tendency for the method which produced a particular result in one instance to have a very different influence in another situation. Thus, a specific approach to toilet training, for example, is not followed necessarily by the development of a recognizable pattern of behavior in the child. Instead, the outcome of the practice is likely to depend entirely upon whether it was instituted within a general interpersonal relationship of love or of hate and upon the degree of correspondence of the child's orientation with the objective reality of the world in which he has to live.

As a result, feelings of psychological safety and orientational congruence with the external world are closely related to one another during the course of the person's ego development. As he gains in confidence, he relates more freely to other people and also is able either to modify his orientation or to re-affirm it with a new and vital sense of involvement. Moreover, not only does he feel comfortable with himself to give love and acceptance to other persons but by means of his orientation, he communicates actively and genuinely, in a way that makes him truly human, his positive regard and respect for the unique contributions and abilities of other people.

SUMMARY

1. A person's feeling of psychological safety is dependent on the degree of love that he has received and his sense of belongingness in a particular group.
2. Love is expressed most effectively in a relationship that allows each person to attain the goals that he desires specifically to achieve,
3. Frequently when a person fails to experience love in such a complete sense, he turns to relationships with organizations, objects, animals,

etc. in order to counteract his inability to find a more meaningful expression of love.

4. A person's sense of belongingness increases to the extent that his uniqueness as a person and his contribution to the development of a social group are recognized.

5. Ideally, as a result of receiving love and affection from other persons, an individual learns to appreciate and love himself, and, in turn, is able to express love and respect toward other people.

6. To the degree that a person feels psychologically safe and his orientation is congruent with the reality of his environment, he develops a more adequate concept of himself, lives freely and effectively, and moves easily toward the attainment of an increasingly wider variety of goals.

EXERCISE 5

Norms and the Individual

The norms existing in a group help determine individual behavior within that group. Your family has developed norms which may be explicit or implicit. The church and the school have developed standards of proper behavior for members of these institutions. Your peer group has probably chosen behavioral norms which are sometimes divergent from all of these. Each group tends to specify such things as proper language, proper dress, attitudes, and a thousand and one things having to do with expectations of group members. All of our behaviors are directly affected by the prevailing norms in particular situations.

Following are several norms for eliciting behaviors in groups that some "experts" feel will either help or hinder effective group participation. Put a plus before each behavior you would prefer to utilize in a group situation and a minus before those you would not choose.

1. _____ Being open—saying what you honestly think.

2. _____ Taking personal risk—experimenting with behavior that you would not ordinarily display.

3. _____ Talking about "there and then"—talking about things that happened at some other time and some other place.

4. _____ Expressing affection—speaking up about your approval of others.

5. _____ Providing feedback—telling others in the group how they are affecting you or how their behavior looks to you.

6. _____ Holding back affection—saying nothing about something you like.

7. _____ Playing it safe—doing in new groups exactly what you have always done before in other groups.

8. _____ Not telling others—holding back the feelings or reactions you have toward other group members.

9. _____ Playing games in the group—doing what you do for effect and holding your real responses back from the group.

10. _____ Insisting on conformity—trying to get everyone to be like everyone else.

11. _____ Distrusting others—deciding beforehand that they are this or that and not letting them speak for themselves.

12. _____ Talking about the "here and now"—talking mostly about what is happening in this group at this time.

13. _____ Trusting others—behaving on the assumption that the other group members are pretty nice people who will allow you to be yourself.

14. _____ Avoiding conflict—crossing no one and swallowing your feelings about what is happening.

15. _____ Expressing conflict—speaking up when you don't like something—getting your feelings out in the open.

16. _____ Respecting individuality—working for conditions so that everyone can be himself.

The desirable behaviors according to some experts are described in items 1, 2, 4, 5, 12, 13, 15, 16. As you think about these you may discover you have some fears about what might happen in a group which established these norms. List some of these in the following spaces.

_____

_____

_____

_____

Frequently, we experience norms as something imposed from outside ourselves. Sometimes this is true. In many situations we have minimum choice about proper behaviors. Conversely, many times the prevailing norms governing our behavior are a matter of choice. Members of groups are relatively free to select their own rules. In these cases it becomes the responsibility of each member of a group to exert his influence in the choice-making procedure.

It frequently happens, however, that in free groups one or two members "run down the dock and jump into the water." The others passively follow and everyone finds himself in the situation imposed by a vocal minority. Discussion of available alternative norms would avoid such a premature consensus. Personal courage is required to speak up under these circumstances. Ask yourself if you are a blind follower or, if in relatively open groups, you do attempt to exert influence.

CHAPTER 7

The Achievement Goals

Once the basic goals have been at least partially attained, the achievement goals may be expected to emerge as a new and integral part of the developing person's hierarchy of goals. Lasswell (1951) has categorized the eight goals or values which man seeks as skill, enlightenment, power, wealth, respect, affection, rectitude, and well-being. In the arrangement of this book, however, affection, rectitude, and well-being have been placed at other levels in the hierarchy of goals from the remaining five achievement goals.

DIFFERENTIATED APPROACH TO ACHIEVEMENT GOALS

When a person moves toward attaining the achievement goals, he has the opportunity to use a lot more highly differentiated and specialized approach than is the case when he is gaining satisfaction of the more basic goals. Thus, the particular method of obtaining goal satisfaction that is uniquely important to him may become very easily distinguishable from the approaches used by other people.

It is important to note also that there are differences in behavior between the individual who achieves his goals to satisfy his own intrinsic needs and the person who sees the attainment of goals only as extrinsically valuable because they lead to the achievement of a further goal which is more important to him. In the first instance, the individual is able to enjoy a degree of satiation and personal satisfaction over his accomplishments that will be likely to provide him with feelings of fulfillment and relaxation. In the second case, however, achievement of the same goal provides little if any satisfaction because it has no real value in itself to the person. Possibly the difference may be illustrated more clearly by the following example.

Perhaps you enjoy playing golf to such an extent that the idea of shooting a round of golf at par becomes tremendously important to you. Despite the inevitable setbacks and frustrating disappointments, each game is increasingly a source of exhilaration and pleasure. Over the years, as your weaknesses are ironed out and your game gradually improves, the chances of playing par golf become better and better. Although you may never achieve this ultimate form of satisfaction, you continue to play golf because you enjoy the game and not because it provides opportunities for satisfying such extrinsic and external factors as impressing your friends, surpassing their performance, clinching a business deal, or being known as one of the smart set.

The importance of the intrinsic value holds true also for all kinds of activities, from reading to playing chess and from displaying social skills to the playing of musical instruments. Without the intrinsic motivation, the same activities become an endless chase on a treadmill, rather in the fashion of the movie, *La Dolce Vita,* which carries people nowhere and leaves them joyless while on the journey.

Many persons in the United States pile wealth on top of wealth and add power to power or knowledge to knowledge in a continuous pursuit of activity. Their behavior is interpreted sometimes as lending credence to the mistaken belief that there is advantage in pursuing one goal exclusively. The intention is not to belittle the practical achievement of goals because reading skill, for example, is a necessary step in the direction of enlightenment, but to point out the limitation of behavior that is motivated only extrinsically toward the accumulation of wealth, power, etc. While it is always preferable to own the objects that money can buy, than not to have them, possession per se never guarantees that a person's need for love, belongingness, and psychological safety will ever be satisfied.

Respect

RESPECT IS NECESSARY FOR ALL PEOPLE

Most people want very much to achieve the goal of respect through having other persons think well of them and recognize them as distinctive individuals. Even very early in life, people begin trying to earn and achieve respect. Children, for example, at the playground or swimming pool, may be heard calling to their parents over and over again, "Look at me, Daddy." "Look at me, Mommy." Later on, the boy walks fences to gain the little girl's attention and the little girl, in turn, wears lipstick for perhaps the same reason. In the course of time, the person learns to make his cry for attention more subtle and, as an adult, he seeks covertly what the child seeks overtly.

If the need for respect is not met, there is a very real danger that the person will undergo severe emotional disturbance. When a member of a social group, for instance, finds suddenly that he is being ostracized and ignored by his friends, he becomes upset quickly and questions his own behavior in an attempt to find out why there has been a change in attitude toward him.

While people are entitled to a minimum of respect because they are human, the extra measure of respect that is especially desirable is gained through the achievement of skill, enlightenment, power, and wealth. If you will think for a moment of some outstanding persons in your home town, probably certain individuals will come to mind immediately as people who enjoy a high degree of respect. In all likelihood, they are the persons who are elected to serve in positions on school boards and other civic organizations, who are selected as the men or the women of the year, and who are bestowed recognition and honors in the form of plaques and testimonials. Their advice is sought frequently on many different problems in the community and generally through a variety of ways they are made to feel important.

Moreno (1945, p. 83) has pointed out that social choice, which is one measure of respect, is distributed in sociometric data in a comparable manner to the distribution of wealth in a capitalistic society. In other words, in the same way that there are only a few extremely wealthy persons but many relatively poor people, a few members of a social group receive most of the recognition and a much larger number of persons are forced to share the few remaining indications of social choice and respect.

Further evidence supporting this position may be found by the fact that, through a phenomenon known as the "halo effect," persons possessing high rankings at the beginning of social interaction are rather consistently over-rated and those people who are not considered initially to be effective or important tend to have their behavior under-rated. Thus, a speech made by Horace B. Trueheart, international expert, is likely to be accorded a different audience from that given to the same speech by George Smith, local citizen, while the opinion of Mr. C. G. Johnson, small town banker and civic leader, is likely to be listened to with greater acceptance than that of Jack Jones, the local plumber. As Gardner (1961, pp. 71-72) has stated:

> It must never be forgotten that a person born to low status in a rigidly stratified society has a far more acceptable self-image than the person who loses out in our free competition of talent. In an older society, the humble member of society can attribute his lowly status to God's will, to the ancient order of things or to a corrupt and tyrannous government. But if a society sorts out people efficiently and fairly according to their gifts, the loser knows that the true reason for his lowly status is that he is not capable of better. That is a bitter pill for any man.

CONSUMPTON OF GOODS AS A SYMBOL OF RESPECT

Weber (Gerth and Mills, 1948, p. 193) has noted that status, the sociological term used to denote relatively constant positions of respect, tends to be related to the consumption of goods while Seeley, Sim, and Loosley (1956, p. 7) found that, "status may be validated in the acquisition and exhibition of material and non-material 'objects': houses, cars, clothes, jewelry, gadgets, furniture, works of art, stocks, bonds, membership in exclusive clubs, attendance at private schools."

An interesting example of consumption as a symbol of respect may be found in the pattern of automobile buying habits over the past few years. At one time, the Cadillac was the ultimate in status symbols. Then later, the possession of European sports cars became the mark of distinction. Recently, while visiting Hot Springs, Arkansas, one of the authors encountered a new trend which may become the latest move to gain respect and recognition: people were purchasing antique cars. It is very easy to see how an old Rolls Royce, particularly when it is driven by a uniformed chauffeur, offers all kinds of possibilities for delineating status and social position.

By and large, consumption appetites are insatiable and the need for expenditure grows as fast as the ability to satisfy it. When a wife says she needs another rug for the living-room floor, she may not mean that the old one is worn out but, instead, that the feelings of respect that her friends have for her are dependent upon the acquisition of a new rug. In her way, she is saying, "Look at me." Her desire for a new rug is not to be dismissed lightly in that her husband, who scoffs at such keeping up with the Joneses, may not hesitate at all to buy a Buick instead of a Volkswagen for a variety of very practical reasons. He needs to be recognized as well and, as the endless chase continues, the family eventually purchases a Volkswagen as well as a Buick in order to express the latest way of crying, "I want to be noticed."

Why do persons need to seek respect through possession and consumption? The harsh fact is that a reputation for excellence in morals, skill, knowledge, etc., is hard to obtain. When a person is respected because he lives better, knows more, or performs more effectively than his neighbors, his achievement speaks for itself. Many people, however, are unable to attain such intrinsic success and respect. To make up for the disappointment of failure or to avoid the demands of study and practice, which are the prerequisites of excellence, they choose the symbols of consumption in the hope that they will pass for excellence in themselves. As Veblen (1919, p. 394) has said, too often the appearance is preferred to the substance of success.

Mumford (1961, p. 379) has commented on this same aspect of life as it has been expressed architecturally. Buildings have been erected primarily to be seen, recognized, and accepted. False fronts in the form of monumental facades have masked pretentiously the insignificant buildings of many cities in the world.

One of the apparent difficulties of a person's efforts to win respect through accomplishment, however, is that society is sometimes quite variable and inconsistent in the way it accords respect. Mumford (1961, p. 23) noted that throughout history, herdsmen and hunters have been heroic figures while the productive peasant has been held in low esteem. Simeons (1961, p. 55) pointed out that material rewards are given to those who pander to the needs of people in society, but those who risk their lives must be content with a medal. Similarly, today the writer of advertising jingles is afforded a great deal more money than the man who writes poetry or composes a symphony.

The inconsistency with which respect is granted may be seen also when a person receives it only in one aspect of his life. A neighbor of one of the authors, for example, is a railway engineer; he is also an expert golfer. As an engineer he is accorded only an average amount of respect. As the winner of the local club tournament, his picture is printed in the paper, an index of respect, and his advice sought eagerly by beginning golfers. The respect he receives is based upon his ability to play very, very good golf. To match his ability would require prodigious effort and most people would prefer to gain a comparable status without expending that much energy.

Occupational groups in American society are composed of both status and economic elements. In recent years, the plumber, for example, has received a fairly high income but his status in terms of respect is much lower. In contrast, the school teacher and the white collar worker have ranked fairly high in prestige but their incomes have been at the lower end of the economic scales. Many people find, however, the dividends of respect to be just as real and meaningful as the financial return and, therefore, they prefer the role of the teacher or the white collar worker to that of the artisan or skilled craftsman.

DENIAL OF RESPECT FOR WOMEN

As a group, women in Western society are still engaged in a battle to win respect in terms of their total personalities and potentialities. Friedan (1963, p. 374) has noted that:

It . . . is time to stop giving lip service to the idea that there are no battles left to be fought for women in America, that women's rights have already been won. It is ridiculous to tell girls to keep quiet when they enter a new field, or an old one, so the men will not notice they are there. In almost every professional field, in business and in the arts and sciences, women are still treated as second-class citizens. It would be a great service to tell girls who plan to work in society to expect this subtle, uncomfortable discrimination—tell them not to be quiet, and hope it will go away, but fight it. A girl should not expect special privileges because of her sex, but neither should she 'adjust' to prejudice and discrimination.

As sexual objects, perhaps women have received exaggerated respect, but as intellectual beings, respect has been denied them. Riesman (1949, p. 140) has commented on this condition by stating that:

> Men today are far too anxious, too lacking in psychological defenses against each other, to tolerate critically-minded women. The women they want must be intelligent enough to flatter their vanity but not to challenge their prerogatives as men. Men once complained to their mistresses that their wives did not understand them; now they would complain if they did.

While many women insist that they would not want the situation to be different, the fact that they refer to themselves as being "just housewives" indicates that they are not completely comfortable with the domestic role. The price of withholding respect from women may be assessed possibly in the overall failure of women to make creative contributions in the areas of science, medicine, philosophy, literature, art, and musical composition.

DENIAL OF RESPECT FOR CHILDREN

Even more tragic are the large numbers of children who suffer from being withheld respect by the people who belong to the "children should be seen and not heard" school. Few people would question that children do not merit the full mark of respect that is given to an adult who is accomplished in some area of endeavor, but to deny children relative amounts of respect, as persons in their own rights, only ensures that it will be difficult for them to utilize whatever capacities and abilities they possess.

The extreme denial of respect which produces aggressive and hostile behavior in children has been described very well by Redl and Wineman (1951, p. 50):

> . . . the quality of the tie between child and adult world was marred by rejection ranging from open brutality, cruelty, and neglect to affect barrenness on the part of some parents and narcissistic absorption in their own interests which exiled the child emotionally from them. Certainly there were also operative heavy mixtures of both styles of rejection, overt and unconscious. One of the things that constantly amazed us when we

would observe the parents and children together was how much like strangers they were to one another. In this connection, we were impressed by how little interest the parents took in what was happening to the children in treatment. Contrary to our expectations that they might become competitive with the treatment milieu on the basis of feelings of guilt for placing the child and for their own inadequacy, they never became involved on any level at all. Their main, unconcealed reaction was: 'We're glad you've got them, not us. Life is so peaceful without them.'

In contrast, when children are shown respect, they become much more capable of sensitive and responsible behavior. Perhaps an incident in the lives of some friends of one of the authors may be used to illustrate the way that even relatively young children are able to respond maturely to frustration and disappointment. For quite a while, the ten- and eight-year-old girls in the family had been looking forward to seeing the circus, but when it arrived in a near-by town it was impossible, because of the pressure of professional responsibilities, for the parents to find time to take the children. Instead of arbitrarily announcing that the trip was out of the question, the mother explained carefully to the children the difficulties involved and pointed out the possibility of going the next year. The ten-year-old responded by saying that a bonus for waiting a year would be that the younger brother would then be old enough to go as well and that he would enjoy it very much. To the mother's comment that she was pleased and proud that the children understood the situation so easily, the eight-year-old daughter responded, "What else did you expect?"

DENIAL OF RESPECT FOR MINORITY GROUPS

The lack of respect in the face of other serious deprivations has caused all minority groups but particularly the Negro to make only a limited contribution to society. This theme may be seen clearly in the writings of Myrdal (1944), Baldwin (1962), Wright (1963), and Griffin (1961). Thus, it may be particularly important for society to remember that despite popular interpretations to the contrary, no group, male or female, old or young, white or black, has a natural monopoly on growth, development, and progress.

DENIAL OF RESPECT IN HUMAN RELATIONSHIPS

Simmel (Wolff, 1950, p. 422) has pointed out that in today's society intimate emotional relations tend to be restricted and man is reduced to a negligible quantity and perhaps is treated like a number or a machine instead of a person. The large corporation or bureaucracy that defines by assigned status the respect that a member of its organization will receive is supporting such impersonality. Thus, the man who is hired as an executive tends to be treated with respect automatically because of his position and his fellow workers are rarely concerned over whether or not his personal qualities justify such an appraisal. The janitor, on the other hand, is much less likely to be shown respect or have his ideas taken seriously, and frequently he is dismissed as a person who is capable of only a limited contribution. Unfortunately, in large corporations there are only a few jobs which guarantee the personal recognition of an individual's ability and, thus, inevitably many people are denied the respect they need and deserve.

Carl Rogers (1961, p. 74) has stressed the importance of the therapist holding within himself attitudes of deep respect and full acceptance of the client as he is in order for the process of growth and therapy to take place. In a similar manner, it is only when a person is shown respect by other people that the potentialities he possesses for creative expression are given a real opportunity to unfold.

Wealth

Since wealth is relatively the easiest to attain of the achievement goals and it is especially desirable in terms of the material goods it will buy, it is not surprising that it has assumed such paramount importance in American society. There are many inequities in the distribution of wealth, however, which tend frequently to be ignored. Sargent Shriver (1965) pointed out, for instance, that America is divided into two clearly distinguishable financial societies. In one group, composed of 35 million people of whom over 15 million are children, life is one of desperate poverty in which the people have less than 70 cents a day for food and less than $1.40 to take care of all their other needs. Some nine million families survive on less than $60 a week, almost two thirds of them receiving less than $40. In contrast, in the other society, more people enjoy more educational and material benefits than any nation in history. At the extreme, Lampman (1962, p. 23) pointed out that the richest 1.6 percent of the population owns nearly one third of the country's total material assets. Moreover, Bazelon (1963, p. 337) noted that the top 1 percent according to wealth own 80 percent of the corporate stock, virtually all of the state and local government bonds, and nearly 90 percent of the corporate bonds.

Russell (Egner and Denonn, 1961, p. 699) has sounded what may be seen as a warning note. He charged that people imagine that they desire to grow rich but that, in his opinion, they desire even more to keep others poor. The point dramatizes effectively the tendency to confuse the goals of wealth and respect. Keeping other people poor may not increase directly a person's wealth, but it so often serves to protect his need for respect and status in a community.

It is doubtful whether these figures concerning the distribution of wealth will change appreciably during the next few years and, since wealth is likely to be one of the goals of every person, whether or not he chooses it, there is real danger that many people, particularly those with grandiose expectations concerning wealth, will be frustrated in their attempts to gain financial success.

The redistribution of wealth would seem to be the most satisfactory means of improving the situation. Although reform is most certainly desirable, another solution that is more practical, as well as less upsetting politically, would be the placing of more emphasis upon the achievement of other goals, thereby reducing the amount of frustration caused by the unrealistic setting of goals concerning the accumulation of wealth.

Power

Power may be defined as the ability to persuade other people to adopt ideas that are different from the ones they possess and to exercise control in such a way that they behave in a manner that is considered desirable by the person who is influencing them. The dramatic nature of the goal for power led the philosopher, Nietzsche, to consider it to be the most powerful motivating state of man.

EXCESSIVE USE OF POWER

Excessive concentration on power, however, not only results in fixation, and the subsequent failure of other goals to emerge, but also in the tendency for the harm done by the fixation to influence negatively other people with whom the person exerting the power comes in contact. Russell's (Egner and Denonn, 1961, p. 673) statement that, "the arguments from history and psychology show how rash it is to expect irresponsible power to be benevolent" demonstrates how often the insatiability of power may be so harmful that nothing short of omnipotence could satisfy it completely. Peckham (1962, p. 251) concurred with this evaluation, stating that, "to be morally responsible, power must be self-limiting." He added, however, that for him, as a consequence, limited power was a contradiction.

In studying ancient history, Mumford (1961, p. 23) hypothesized that certain persons within a group were given the power to protect the other members of the group from the danger of attack from animals. In time these people were not content with the role of guardian alone and they demanded money in return for taking care of the persons they were expected to protect. In a similar way, royalty, church officials, military leaders, etc., have used power on occasion to the disadvantage of the majority of people in order to forward their own particular interests. More recently, President Eisenhower's final warning to the American people concerned the growing concentration of power in America's peacetime military-industrial complex (Cook, 1962, p. 3) while the themes of two novels, *Dr. Strangelove* by Peter George (1964) and *Seven Days in May* by Fletcher Knebel and Charles W. Bailey II (1962) have pointed out rather vividly the danger of the misuse of military power leading to world destruction.

DANGERS OF THE ABUSE OF POWER

When a person begins to use his power or influence to dominate a social situation to such an extent that he will not permit other members of the group to express their feelings and exchange ideas, there is inevitably a loss of vitality in the relationship. No doubt, some time in your high school or college career, you have been exposed to the dreadful apathy that overtakes a classroom when a teacher rambles on in a monotone, reading from his yellowed notes, without making any attempt to relate the subject matter to the concerns and interests of the students. Unfortunately, this situation occurs in many other areas of life as well. Officers in social organizations dominate the business meetings of these groups while presidents, deans, and senior professors have a great deal more influence on faculty and committee meetings than younger instructors. Executives tend to monopolize staff business meetings at the expense of the contributions of other employees while often physicians do far more talking at case conferences than nurses and other staff members.

Mumford (1961, p. 125) has pointed out that within a couple of centuries the Greeks found out more about the nature and potentialities of man than the Egyptians seemed able to discover in as many millennia. He deduced that this condition was at least a partial result of the fact that in the Greek society there was less opportunity for one-sided exploitation, less need for strict control of its citizens, and generally a more diffuse distribution of power.

The system of checks and balances indicates that there has been recognition in American life of the importance of the relationship between the diffusion of power and growth and development. At the same time, however, certain persons and groups within American society have allowed the goal of power to become so predominant in their lives that the struggle for control takes place daily in places of business, legislative halls, universities, social clubs, and in various other aspects of life.

IDENTIFICATION WITH ATHLETIC TEAMS

The phenomenal increase in spectator sports and particularly in professional football reflects also a preoccupation with power. People identify with the various athletic teams so that when the Chicago Bears or the New York Yankees win, it is not just one team beating another team, but a personal victory for the individual identifying with the successful team. Thus, if power may not be gained through specific accomplishment, it may be experienced vicariously through identification with the strength of a team, frequently represented symbolically by such nicknames as Giants, Bears, Rams, Lions, Tigers, etc. In actuality, however, the victory belongs to someone else and, consequently, as in the case of all attempts to by-pass actual goal achievement, it is doomed to be only partially successful.

IDENTIFICATION WITH THE CITY AS AN EXPRESSION OF POWER

Mumford (1961, p. 68) has stated that many city dwellers identify with the city and all of its power. Thus, many of the people living in New York are most comfortable when they consider themselves to be part of the strength and blatant power of the large city and they would not consider living in some more modest hamlet.

THE DISTRIBUTION OF POWER

Studies indicate that power may not be distributed as broadly as has been supposed. Bazelon (1963, p. 194) noted a study by the Federal Trade Commission which reported that 113 corporations with assets of over 100 million dollars held 46 percent of the total resources of manufacturing firms. Another study by Thometz (1963, p. 31) indicated that power in Dallas, Texas, a city with a population of 800,000 people, was controlled in essence by only seven men: three bankers, two utility executives, one man from the retail trade, and one man in industry.

THE INFLUENCE OF THE ABSENCE OF POWER

The fact that many people are not satisfying their needs to achieve power may be seen perhaps in the great appeal that cartoons and comedies have for the American public. The typical theme which never seems to grow old is that of an innocuously weak person becoming strong and powerful. In the cartoon, if not in real life, the mouse clobbers the cat, the cat the dog, the rabbit the hunter, and so on. Certainly children, who are the weakest and smallest of all, never seem to tire of watching this re-alignment of power.

Rolo's (1958) analysis of the meaning of the fantastically high sales of a series of books written by Mickey Spillane is instructive also concerning the degree of absence of power in the lives of people in American society. In the face of feelings of helplessness engendered by the complications of modern life, these books provide a welcome and necessary relief. In the words of Rolo, Mike Hammer, Spillane's hero, has appointed himself detective, judge, jury, and executioner. The titles tell the story: *I the Jury, My Gun Is Quick, Vengeance Is Mine.* Hammer is not a helpless person like so many people in society but, instead, he is a powerful enough figure to counteract injustice, crime, corruption, and so forth. The fact that he is successful by undermining lawful government does not seem to make any difference to his reading public, although it does raise a question about the potential danger of the legal form of government in American society being disrupted.

Furthermore, it is worth noting Dunham's (1964, p. 9) warning, that the self-justification of power is almost certain to be corrupt, simply because it is self-justification. To survive in a world where power is pursued too openly is often to become brutal. Many times in history, even those forces that were first gathered together to right a wrong have been guilty of perpetuating the very wrong they set out to correct.

BASES FOR POWER

French and Raven (1959) have described the following five bases upon which interpersonal power is conferred: (1) the ability to mediate rewards, (2) the ability to mediate punishment, (3) referent power or attractiveness, (4) expert power, and (5) legitimate power.

Ability to Mediate Rewards. The teacher, for instance, who is in a position of passing or failing students, the supervisor who evaluates the effectiveness of the people working under him, and the wealthy person who by his decisions is able to affect either directly or indirectly the lives of thousands of people, all are in a position of exerting power and consequently of having their wishes and opinions treated with deference.

Ability to Mediate Punishment. On a simple level anyone with superior size and strength has the ability to mediate punishment. In most situations, therefore, men have more power than women and adults more than children. Certainly those persons who are able to control the lives of other people by threatening them with the possibility of punishment are in a position to exert power and influence.

Referent Power or Attractiveness. Being attractive or aesthetically pleasing to the eye provides the person who possesses this characteristic with more power than accrues to the physically unattractive person. Thus, for example, a little girl may use her prettiness as a weapon for controlling her parents and attractive boys and girls may rely upon their physical attributes to gain followers.

Expert Power. Those persons who possess superior knowledge or skill find themselves quite often in positions of influence over other people. Scientists and engineers who are the source of new technological ideas, for example, are one of the most potent power groups in today's society.

Legitimate Power. Legitimate power is the authority that is wielded as a recognized right. The general in the army has legitimate power over all persons ranked below him while, on a less formal basis, the power of parents over children is prescribed by the mores of society.

One of the drawbacks to the possession of power is that leaders are forced to live in a relatively isolated and unapproachable fashion and a degree of loneliness may result. In wartime particularly, the captain of a ship or of an aircraft must bear responsibilities and make decisions which he cannot share with the members of his crew. In *The Making of a President 1960,* White (1961) has indicated very clearly the loneliness that comes with assuming the awesome power of the Presidency.

THE ABILITY TO EXERCISE CHOICE AS AN EXPRESSION OF POWER

The ability to exercise choice is a relatively accurate index of power in that the greater the opportunity for selection a person possesses, the stronger is his power status and, correspondingly, the fewer the choices that are available to him, the less significant is his influence and power. The loss of opportunity to make up one's own mind and to exercise the power of choice leads inevitably to demoralization and unconcern. The absence of interest in public affairs by young people, for example, may be explained by the fact that they are too young to qualify for the right to vote.

POWER AS A LEGITIMATE SOURCE OF INFLUENCE

While no one but a blindly optimistic Pollyanna would deny the inherent danger of excessive power, there is still value, of course, in its use as a legitimate source of influence. The writing of this book, for example, is in part a power goal-directed activity. The authors believe in the importance of enlightenment and, because they feel that ultimately it is in your best interest to move toward the achievement of this goal, they want you to have an opportunity for deciding realistically to what extent it should become a value for your life. Perhaps in this way the authors are exercising power beneficially.

Skill

Skill represents the ability to do something well. Without a large repertoire of skills, the person is handicapped in his attempts to earn a living, gain the respect of other people, and generally achieve the goals that are important to him. In addition to performing effectively in order to obtain a goal, people like to be skillful enough to be efficient because it is intrinsically more satisfying than being inefficient. In most cases it is more satisfying to do an effective job even when a mediocre one would suffice to accomplish the same end.

A complete skill involves the control of behavior in both direction and execution so that there is a pattern of sequential acts. The importance of execution in skillful behavior is evidenced by the statement, "He has the knowledge but he lacks the skill." The list of skills is endless but some of the more basic ones are related to motor activities, thinking, communication, social life, and aesthetics.

INDIVIDUAL DIFFERENCES IN SKILLS

People differ greatly in their potentiality to be skillful. One person may have the muscle coordination of the "natural athlete" while another person may possess an ear for music or find that mathematics or science is the field in which he can perform most easily. Some individuals are fortunate enough to be more gifted in every one of these areas than are other people.

DIFFERENCES IN OPPORTUNITIES FOR DEVELOPING SKILLS

In addition to the differences in potentialities among people, the opportunities for the development of talent vary widely as well. Individual A, for example, may grow up in a large city as a member of an active family, with numerous opportunities for engaging in a wide range of social and aesthetic experiences literally thrust upon him. On the other hand, individual B, with the same potential, may be raised by passive parents on an isolated farm where the opportunity for a variety of activities is lacking almost entirely. If these two persons are placed in the same environment on a large university campus, life is relatively easy for A but probably a lot more difficult for B. A has a surplus of skills which enable him to achieve his goals while B is handicapped by possessing only the barest minimum of skills necessary for life at a university. It would be very easy for anyone meeting the two boys to conclude that A has superior abilities to B. In terms of actual performance such an evaluation would be correct, but, of course, the potential ability of B has been obscured totally by the absence of suitable opportunity. Consequently, because of his initial lack of skill as a university student, B's development is likely to fall further and further behind that of A. In fact, if his attempts to acquire the minimum basic skills are too painful, he may retreat from the new environment entirely by dropping out of school and thereby causing his potential not only to be lost to himself but to society as well.

Many males have known perhaps the experience of secretly envying the young man at the swimming pool who dives gracefully from the high board, twists and turns, and enters the water with hardly a splash. Perfection of this ability depends obviously upon the availability of a diving board, a pool, and usually some form of instruction. Some families and communities have swimming pools; others do not.

A surprisingly large number of college students express the desire to be able to play the piano. Perhaps they see it as a means of winning respect and belongingness, perhaps as an intrinsic expressive activity. No doubt some of these students had the opportunity to learn to play the piano but passed it up, but for others piano lessons were as unavailable as a trip to Europe.

Some students live in communities where libraries, art galleries, theaters, concert and lecture series, and movie theaters are important aspects of life. Tennis courts, golf links, and riding stables are available to them and they are provided with dancing, music, and bridge lessons. Their parents speak fluently and are adequate adult models from whom the children may learn skills. Other children have none of these opportunities. They spend their spare time working and are exposed only to the influence of television, comic books, and parents who are woefully inadequate models for identification.

Thus, it becomes increasingly important for society to provide each person with experiences that encourage the development of a reasonable proportion of his potential talent. With such opportunities, the person may continue to grow and move on toward further goal achievement; without such opportunities, his behavior becomes fixated and there is a likelihood of his behavior becoming destructive.

Mass production and the development of the current bureaucratic and economic organization have made it difficult for a person to obtain a job in which an intrinsic skill is required. Consequently, today's worker has been forced to seek avocationally what yesterday he was able to find vocationally. Possibly the following illustration will help to clarify what is happening in society.

Perhaps you can imagine that you know a man who, together with three or four other workers, has built ten or twelve homes in a community every year for several years. Whenever this man drives around the residential areas where his homes are located, he observes the results of his skill and ability and he enjoys feelings of satisfaction and accomplishment. Contrast his experience, however, with the worker in a large modern construction gang, whose job involves the repetitious sawing of certain lengths of lumber which go to make up the identically alike one hundred new houses of a suburban subdivision or, even less meaningfully, comprise the packages for prefabricated homes which are shipped all over the state or even the nation. There can be no question that in a modern society the latter method is the more effective way of building houses. The subsequent loss in the satisfaction of having developed a high degree of diversified skills, however, makes it especially necessary to provide a wide range of opportunities for workers to engage in avocational and recreational skills.

It may be that some of modern man's preoccupation with production at the expense of recreational, aesthetic, and personally satisfying motor skills is only an expression of his present orientation. Certainly during the past, man has expressed his perceptions decoratively and imaginatively. According to Hawkes (Hawkes and Woolley, 1963, p. 194):

> The cave and the home arts together include drawing, stencilling, engraving, painting, modelling in relief and in the round, sculpture in relief and in the round. Thus almost every process known to us today was developed during the first flight of the visual arts between ten and thirty thousand years ago.

The growing importance of including arts and crafts in the secondary school curriculum has been stressed by Hutchinson and Young (1962, p. 51) who use the following quotation from the Crowther Report (15 to 18, 1959, p. 392):

> A boy or girl may be asking that he should be taught to do as well as to appreciate what others have done. He wants, perhaps, to play in an orchestra, and not merely to listen to one; to paint and not only to receive lessons in art appreciation. He stands in a tradition many thousands of

years old, an educational tradition, though not historically a school or university tradition. It is a task of importance to make this other tradition of artistic or creative education (historically a matter of professional or technical training) as much a respectable part of the general educational system as the largely analytical tradition of the schools. It is right to add that some of the most encouraging educational achievements of our time have been precisely in this sphere.

Hutchinson and Young go on to state that when a child is equipped with skills of this kind, he has resources which will stand him well in the future. Not only will he be capable of adding color and variety to his surroundings, but he will be able to use more effectively the leisure time that is increasingly likely to be available to him.

PRACTICE AND LEARNING ARE NECESSARY IN THE DEVELOPMENT OF SKILLS

As is the case in the development of all skill, a great deal of practice and learning is necessary for reaching a high level of aesthetic achievement. This point is illustrated most effectively in a story that is told about Sviatoslav Richter, the Russian pianist, who presently certainly must be included among the greatest artists of the concert stage. In the late afternoon, prior to giving a recital, he will rehearse the concert that is to be presented. Then he will play the actual concert and, after the completion of the performance, when the concert hall is empty, he will play the music a third time, correcting the mistakes that were noted in the live performance.

Although the appreciation of music, painting, and writing may come easily to a few people, it requires in most cases a great amount of study and preparation. In the field of music, for example, the experience of listening to counterpoint, that is attending to a minor melodic theme as a figure, rather than concentrating solely on the first theme that dominated the perception, may change almost entirely the experience of hearing a piece of music. Similarly, a person who has little knowledge of art may dismiss modern painting as gobble-de-gook and thus completely miss the artist's attempt to help him find a new orientation toward some aspect of life.

THE FRACTIONIZING OF MAN

Mumford (1961, pp. 166-169) has commented on a period in the history of Greece when the ways of the gods, the ways of nature, and the ways of men came close to one another. Men were athletes, soldiers, thinkers, common citizens who were active in public affairs, business men, and participants in the arts. One aspect of their lives flowed into another part so that no phase was segregated, monopolized, or set aside from the rest. Modern man, however, has so fractionized this integration of activities that such functions as the production of goods, talking, worshipping, playing, and educating the children have been turned over at least partially to full-time professionals and the events of life which were once integrated in a single building are now distributed among factories, market-places, hotels, churches, and schools. As a result, many people feel that the home has nothing to do with the school, the school, in turn, has nothing to do with the church, the church nothing to do with the business, etc., and it has become vitally important for man to find some activity in which he can express himself wholly and completely. It is quite possible that in the days of increased leisure time which are to come in the future, the development of recreational and aesthetic skills offers man the best opportunity for regaining his lost sense of completeness.

Enlightenment

ATTITUDES TOWARD ENLIGHTENMENT

Enlightenment is the value which represents man's desire to know and to understand. The man whose overriding goal is enlightenment will undergo relatively severe deprivations of the other values in order to gain the understanding he seeks. Perhaps Figure 6, adapted from Townsend (1953, p. 4) will clarify the meaning of enlightenment as a motivating force. Area A represents what the person is expected to learn either formally or informally as a member of society. The area contains society's accepted "truths" and understandings, most of which are passed along to the child by the family, the school, the church, and other social institutions. Area B of the same figure represents the unanswered questions which attract the attention of a limited number of the members of society. The search for a cure for cancer is an example of behavior which is best represented by Area B. Area C represents knowledge that is believed to be inaccessible to society and incapable of solution. Area C, in turn, will draw the attention of a limited number of people in society who will not accept no for an answer and who reframe questions in a form more conducive to the discovering of answers. One hundred years ago, those persons who toyed with the idea of man going to the moon were operating in Area C. Today this accomplishment is represented in Area A. What was impossible yesterday is today's accepted fact.

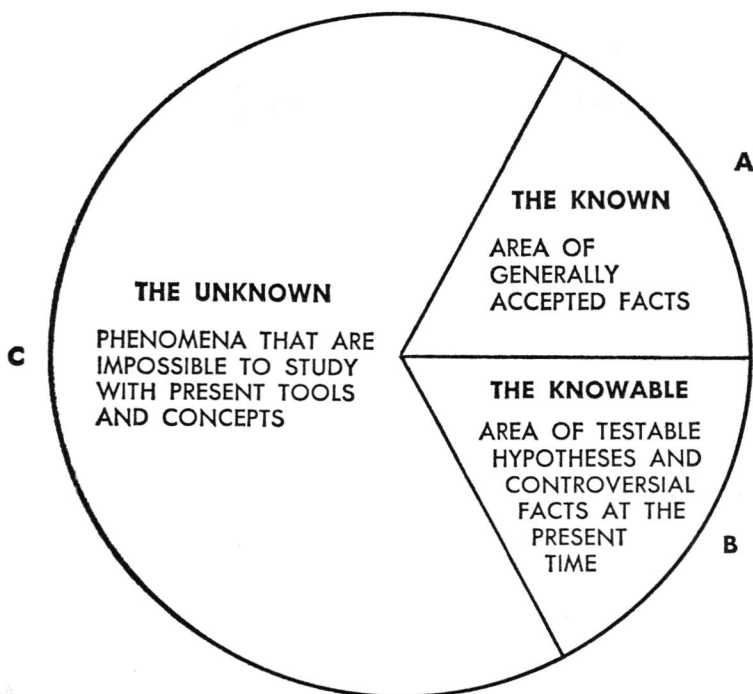

FIGURE 6. Society's orientation toward enlightenment.

Figure 7 represents an individual's orientation toward enlightenment in which Area D contains what the person knows. It may vary from a small part of what is known in society (Area A, Figure 6) to an amazingly complete understanding of knowledge. Area E denotes the knowledge which society possesses which the person does not know. Area F represents aspects of life which no one understands. Unfortunately, it is sometimes difficult to distinguish people with creative abilities from those persons, often referred to as crackpots and cranks, who are preoccupied also with the same questions but who do not possess the underlying wisdom, intelligence, and knowledge to remain in touch with communicable reality.

It would seem that a large majority of persons in American society are content to live with a limited amount of knowledge. Frequently, they blow up to balloon-like proportions what little understanding of life they possess and refuse steadfastly to recognize the immense area of learning represented by Areas E and F. Evidence for this point of view may be found in the general down-grading of intellectual achieve-

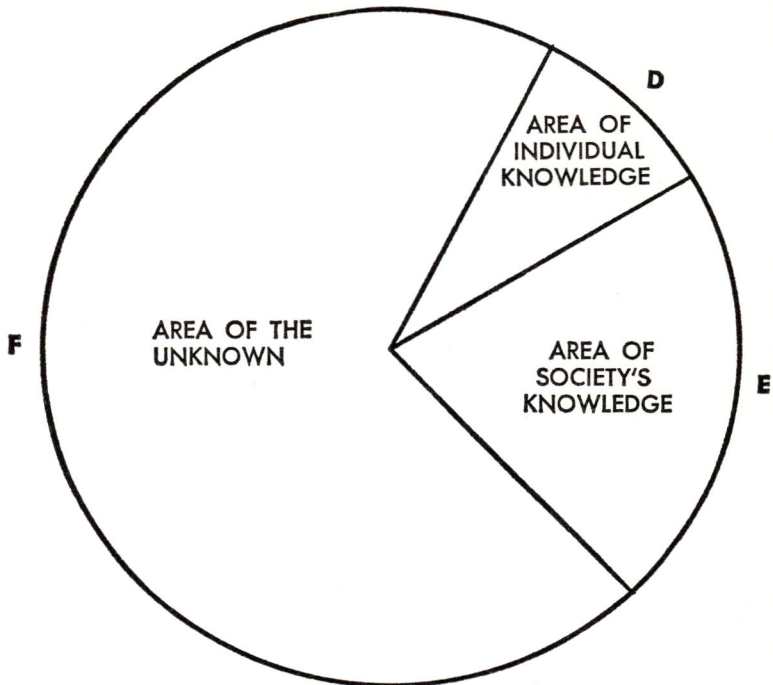

FIGURE 7. Individual's orientation toward enlightenment.

ment that still exists despite the leadership that the late President Kennedy gave to the academic life. Prior to the days of the Sputniks, at least, the word "egghead" was a term of derision. The intellectual was suspected by people with little knowledge who found it easier to attack his insight and understanding than to attempt to make some of his learning their own. Although held somewhat in awe, it was more comfortable to dismiss him as being impractical, unrealistic, an ivory-towered dreamer, or a Harvard bureaucrat than to try to understand him. Probably society expresses its evaluation more deeply when it pays movie stars, baseball players, advertising copy writers, and rock and roll singers far greater material rewards than its scholars. It is interesting to note in passing that in the U.S.S.R., where a person's salary depends in part on his contribution to the state, the university professor enjoys the highest salary and status of all workers.

CHARACTERISTICS OF ENLIGHTENMENT

Curiosity. In Chapter 4 curiosity was posted as being one of the basic physiological goals that accompanies growth and change and, consequently, it is easy to appreciate why it would be the outstanding characteristic of the person attempting to achieve the goal of enlightenment. The following paragraphs by Fillmore Sanford (1964, pp. 6-9) express some of the excitement that accompanies the development of curiosity:

In your intellectual work, seek the thrill of discovery. Seek the great and consummately human satisfaction of noticing relationships, of seeing good analogies, of finding the elegant simplicities that lie behind all the complex things you are learning. You may have to wait through many introductory courses, concerned as they must be with facts and vocabulary, before you earn the right to this thrill of discovery, of creation, of bringing into the world an effective surprise. Some of your teachers will not help you very much along this road. Some will not be gifted at the art of intellectual temptation, thus helping *you* make discoveries. Many will want to talk instead about their own discoveries; but they still can teach you something, and a little deliberate obedience will not hurt you. Unless it insults too severely your sense of independence, learn well what they ask you to learn. Ignorance does not contribute to invention or discovery—or to wisdom.

Don't let your grades interfere with your education. In almost every college in America, especially since the advent of Sputniks, there has been a tremendous emphasis on grades and a tremendous competition for them. Certainly you should get good grades. They have them there. They are meted out according to rules. The rules are learnable and not too stringent, and good grades are obtainable. So get them. They will be mighty convenient to have, especially for those people who do not bother to learn about you but judge you on the basis of the papers you carry. And they obviously will be convenient if you choose to go on into graduate work. But grades—and there is considerable evidence to support this—do not always by any means measure the benefit an individual can get from a course or a curriculum or a college. Also, it may be well for you to remember the recent research evidence showing that creativity of a high order is not closely related with the kind of intelligence necessary to make good grades.

Do not be afraid of ideas. You very likely will encounter in your reading, in your classes, in your bull sessions in the dormitory, many ideas that seem to you not only erroneous but perhaps even abhorrent. I hope so, for even with your 'fabulously enlightened upbringing,' you obviously have not encountered all the significant ideas that have come to and from the minds of men. There is a great likelihood that you arrived at the university with a pretty definite readiness to accept ideas you find cozily compatible with your present view of things and to close out those that do not agree with your existing view of the world. Anyone who remains so neatly and comfortably selective throughout four years of so-called education will emerge with nothing more than a naked diploma and a fancy set of slick and pseudo-sophisticated techniques for protecting, preserving, and propounding the half-baked ideas with which the whole adventure was started. Simple-minded and whole-bought biases, when embossed and trimmed with selected quotations from the Bible, Shakespeare, Kirkegaard and Ciardi, are even more dangerous than mere ignorance.

Whatever else you do in the university, learn to learn. As sure as death and taxes is the coming explosion of knowledge. Almost surely the substantive content of what you learn in college will soon be outmoded—outmoded at least as much so as Newtonian physics when applied to the inside of an atom, or as outmoded as a blacksmith shop on the freeway. Scientific and technical knowledge will of course accumulate more rapidly than knowledge in other fields. But there is an inherent interconnectedness of all knowledge, and advancing scientific techniques will have an effect on all forms of scholarship. Knowledge will grow geometrically, will snowball. All of us must keep on learning or else the aged will become useless and the young will be old fogeys at 40.

I once knew a man who made it a practice to preface most of his declarative sentences with the words 'Today.' 'Today, I believe,' 'Today, I think.' By placing 'Today' in subtle italics, he seemed to be saying to himself and others that while he was ready for today's decisive action, he still maintained the right to change his mind on the basis of tomorrow's new evidence. Can one live with such tentativeness? I think so. And I think in many areas of human endeavor, tentativeness is blessed, for it prevents the ossification of mind, avoids the paralytic dangers of facing tomorrow's problems with yesterday's casts of thought.

In all your endeavors, seek for ways to reward yourself for your own good performance. Do not let other people do all of your judging of you for you. Make neither too much nor too little of the approval of your teachers, expressed by grades or in other ways. Teachers, like parents, will not long be with you. You will be around *you* all your life, and you have to be the final and often lonesome judge of the quality of your behavior. Some people have a capacity to enjoy learning, to enjoy creating, to enjoy living life for its own sweet savor; they don't have a desperate need either for the kindly uncle's daily pat on the head or for the explicit approval of 'the group.'

Don't overdo the search either for the factual or the practical. One crucially important function of higher education is that it helps us learn both effective and human ways to deal with our life of impulse. Here's where the study of non-factual, non-practical poetry and drama and art come in. Through the study of O'Neill or Shakespeare or Dylan Thomas or Georgia O'Keefe or Thomas Mann or Debussy, we can not only add a dimension to the sheer enjoyment of life but we also can learn about the nature of our own impulses, and perhaps we can learn new and good ways to express them, ways that can be truly human rather than humanly animal. Hopefully, we can come to deal with impulse in ways that can be creative and artistic rather than merely primitively gratifying, ways that are more intricately human and closer to life than are the over-simplified, black-white, standardized fantasies of either soap or horse opera.

Concern for All of Man's Experience. The person concerned with true enlightenment holds the position that all of man's experience is a legitimate object for study and that no limitation should be placed on any area that shows potential for providing new insight and understanding. One aspect of Gardner's (1961, p. 134) conception of excellence, for example, is a pluralistic approach to values in which people "honor the many facets and depths and dimensions of human experience and . . . seek the many kinds of excellence of which the human spirit is capable." Thus, the concern of the enlightened man is not only with the traditional areas of academic study but extends also to the important task of relating himself meaningfully to the question of religion, the formation of a philosophy for his life, and generally the selection of a value system for his behavior.

When a student is interested genuinely in achieving enlightenment he assumes a great deal of responsibility for his own educational experience and invariably he reads and studies far beyond the instructor's expectancies for credit in a particular course. Because he is devoted seriously to gaining new understanding as a reward in itself, he provides tremendous stimulation for the sincere educator. At the same time, because he is not interested in regurgitating innocuous facts and clichés, he is frequently a very serious threat to the instructor of the "Mickey Mouse" type of course whose objective in teaching is more likely to be concerned with maintaining power and control over the members of the class.

Conflicts in Goals. Most college students presume that enlightenment is one of their predominant goals but examination of their behavior, however, does not support necessarily this assumption. Many students are oriented toward achieving wealth and they find a course in accounting, which has obvious value to an economic career, to be considerably more exciting than a history class which is best sat through with a minimum amount of time and effort.

Other students are seeking respect. In all probability they couldn't care less about enlightenment and their academic behavior is directed primarily toward winning the respect of teachers, parents, peers, etc. They study continually and industrially memorize assignments in order to obtain the high grades that are so essential to their well-being.

Still other students study in order to win love or refuse to study in the hope of winning approval and affection from the group that disapproves of the academic life. For these students college life is a more-or-less continuous round of social activities, parties, dances, football games, and bull sessions.

No matter what the type of educational institution, whether it be a large state university, small liberal arts college, or a teachers college, it is expected to ensure that its students, who possess a wide variety of reasons for attending college, are graduated with enlightenment as a predominant value in their lives. Every professor knows, however.

that it rarely occurs that way. As the Jacob (1957, p. 5) study indicated, many students leave college with about the same values they possessed when they began as freshmen.

As the reader of this book, you are most likely to be a college student or, at least, a person of a comparable level of academic endeavor. You might think carefully about your own reasons for attending college and give some thought over the extent you find enlightenment intrinsically satisfying in its own right. If you have not known the experience of learning for the sheer pleasure of gaining in understanding, then you are forfeiting one of life's experiences that other people use to enrich their lives.

In 1942, when England was still withstanding bombing attacks from the German Luftwaffe, and the tide of World War II was just beginning to turn, the late Sir Winston Churchill made one of his most memorable speeches in which he said, "Now this is not the end. It is not even the beginning of the end. But it is, perhaps, the end of the beginning." As a student, you have a decision to make concerning your academic career and quest for enlightenment. Possibly you have reached the end or the beginning of the end, but what is much more exciting, you may just be coming upon the end of the beginning. The choice is yours.

SUMMARY

1. A person approaches the attainment of the achievement goals in a way which is related closely to his own particular value system.

2. A person tends to turn to the excessive accumulation of wealth and the valuing of status and prestige positions when he is unsuccessful in gaining respect and recognition on the basis of his personal accomplishments.

3. It is necessary for a person to be shown respect, regardless of his age, sex, position, and general background, if he is to grow and develop to the point of realizing his potential abilities.

4. The accumulation of wealth is a goal that is actually achieved with any degree of success by only a very small percentage of the people in American society and, consequently, many people would find life much less frustrating if they concentrated instead on attaining the other achievement goals.

5. Although a person may use his power beneficially, there is always a danger that he will attempt to influence the lives of other people in a way that is most advantageous and comfortable for him.

6. If people are to live fully and creatively, it is necessary for them to experience a wide variety of opportunities for developing skillful behavior.

7. There is a tendency for many people in American society to exaggerate the limited amount of knowledge with which they are content to live and, at the same time, to ridicule anyone who seriously tries to find enlightenment.

8. The person who is genuinely interested in moving toward the goal of enlightenment assumes the major responsibility for his own learning experiences.

EXERCISE 6

The Self in Groups

It may help you to achieve the goals you have set for yourself if you develop skills in self-observation. One important aspect of behavior is the way you function in groups. As honestly as possible, quickly check the following items to best describe yourself in a *general way*.

Check one:

YES   No

1. Do I feel free to express myself in groups?

2. Am I honest when I choose to be?

3. Are there often persons within groups who inhibit me from expressing myself?

4. Do I often feel considerable hostility toward individuals who are with me?

5. Do I often have strong positive feelings toward individuals who are with me?

6. Do my feelings about some members often change during the course of the interactions from either negative to positive or positive to negative?

7. Does the size affect me? (Am I more comfortable with small or with large groups?)

8. Am I satisfied with the way groups function?

9. Do I often attempt to assert myself as to how the group should function?

10. Am I satisfied with the amount of my participation?

11. Am I satisfied with the quality of my participation?

_____ _____ 12. Do I feel accepted by groups—feel I belong?

_____ _____ 13. Do I ordinarily formulate goals for what I hope to get from each group with whom I participate?

_____ _____ 14. Do I often say what I think the group wants me to say instead of what I really think?

_____ _____ 15. Do I ordinarily seek out persons in the group who make me feel comfortable and avoid those who make me uncomfortable?

_____ _____ 16. Do I prefer strong leaders?

_____ _____ 17. Do I ordinarily feel secure in group situations?

_____ _____ 18. Do I ordinarily feel defensive or shy in group situations?

_____ _____ 19. Do I resent group situations?

_____ _____ 20. Do I often gain new insights into others after participating in groups?

_____ _____ 21. Do I often gain new insights into myself after participating in groups?

_____ _____ 22. Do I believe there is any relationship between preconceived attitudes toward and what can be learned from participation in groups?

_____ _____ 23. Do I like myself as I ordinarily act in groups?

_____ _____ 24. Do I want to change the way I act in group situations?

Now go back over the 24 items you have checked and select the five that seem most significant to you. List them in order of their importance.

1. _____

2. _____

3. _____

4. _____

5. _____

What does this exercise tell you about yourself and your group behavior? Are you active or passive? Are you a leader or a follower? Shy? Outgoing? Are you satisfied with yourself? If not, in the following space list things you might do that would facilitate your becoming more the person you would like to be.

_____

_____

_____

CHAPTER 8

Well-Being Level I

The achievement of personal satisfaction, meaning, and well-being in one form or another is the goal of all people. What provides satisfaction for one person, however, is not necessarily appropriate for other people because every individual lives according to his own somewhat unique system of values, regardless of whether he has deliberately worked out and decided what is important to him. This system of values, moreover, is invariably being modified and changed so that the behavior that provides satisfaction at one time in a person's life may be quite unsatisfactory at a later stage in his development.

It is probably necessary to distinguish between what is meant by satisfaction and the hedonistic concept of pleasure. The martyr, for example, may find great satisfaction in suffering for a cause which is important to him, but at the same time, he gains little pleasure from his behavior. The soldier at the battle front is hardly likely to find life pleasurable and yet he may obtain considerable satisfaction from overcoming his nervousness, fighting bravely, and generally behaving in a way which is consistent with his value system. The person, on the other hand, who actively pursues the attainment of pleasure usually finds life to be relatively empty and meaningless and he experiences only fleeting moments of happiness, contentment, and personal satisfaction.

Historically, mental health or the finding of personal satisfaction and well-being has been studied primarily in terms of the absence of negative or pathological symptoms and, as a result, healthy and normal people have been defined as those persons who have not displayed psychotic or neurotic symptoms. From this type of emphasis on mental health, the following continuum has resulted:

←——— Psychosis ——— Neurosis ——— Normal ———→

Whereas differences in the degree of sickness have been recognized, variations in the degree of health have been slighted. The situation would be the same if people had been classified according to height as very short, short, and normal.

Menninger (1963, p. 2) has expressed discontent with the existing classifications of mental health and has stressed the necessity for a scale which would measure the "success of a life" or the "satisfactoriness of the individual and his environment of their mutual attempts to adapt themselves to each other." In enlarging upon the need for such a scale, he makes the point that gone forever is the notion that the mentally ill person is an exception. Instead, it is becoming generally accepted, just as with physical illness, that most people have some type of mental illness at one time or other during their lives. Menninger (1963, p. 41) then, sees disease, whether it be mental or physical, as a characteristic of life under altered conditions and not a departure from life itself. Health, in turn, involves the capacity of the person to maintain a balance in life which is free from undue pain, discomfort, disability, and limitations in behavior and social effectiveness.

The continuum that is proposed below emphasizes both of these positive and negative characteristics to the same extent:

←— Psychotic—Neurotic—Over-Conforming—Integrated—Actualizing —→

As this scale of well-being suggests, it is quite conceivable that in any given population there are as many individuals who are very superior (actualizing) in their functioning state of mental health as the number of persons who are very inferior (psychotic). Similarly, there are likely to be as many people who are superior (integrated) as inferior (neurotic). In the middle of these groups are the persons who are neither superior nor inferior (over-conforming). Although they are certainly not seriously ill and they make many important contributions to society, because they primarily conform to the expectations of the particular community in which they live, they fall far short of realizing their full potential.

The degree of well-being that is characteristic of a person at any given point in time may be located somewhere on the scale. As the person grows or regresses, the position moves accordingly on the continuum. Failures in continued growth, lack of personal satisfaction, and maladjustment to the environment characterize a position at the left end of the scale. Conformity, over-adjustment to society, accompanied by arrested growth and lack of deep satisfaction are typical of the people located in the middle segment. Adjustment to society, continued growth, higher goal emergence, and greater degrees of personal satisfaction distinguish the people at the right end of the continuum. In general, a person's well-being is proportionate to his overall success in achieving his goals. Thus, the person who has been able to attain the goals he values is more likely to be moving toward actualization than the person who has failed or has been severely frustrated in his attempts in goal achievement.

Psychotic and Neurotic Behavior

It is never possible to draw a clear line of demarcation between any of the adjoining categories on the well-being scale, but primarily the person placed at the psychotic end of the continuum is distinguishable because of the fact that he suffers from a severe degree of personality disintegration. His contact with reality is impaired and his ability to function in everyday social situations is drastically retarded. Although the same symptoms may be found in the neurotic, the degree of disturbance and loss of contact with reality is much less serious. Coleman (1964, p. 264) has distinguished between the psychotic and the neurotic in the chart that is presented below:

FACTOR	PSYCHOSES	PSYCHONEUROSES
General behavior	Severe degree of personality decompensation; reality contact markedly impaired, patient incapacitated in social functioning	Mild degree of personality decompensation; reality contact and social functioning impaired
Nature of symptoms	Wide range of symptoms with delusions, hallucinations, emotional blunting, and other severely deviate behavior	Wide range of psychological and somatic symptoms but no hallucinations or other extreme deviations in thought, feeling, or action
Orientation	Patient frequently loses orientation to environment	Patient rarely loses orientation to environment
Insight	Patient rarely has insight into the nature of his behavior	Patient often has some insight into nature of his behavior
Social aspects	Behavior frequently injurious or dangerous to patient or to society	Behavior rarely injurious or dangerous to patient or to society
Treatment	Patient usually needs institutional care	Patient rarely needs institutional care

It has been estimated that at any one time there are around 1,000,000 persons in the United States who may be considered to be psychotic, about two-thirds of whom are hospitalized, and about 10,000,000 or more people who may be classified as being neurotic (Coleman, 1964, pp. 193 and 262-263). Generally these people act in a way which indicates they they are emotionally disturbed. Probably more serious for American society, however, is the much larger number of people, described below, who feel something is wrong with their lives even though for the most part their behavior conforms to the expectations and norms of society.

The Conforming Person

Burrow (1927) has taken the position that the problem person is but a symptom of the problem society which, stated even more directly, means that people become sick because they live in a sick society. In the behavior of many people there is evidence of the hideous distortion of human values embodied in the repressive subterfuge and truth of our so-called moral codes and conventions. The inconsistency of "saying one thing" and "doing another" results almost inevitably in disturbed patterns of behavior and a general level of social malfunctioning among the members of society.

As described in Chapter 4, a person develops an orientation which is an internalized version of what he has experienced or been taught to value. To the degree that this orientation is shared by a large proportion of society, it is believed to be appropriate and ideal. It may begin to dominate patterns of behavior and in some societies be followed blindly and even worshipped.

Unfortunately, only too often such orientations provide a caricature of man and his potentiality. The individuals who have the courage to question the accuracy of the orientation and refuse to conform to its false cultural demands are rejected and even ridiculed by the larger number of people who find a false type of safety in going along with the orientation willingly and passively. Quite frequently the people who conform to the orientation are living only in terms of their own self-interest. They intend to "get ahead" at any cost to both themselves and their fellow men and they do not intend to "rock the boat" or in any way jeopardize the possibility of personal advancement.

Furthermore, people in American society are exposed to a wide variety of orientations, many of which are in conflict with one another. The daily newspapers, popular magazines, and news programs on radio and television tend to deal superficially with scattered and unrelated events that have no connection, except that they occur at the same time. Fashions and styles, from hairdos to automobile designs, change regularly, thus fragmenting even further man's experience of his world. When a person is unable to find any way of integrating these diverse elements, he begins to feel inwardly the sense of division and separateness that surrounds him externally. Because of his inability to find meaning in his experiences and his mixed and ambivalent reaction to such uncertainty, he turns to and begins to follow obediently the expectancies and orientation of whatever is the most powerful influence in his life.

Caught in the web of judging himself and other persons in terms of a particularly dominant and idealized orientation, an authoritarian person is forced into devoting a great deal of energy to making sure that the people with whom he is associated fit into the mold of his orientation. Such a person displays his disturbance in a variety of ways but particularly in his complete inability to conceive of the destructive effect his behavior has upon the people around him. Presthus (1965, pp. 22-23) has commented on the negative influence that such a destructive orientation has upon the academic life in the following way:

> Another unhappy result of administrative imperialism is the displacement of intellectual values by those of the marketplace. Power, publicity, consulting service to powerful groups, and 'practical' research compete strongly with traditional goals. The notion that administrators alone really speak for the university, the ramifications of their roles by all kinds of ceremonial paraphernalia, their monopoly of initiative in university affairs—all tend to weaken academic roles and values. Administrators prefer charming, sensitive, dependent, loyal faculty members and such criteria now compete with professional standards in appointments and promotions. The effects include a subtle demoralization among the most committed of faculty men. Faculty disenchantment weakens the desire to do hard, disciplined work.

The preservation of such an orientation thus can be accompanied by decay, disorder, and, on occasion, downright cruelty of man toward his fellow men. Today's factory worker, for example, is often a uniform and replaceable part of a complicated production system. If he fails to do his job, another person can be found to take his place, usually with a minimum amount of difficulty and negligible effect upon production.

Another more subtle form of conformity is expressed by the person who refuses to go along with normal social expectations and conventions and who chooses instead always to act and think differently from the people with whom he is in contact. Such a person simply cannot stand to behave in the same way as other people and therefore he turns to what seems like inappropriate and even unusual and strange behavior patterns in order to express what he considers to be his individuality. The very fact that he can never be satisfied with behaving in the ordinary, routine, and socially acceptable way and that he finds it necessary to rely on such extreme measures, almost as if to justify his uniqueness, indicates that he feels considerable uncertainty about his worth as a person. As a result, he is not free to be the sort of person he really wants to be but, instead, is forced to conform to the expectation that he must be different from other people if he is to be recognized and respected.

Frequently, his behavior takes the form of refusing to observe the usual social amenities and courtesies. While a rigid conformity to good manners and acceptable behavior is more likely to be an expression of self-centeredness than of social sensitivity, it is true, nevertheless, that the boy who does not bother to open a door for his date, or who does not feel the necessity of wearing a tie at a formal occasion, is more likely to be expressing his unconcern for the feelings of the people around him or his need for attention than his own uniqueness and individuality. In time, his friends begin to tire of his behavior and as they tend to reject him, he is forced into more unusual attempts to show that he does not need to conform to normal social expectations. Unfortunately, such behavior leads inevitably to failure, for it is only when the individual is secure enough to behave like other people when the occasion warrants it that he is able to begin to formulate the integration of his experiences, not in a rigid and unchanging manner, but with an orientation that is uniquely his own and characterized by a constantly growing and re-structuring process that is typical of the integrated and actualizing person.

Patterns of Conformity

In order to understand the damage and harm that may result from an undue emphasis upon conformity, a discussion of its impact upon life in Germany and in the United States and upon higher education in the United States today is presented below.

GERMANY

The influence that the presence of a large and conforming population may have upon a modern state or nation is illustrated frighteningly by what Arendt (1963, p. 15) referred to as the complicity of all German offices and authorities, including the civil servants in the state ministries, members of the regular armed forces, the judiciary, and the business world, in the massacre of millions of Jews. In short, an entire nation, with far more people participating, either actively or passively, than opposing, went along with these terrible events. As Arendt (1963, p. 143) pointed out, there "existed not a single organization or public institution in Germany, at least during the war years, that did not become involved in criminal actions and transactions."

Many respectable German citizens, who were neither psychotic nor neurotic and who played their role in the slaughter, never felt anything whatsoever against the Jews personally. In Germany, and no doubt in other parts of the world, there were average or normal people who were not concerned about behaving ethically. The presence of this attitude among so-called normal people is attested to further by the role of the Jewish leaders in the destruction of their own people. Almost without exception, the leaders cooperated for one reason or another with the Nazis (Arendt, 1963, p. 111). Frankl (1963, p. 4) has described, moreover, how the Capos, prisoners in the concentration camps who acted as trustees, not only were often harder on the other prisoners than were the guards but also beat them even more cruelly than did the SS men. In fact, this pattern of behavior was one of the darkest chapters in the whole bitter story. Unfortunately, the youth in Germany today is surrounded on all sides and in all walks of life by men in positions of authority and in public office who, although to some extent are guilty for these events, feel little remorse (Arendt, 1963, p. 229).

The pattern of over-conformity may be recognized as well in the men who become Nazi leaders. Eichmann, for example, was a joiner who stated that he sensed he would have a difficult individual life. He did not enter the Nazi party out of conviction, for he did not know the program and he had not read Hitler's *Mein Kampf*. Eichmann was said also to have been incapable of uttering a single sentence that was not a truism, causing him to develop a different cliché for each period and activity of his life. To some extent the entire German nation may have been taught to distort reality by deceptions similar to those so deeply ingrained in Eichmann's way of life. This belief is supported by a study by Ansbacher (1948) of the attitudes of a group of German soldiers who were captured in September, 1944. Of the 65 percent who expressed confidence in Hitler, only a minority agreed with all of his views, the majority being in opposition to the policies that Hitler proclaimed. Ansbacher (1948, p. 18) interpreted the confidence in Hitler, despite the presence of a basic disagreement, as occurring because "the object of the confidence was no longer the real totalitarian leader as manifested in his writings, speeches, and deeds, but a leader of the followers' own creation."

Klineberg (1965, p. 62) emphasized that the rise of a leader to power must be understood not only in terms of his particular abilities, but also in relation to the willingness of the people to accept the type of leadership that was being offered. The prevalent attitude in Germany that obedience was a virtue and disobedience a sin pointed to a pattern of over-conformity in which many people believed that all that was necessary to fulfill the function of a human being was to obey and follow instructions. Thus, the notion of open disobedience was a fairy tale for "nobody acted that way." It was unthinkable not to follow instructions and, as Arendt (1963, p. 88) pointed out, most Germans were always extremely careful to be covered by orders. Because so many Germans were unable to discriminate between right and wrong in individual as well as collective matters, they remained unaware of the serious implications of their behavior, which were so readily apparent to the outside and neutral observer.

THE UNITED STATES

In synthesizing the relevant insights on American values advanced by a number of writers, Du Bois (1955, pp. 1237-1238) included conformity as one of the three dominant values. She noted, moreover, that in America:

> Doors need not be closed to rooms; fences need not be built around properties. The tall hedges of England and the enclosing walls of France are not appropriate to the American scene, where life faces outward rather than inward. If every individual is as 'good as' the next and all are good citizens—what is there to hide? The open front yards, the porches, or more recently the picture windows that leave the home open to everyone's view, the figurative and literal klieg lights under which our public figures live are all evidence of the value placed in American life on likeness and the pressure exerted for conformity. This is very different from saying that American middle-class individuals are in fact all alike. It means merely that likeness is valued.

The signs of conformity are recognizable elsewhere in American society. Mumford (1961, p. 495) has noted that compulsive play has rapidly become the acceptable alternative to compulsive work. The average person literally has "fun" even if it kills him and fun, of course, is that activity which public opinion has told him he should enjoy and not the activity in which he really wants to participate.

According to Mumford (1961, p. 231) the need for mass entertainment is imperative in direct proportion to the futility of the rest of existence. Today in America, as people lose their individual autonomy, they console themselves with frantic play, compulsive work, or the possession of the numerous material objects and things which are available to be bought and put on display.

As mentioned in Chapter 4, Henry (1963, p. 50) has pointed out that there exists in America today a pecuniary truth which is not intended to be believed. The housewife is not really expected to be persuaded that her washer will wash as if it were ten feet tall. Her husband is not actually going to obtain limitless shaves from blade X. No proof is ever offered that such statements are true and, even more tragically, none is ever demanded.

The danger of such blind conformity to the advertiser's slogans may be seen in the fact that in 1960, as noted by Henry (1963, p. 58), Congress appropriated only 33 million dollars for the Federal Trade Commission, the Federal Communication Commission, and the Food and Drug Administration, all of which serve as restraints upon the "pecuniary truth." This figure was about three-tenths of one percent of the sum of money that was spent for advertising that year. Mumford (1961, p. 538) observed, moreover, that something like twice the amount of money was spent per family on advertising as that allocated for primary and secondary education. Thus, economic ends have been allowed to take precedence over personal welfare, and national and group interests of all kinds have assumed priority over individual interest. Heilbroner (1961, p. 358) has charged that:

> Our society is an immense stamping press for the careless production of under-developed and malformed human beings, and that, whatever it may claim to be, it is not a society fundamentally concerned with moral issues, with serious purposes, or with human dignity.

Perhaps you will find the preceding paragraphs overly pessimistic and even cynical. It is true that modern life is infinitely better than life 300 to 1000 years ago and that in the present technological society, man lives longer and better and, despite his shortcomings, he is healthier and wiser. Jarrell (1962, pp. 64-89), however, has accused the modern conforming person of giving other people what they think and want, instead of stubbornly or helplessly sticking to what he sees and feels, to what is right for him and true to his reality. The price of such conformity is a loss of feeling for himself and for others and a state of uneasiness and dissatisfaction with his failure to realize his potentiality.

HIGHER EDUCATION IN THE UNITED STATES

Additional evidence of the conforming person may be found in a study of the mental health of a group of students primarily composed of co-eds at the University of Texas. Only five or six students out of one hundred and three were considered to be seriously disturbed but, by the same token, no more than half a dozen were found to have optimum mental health. The great majority of the students had neither suffered from a severe loss of mental health nor had attained it to any marked degree. They were described by Peck (1962, pp. 174-186) in the following way:

1. They are dependent social conformists. Their life experiences have unavoidably left them with little practiced skill at thinking for themselves, and not much impressive self-assurance or faith to motivate them to try.

2. They get along half-ineptly, on a rather thin diet of human happiness and healthy pride. . . .

3. Most of them show a pervasive anxiety, of a tolerable but uncomfortable kind. . . . Much of the anxiety seems rather to stem from a quite accurate perception on their part that their lives lack shape and purpose. . . . They often try hard to hide this painful sense of meaninglessness from themselves, but it becomes evident when they seriously contemplate where they are going in life, and what they hope to find. . . . Their anxiety is essentially a realistic one. They do, in fact, lack the purpose or the skill to set and pursue worthwhile goals.

4. They have the desire and courage to keep going . . . do achieve occasional visions of what a fully realized life could be. . . . Perhaps, above all, they have a hope that the future will somehow be better.

Perhaps a more detailed description of some of the students in the average mental health group may help to clarify these patterns of behavior. One of them, referred to as "The Nice Young Thing" is seen as trusting authority figures completely and almost fatalistically accepting their directions. Basically she is an extremely passive person who is happy as long as she can earn the pleasure of personal approval by doing what others ask.

Another girl, "The Well Equipped Operator," loves the limelight and devotes "most of her effort toward achieving high social visibility and personal recognition." She tends "to be quite lazy in her thinking and prone to biased, subjective judgments. . . . .Primarily expedient in her character type, she has the intelligence and surface attractiveness to be a rather successful operator in casual social interaction."

A third girl, "The Shy Good Girl," is "not really very happy, partly because she is so restrained that she does not have too many effective ways of initiating action to achieve the effects she very much wants to accomplish. . . . She feels quietly disappointed in a low-key way, and there is a distinct possibility that unless she is reassured by genuinely interested, personal attention from people she likes and respects, she could easily become progressively disillusioned with life in the years ahead."

The salient characteristics of the students in the average mental health group were summarized in the following way (Peck, 1962, pp. 191-192):

This middle majority of students ask overly simple questions of life and expect overly simple formulae by way of answers. Their relatively stereotyped habits of thinking appear to be due to inadequate parental training. With the best will in the world, they cannot quickly and easily alter this state of affairs. They memorize, they do not question. They take notes and they write, but they do not necessarily understand, nor do they long remember. . . . It is a basic fact about these students that before they can learn to care about a new set of ideas, they have to feel a personal interest toward, *and from,* the person who is trying to communicate the ideas. Put negatively, this characteristic reaction can be termed dependent conformity, or subjective, personalistic thinking. Viewed positively, if they are approached on an individual level with genuine interest in their personal thoughts, feelings and concerns, such an interest awakens a strong response in them. At the beginning, it is largely an emotional response, a hunger for personal attention; but with patience and clear purpose, students like this can slowly be led to assume modest but increasing amounts of independent thought and work.

It is no use trying to force the pace with these young people. To give them wide freedom of choice at first, without detailed guidance, usually is to paralyze them with anxious indecision. . . . What would look like a wonderful freedom to mature students looks like frightening chaos to these average students, at first. They need to be led toward more autonomous habits of thought by small degrees, with plenty of personal encouragement, if they are ever to achieve much growth in this direction.

This description corresponds almost perfectly with the idea that the satisfaction of the safety, love, and belongingness goals must take place before the higher goals in the hierarachy are able to emerge. These so-called average or normal students have never received sufficient love for them to feel safe enough to launch themselves on the demanding struggle of becoming a person. Thus, they are forced to be content with hiding their uniqueness behind the masks of conformity and expediency.

Collaboration of this viewpoint has been presented by Nevitt Sanford (1962, p. 253) who described the typical freshman entering Vassar College in the following way:

She is oriented primarily to the social group, and her very considerable social skill is freely displayed; she is friendly, cooperative, polite and—at least in her external aspect—poised. She participates comfortably and uncritically in the values of her family and home community, has high respect for our social institutions and, toward the powers that be, she is deferential and uncomplaining.

Her reliance upon the family and the community is evidence of the need for external support for her system of values. As Peckham (1962, p. 355) stated, "The effect of conventions in a cultural tradition is to limit the individual to experiencing those emotions which the conventions signify." Thus, the person is told what to look for in the real world and he feels only what he thinks he ought to feel. In *The Brothers Karamazov,* Dostoevsky's Grand Inquisitor may have been right when he said that for the great majority of man, the freedom of choice offered by Christ is an intolerable burden; what they want and need first of all is bread, and then, "miracle, mystery, and authority."

Sanford (1962, p. 253) pointed out that as the college student encounters the complexity of critical thinking and difficulty of realistically supporting the blacks and whites of childhood, her externally imposed and supported certainty may be replaced by a college-induced doubt. It is likely that she will feel rather confused, frustrated, and anxious by midway through her senior year and that she will look back on her freshman year as a remote and happy time. Growth toward a greater degree of well-being is never a painless task, but all people may experience it, provided they are surrounded by social situations in which it is safe for a person to be himself, express what he feels and values, and find out what he and other people really do experience in the process of life.

SUMMARY

1. The achievement of personal satisfaction and well-being is related closely to the person's value system and philosophy of life.
2. Although historically in psychology the absence of serious illness has been considered to be an indication of normality, currently there is an increasing awareness of the necessity of viewing mental health in terms of the constructive aspects of a person's behavior.
3. As a result, it is helpful for mental health to be considered in terms of a continuum which has the psychotic or very seriously disturbed person at one extreme and the actualizing person with a high degree of social sensitivity at the other end.
4. The vast majority of Americans, however, live in terms of a pattern of conformity which fits the orientations of the more authoritarian persons and groups in society.
5. A subtle form of conformity to the reactions of other people is expressed through the behavior of a person who, in order to gain attention and recognition, invariably chooses to be different.
6. The history of Germany under the Nazis is a frightening example of what can happen to a group of people who follow blindly a prescribed pattern of behavior and thereby fail to assume responsibility for their own lives.
7. In the United States there are a number of serious signs of conformity in higher education, interpersonal relationships, and social life generally.
8. The tendency toward conformity is counteracted most effectively by allowing people to have experiences in which they are free to express whatever they feel and consider to be important.

EXERCISE 7
Leadership Styles

Individuals utilize many different styles of leadership. Following are a number of statements, some with which you may agree and some with which you may disagree. Check the 15 with which you agree most.

_____ 1. The leader serves the group best when he is direct, real, open, spontaneous, permissive, emotional, and highly personal.

_____ 2. The leader should be ready to give negative criticism where warranted and to appraise performance frequently, fairly, and unequivocally.

_____ 3. The leader must set clear goals for himself and for the group or institution.

_____ 4. Ultimately, the responsibility for the outcome of the enterprise rests in the hands of its leaders.

_____ 5. People can be trusted independently to put out a great deal of effort toward achieving organizational goals.

_____ 6. The leader should reward good performance and learn effective ways of showing appreciation.

_____ 7. People tend to want to cooperate with others.

_____ 8. Good leadership requires good fellowship.

_____ 9. Leaders are born, not made.

_____ 10. The best leader brings out group strength, individual responsibility, diversity, nonconformity, and aggressiveness.

_____ 11. Leaders are disposable and quickly replaceable to the enterprise.

_____ 12. People are frequently creative and imaginative.

_____ 13. People grow, produce, and learn best when they set their own goals and are free to choose self-related activities.

_____ 14. The leader must command strong discipline, not only because people respect a strong leader, but because strength and firmness communicate care and concern.

_____ 15. Finding the right leader is a critical variable in the success of the enterprise.

_____ 16. People should have freedom of choice in all parts of their lives.

_____ 17. The leader must make policies and rules and see that these are administered with justice, wisdom, and compassion.

_____ 18. The leader's job is to help the group to grow, to emerge, and to become more free.

_____ 19. While the leader must listen for counsel before making decisions, the decisions he makes are ultimately his responsibility.

_____ 20. The good leader tends not to lead but permits, feels, acts, relates, fights, and talks—in short, is very human.

_____ 21. Leadership is only one of several significant variables in the life of enterprise.

_____ 22. People tend to follow good leaders.

_____ 23. People perform best under leaders who are creative, imaginative, and aggressive—under leaders who lead.

_____ 24. The most effective leader is one who acts as a catalyst, a consultant, and a resource to the group.

_____ 25. The leader should keep an appropriate social distance, control his emotions, command respect, and be objective and fair.

_____ 26. Under most conditions people are highly motivated.

_____ 27. It is the responsibility of the leader to marshal the forces of the organization, to stimulate effort, to inspire people, and to coordinate efforts.

_____ 28. The best leader is an effective group member.

_____ 29. People like to take responsibility.

_____ 30. The quality of an organization is best judged by the quality of the leadership.

Agreement with the following 15 statements indicates a preference for a traditional authoritarian leader. Color out those you agreed with.

2	3	4	6	8	9	14	15	17	19	22	23	25	27	30

Agreement with the following 15 statements indicates a preference for a more permissive, non-authoritarian leader. Color out those you agreed with.

1	5	7	10	11	12	13	16	18	20	21	24	26	28	29

Is your preference clear-cut? Uncertain? Do the results tell you more about how you would perform as a leader or about the kind of leadership you prefer to follow? In the following space, list as many advantages and disadvantages as you can for each style. Refer back as frequently as necessary to the 15 statements describing each.

Authoritarian Leadership

Advantages

Disadvantages

Permissive Leadership

Advantages

Disadvantages

Assume your teachers are examples of leaders and observe the styles of different ones. Which types do they seem to be? How does the way they lead make you feel? Which style motivates you best? Is it fair to generalize from this? Should leadership styles vary with situations?

CHAPTER 9

Well-Being Level II

As mentioned in the previous chapter, the behavior of the people on the right of the mental health continuum is characterized by integration and actualization. Generally they are distinguishable from the over-conforming persons in the degree to which they tend to think and feel differently from other people and relate to the environment in a way that is uniquely their own.

In the presentation of this description of Well-Being Level II, the authors have drawn particularly from the writings of Rogers (1961), Allport (1961), and Maslow (1962). On the whole, however, it is hypothesized that integration and actualization occur to the extent that the person is able to (1) grow and develop continuously throughout his life; (2) become more integrated, autonomous, and self-directing; and (3) experience rich and satisfying interpersonal relationships.

Continuous Growth and Development Throughout Life

Continuous growth and development throughout life seems to occur more frequently among people who tend to have been gratified rather than deprived. A study by Nichols and Davis (1964) of the National Merit Scholarship winners, who represented academically the top one percent of America's youth, pointed out the following characteristics in the backgrounds of these students:

(1) They tended to come from homes of high educational and socio-economic status.

(2) They lived more frequently in the suburbs of large cities and less frequently in farm areas.

(3) There was a larger proportion of males among them than is found in the general population.

(4) They were almost exclusively white.

(5) They had significantly more younger than older siblings and tended to be the oldest child in the family. They had fewer brothers and sisters than is the case with average students.

Each one of these factors may be interpreted as pointing to a life in which gratification was more typical than deprivation. Obviously, for instance, parents who are relatively wealthy are able to provide more opportunities for gratification of their children's needs than parents without such an advantage. The sons and daughters of the wealthy are much more likely to be respected than looked down upon, and parents with strong educational backgrounds tend to be more acceptant and less punitive toward their children than parents with little formal education. The suburban environment clearly provides more diverse opportunities for experience than the rural area. Generally, males have fewer restrictions placed upon them than females and white persons are obviously more gratified and goal satiated than Negroes. The oldest child tends to obtain the most attention in the family, if only by virtue of the fact that probably for at least a year or so he has the parents exclusively to himself. On the same basis, it may be assumed that children in small families tend to receive more attention from their parents than the members of large families. Altogether, then, it is felt that gratification, rich diversity of background, and acceptance are the influences which make it easier for a person to continue to grow and develop. Although it may take form in a number of different ways, such behavior is seen as primarily occurring when a person becomes motivated intrinsically, remains open to his experiences, emphasizes rational morality or rectitude, and establishes an integrated value system or philosophy of life.

INTRINSIC MOTIVATION

When a person's need for love, belongingness, and psychological safety is being satisfied more or less continuously, he no longer finds it necessary to use the achievement of his goals as a means of gaining recognition and feeling safe. As a result, his energy is expended toward the attainment of his goals because the experience of doing so is important in and of itself. Thus, for instance, in the ideal educational setting, the student is encouraged to move beyond the mere requirements of courses and he is provided with opportunities for assuming responsibility for his own educational experience.

It appears that such learning occurs most readily when the student experiences a close and meaningful relationship with his teacher. After studying an average group of college students, for example, Peck (1962,

p. 191) concluded that, "it is a basic fact about these students that before they can learn to care about a new set of ideas, they have to feel a personal interest toward *and from* the person who is trying to communicate the ideas." This viewpoint is expressed also in the following excerpt from a paper written by a student of one of the authors:

> One of the really good things this semester for me is the real feeling of friendship, confidence, and mutual respect that I felt we had. I do not really understand what my need for the respect and closeness with my teachers means psychologically, but the expectation and good will that you communicate to me has been a considerable motivating and energizing factor.

In writing about teachers, Adelson (1964) referred to the work of the altruistic teacher as "a model-less approach to teaching; the teacher points neither to himself or to some immediately visible figure, but chooses to work with his student's potential and toward an intrinsically abstract or remote ideal." Perhaps the secret of helping people to continue to grow and develop on their own is to be found in such treatment of every person as the very special individual that he is. In this way, he is given the opportunity to be what he wishes to be, thus becoming more self-propelled and less driven and, consequently, much more motivated intrinsically.

Openness to Experience

Once they become adults, many people consider the need for any further change unnecessary and unnatural. For them, the developmental task has ended and there is a tendency to approve the status quo and to maintain the same attitudes and experiences. The actualizing person, however, attempts to increase his understanding of life through association with ever enlarging segments of his environment. Thus, for him, to stop growing at 20, 30, 40, 50, 60, 70, 80, or even 90 years of age would be seen as the same as the behavior of a child who refuses to go to school.

It is important to realize that the process of gaining in understanding, enlightenment, and sensitivity is much broader than mere participation in formal education. The cultural attaché at an embassy overseas, for instance, is offered a wide variety of experiences that may be used to enrich his perception and appreciation of life. Similarly, the cab driver, who truly observes the persons with whom he comes in contact during the course of a day, has many opportunities to learn about the way people think and behave. In this way, growth and development in knowledge and enlightenment may take place through such activities as travelling, meeting people, and listening to their ideas, as well as by means of the more traditional experiences of reading, listening to music, attending the theater, visiting art galleries, etc.

An adult's behavior may be compared to that of a child who goes to school gladly with the expectation of learning. Provided the school program is at least adequate, the child participates in experiences that bring a new world to his fingertips. However, he may choose not to take advantage of these opportunities, in which case he gains very little and probably will remain basically the same sort of person for the rest of his life. Similarly, the adult may profit from his experiences or he may restrict himself to the area of life in which he is told what he wants to hear and in which, consequently, he feels comfortable and at home. By concentrating on the familiar and superficial, even the usually broadening experience of travel may fail to challenge him into developing a new perspective on life. He may vacation in Europe, for instance, but ignore the local people and socialize primarily with Americans. Although he may spend on the average of only two days in every major city and give more time to taking in the night life than in exploring the cultural and aesthetic opportunities that Europe provides, he announces naively and proudly upon arriving home that he has "done" Europe.

Perhaps the importance of being open to change and new experiences may be seen even more effectively on the cultural level because social groups also face the alternative of either growing through new experience or stagnating. As Muller (1958, p. 15) noted, the curious spirit of the Greeks "led them to borrow more copiously than any people before them." Through the acceptance of what was new, there was expressed a willingness to let go of the traditional and develop a new way of thinking.

A study by Terman (1954) may be used to illustrate how the activities of only a few persons may cause other people to develop new orientations. Over a thirty-year period, he studied the progress of a group of 1500 college students with an average I.Q. of 150, which means that they were among the intellectually gifted. At the average age of 40 the 800 males in the group had published a total of 67 books, over 200 short stories and plays, 236 miscellaneous articles, and 1400 professional articles. Eighty-five of them earned law degrees, 78 were awarded Ph.D. degrees, another 48 obtained medical degrees, and 104 received engineering degrees. Seventy-four members of the group were teaching in colleges and universities and 51 completed some basic research in the physical sciences and engineering. As may be appreciated, the combined contribution to knowledge of these persons was overwhelmingly significant and the extent of the impact of their activities upon the lives of people in America and the world is open only to conjecture.

Nichols and Davis found, moreover, that the Merit Scholarship winners were capable of change and continued growth and preferred to be involved in more than one activity to a greater extent than a group of average students. The scholarship winners tended more than the average students to be less conventional in their opinions and more favorably inclined toward modern art, thus indicating a greater readiness to break down old orientations and discover new answers to the questions that were concerning them. They valued security as a goal far less than the average students, preferring instead to be "living and working in the world of ideas, opportunities to be original and creative, and freedom from supervision." (Nichols and Davis, 1964, p. 798)

Rokeach (1960, p. 253) has pointed out that "closed-minded" subjects persist twice as long as "open-minded" subjects in the belief that there has to be a solution to a problem that was designed to have no solution. The same characteristic may be observed in people who lack a high degree of well-being in that they are often searching for precise answers to questions about life that simply cannot be obtained.

Russell (Egner and Denonn, 1961, p. 694) noted that "one of the painful things about our time is that those who feel certainty are stupid, and those with any imagination and understanding are filled with doubt and indecision." As José Ortega y Gasset (1964, p. 733) pointed out as well, "life is a petty thing unless it is moved by the indomitable urge to extend its boundaries. Only in proportion as we are desirous of living more do we really live."

The person who has reached Well-Being Level II, however, possesses what Peckham (1962, p. 278) referred to as a "tough-minded power to look at things as they are, and oneself as one really is." Orientations always conceal as well as reveal and a person must be willing on occasion to set aside momentarily his current outlook on life if he is to explore the reality of another orientation. Being emotionally healthy, therefore, involves the ability to question, search, and doubt continually and the willingness to attempt to find a way of resolving the doubt.

It is important to note, however, that doubting and questioning do not consist of the wanton flying in the face of the environment or the expression of nonconformity and rebellion. Instead, what is involved is the utilizing of many aspects of the culture as opposed to few of them so that the person attempts to live in harmony with more and more of its diverse orientations. As Jung (1961, p. 405) has warned, unless man "can atone by creative ability for his break with tradition, he is merely disloyal to the past."

Emphasis on Rational Morality or Rectitude

The person who achieves a high level of well-being questions all of the "do-nots" that come his way and accepts or rejects them as they are appropriate to his own experience. Thus, instead of having other people impose their value systems upon him, he decides himself what is right and wrong and assumes responsibility for the control of his own behavior. He is aware of the consequences of his actions upon himself and the people around him and he attempts to live in terms of becoming the sort of person he desires to be. In this way, what may be called rational morality or rectitude replaces childlike faith and obedience. Shoben (1957, p. 183) has observed that the agents of socialization, parents, schools, the church, and so forth, must not be expected merely to minimize the development of anti-social behavior but instead must accept the responsibility for fostering positive growth through the relationships and experiences provided for youngsters.

The person who attains this level of rational morality becomes increasingly capable of controlling his behavior by developing the ability to project the consequences of present actions upon his future being. As in the case of a person who begins to allow himself to be open to experience, the first step in evolving such behavior is often exceedingly difficult and painful. The child, or the adult who acts like a child, is "safe" in an immature sense because his behavior is approved by the prevailing authority. Similarly, the person who rebels against all roles has little difficulty in choosing his behavior because every decision is made on the basis of moving in the opposite direction from what other people expect. The actualizing person, on the other hand, who examines every rule and regulation in order to discover what meaning it has for him, not only exposes himself to the criticism of external authority but also subjects himself to the harshness of his own appraisal and evaluation. He knows that he is liable to be mistaken in his judgment and that it is necessary to live with the consequences of his decisions. At the same time, his errors of omission may be even more serious than those of commission and invariably questions are raised as to what might have been accomplished had he carried through with the plans that were considered.

As the healthy person moves toward a more positive concept of morality, he begins to release other people from the constrictive influence of "don'ts" in the same way that he has removed himself. He gives up his desire to direct other people toward a particular orientational reality and, instead, lives as a model for other persons to see and copy. His behavior exemplifies how he chooses to construe reality, and he leaves the other person free to emulate, ignore, or recreate from his example.

Such behavior is difficult to achieve because it is much easier for a teacher, for instance, to tell children how important the role of reading is in their lives than to be an example of what a person may become as a result of reading widely. Unfortunately, too few teachers provide such a source of identification. It is easy to understand, therefore, why so many students are suspicious of the benefits to be gained from reading and other similar activities and why they prefer, instead, to copy the patterns of behavior of the people with whom they are in contact.

Despite its demands, rational morality is less frustrating than the morality that is governed by a relentless type of prohibition. The insatiability of such a system is illustrated very well in the writing of Ko Hung (De Bary, 1960, p. 304) who pointed out that "those who aspire . . . should accomplish 1200 (good deeds). But if the 1199th good deed is followed by an evil one, they will lose all their accumulation and have to start all over." With such a harsh judgment there is no room at all for human frailty and consequently, frustration and disappointment must inevitably result.

The emergence of rational morality and its control over the destructive and aggressive demands of man was evident in a number of European countries during the German occupation in World War II. In Denmark, for instance, the Nazis were met with open resistance and the wanton killing of millions of innocent victims was checked. It is interesting to note, moreover, that the Germans who were confronted with this attitude no longer treated the extermination of human lives as a matter of course (Arendt, 1963, p. 157).

VALUE SYSTEM AND UNIFYING PHILOSOPHY OF LIFE

During the course of a lifetime, the actualizing person is continually in the process of formulating and revising the value system or philosophy of life that is the basis for his behavior. In so doing, he is forced to give serious thought to the place of the family, education, religion, work, play, personal relationships, aesthetics, politics, and other key social institutions and values in his life. It may be that he finds some of them to be relatively unimportant, but regardless of what he comes to value, his decision is made in terms of what is important to him, and not because it is simply easier to go along with someone else's ideas and avoid the effort that is necessary in establishing his own value system or philosophy of life.

In addition to determining the extent that the values are important to him, the actualizing person attempts as well to integrate them into a meaningful whole. In this way, he is able to avoid a basic or obvious conflict between what he does as a religious person, for instance, and the way he conducts his business. He is not bothered, moreover, with being expected to behave one way in a particular social situation and just the opposite in a different setting. Because he has a clear conception of what is important to him, he is able to avoid the trap of being pulled in a number of different directions and, consequently, his behavior remains consistent with his image of himself as a person.

Integration, Autonomy, and Self-Direction

Traditionally there have been two different points of view concerning the relationship of the individual to his culture. One position has emphasized that the primary virtue of man lies in his subservience to the customs and values of his social group; the other position has recognized the unique characteristics of the individual. According to Campbell (1964, p. 236), most of the world's cultures have subscribed to the former point of view, but the Greeks were a notable exception. He pointed out that:

> Elsewhere the particularities of the individual, novelties of his thought, and qualities of individual desire and delight were sternly wiped away in the name of the absolute norms of the group; but in Greece the particular excellencies of each were at least theoretically . . . legally and pedagogically respected.

One of the consequences of such recognition of individual development and personal autonomy was a flowering of human thought and accomplishment that has been largely unmatched throughout history.

In general, the development of integration, autonomy, and self-direction may be seen to take place to the extent that a person is able to (1) grow in rational thought; (2) develop a broad perspective toward time; and (3) live spontaneously and creatively in a way that allows him to be free to express his impulses.

RATIONAL THOUGHT

The actualizing person becomes capable of disengaging himself when necessary from thinking that is oriented toward the personal satisfaction of his own goals. Frequently, he asks himself how he would look at a situation if he were not personally involved and had nothing of interest at stake. By reacting impartially, he is better able to realize that what is good and desirable for him is not necessarily beneficial to other people or to mankind.

An example of this ability, as it may be applied to international relationships, is presented in the following description of Hawaii's East-West Center (Bartlett, 1964, p. 45).

East-West Center programs are "founded on the assumption that we (Americans) do not have the answers, and that we need to know more about the conditions in these countries if adaptations are going to be made to their special conditions," in the words of a Center administrator. Accordingly Americans and Asians working on research and training projects are brought to the Center as collaborating equals.

Here, at last, Uncle Sam's condescending stance as mentor to the under-developed countries of Asia is altered. For the word "interchange," as it appears in the formal title of the Center, contemplates a two-way flow of technical and cultural thinking, wherever possible on creative levels, frequently promoting synthesis. If honestly implemented, the idea of interchange constitutes an acknowledgment that Uncle Sam has something to learn from Buddha and Confucius, or from a Burmese rice farmer, and a Japanese businessman.

Klineberg (1965, pp. 144-146) described the difficulty involved in causing nations to gain a rational understanding of their differences and stated that the reaction of almost any American commentator on a Soviet proposal and almost any Soviet commentator to an American proposal is that "it's the same old stuff; nothing new or constructive in it." As an alternative, he suggested an approach to encourage negotiations and the development of rational thought around the international conference table which would have the following four characteristics: (1) a flexibility that would avoid the rigidity shown in the previous quotation; (2) an understanding which would take into account how the situation appears to both sides; (3) a willingness to be less suspicious of the motives of other people and to take the chance on the possibility that the sincere desire for peace is not the monopoly of one side; and (4) a readiness to find a solution that is reasonably satisfactory to both sides.

BROAD PERSPECTIVE OF TIME

It is characteristic of the conforming person that he tends to over-emphasize the past, the present, or the future. Members of the upper class, for example, often express their orientation toward the past through the importance they attach to tradition, family background, and genealogical studies. Similarly, older people and persons who no longer enjoy their former level of effectiveness find satisfaction in turning back the clock to the "good old days." Such an emphasis on the past may be seen very clearly in Serling's story, *Requiem for a Heavyweight* (1962). Mountain Rivera, a punch-drunk prize fighter who has difficulty securing employment when his boxing days are over, finds some feeling of importance by reminding his friends that at one time he was "almost the Heavyweight Champion of the World."

Other people live primarily for the present and the immediate future. Persons in the lower class are sometimes so restricted to the present that they will not consider working while they have enough money in their pockets to satisfy their immediate needs. In a study of suburban life, Seeley, Sim, and Loosley (1956, p. 69) found that, "the tempo and the emphasis on the present result in a pervasive feeling that *time is running out;* and there is a tendency for the child to push experience forward in advance of physiological development." This pattern of behavior may be seen in the growing trend for fifth and sixth graders to attend formal dances and for freshmen to arrive on the college campus, having already experienced and grown weary of most of the social activities that the college is prepared to offer.

Still other persons live for the future and, like Wilkens Micawber in Charles Dickens' *David Copperfield*, rather naively they wait in case anything turns up. In the context of present day life, such behavior is seen most clearly in the members of the middle class who are extremely conscious of the importance of security and providing for the future. Personnel directors of major corporations have noted that the strength of retirement programs is one of the primary reasons why newly graduated college students join their companies.

In contrast to these three approaches to life, the actualizing person is concerned primarily with living richly and fully in the present on a level that is appropriate to his social situation and emotional development. He has respect for the rich heritage of his past and he tries to avoid repeating his earlier mistakes. At the same time, he realizes that by taking advantage of his present opportunities, he will have a better chance of achieving a number of his goals in the future. Thus, instead of dreaming about how wonderful life will be when he is graduated from college, he studies hard and strives to gain the enlightenment and sensitivity to life that will help to ensure his future happiness.

SPONTANEITY, IMPULSE FREEDOM, AND CREATIVE LIVING

The actualizing person lives and acts spontaneously. Campbell (1962, p. 495) noted that the great athlete or artist performs without any conscious awareness of his form. It is difficult to imagine, for instance, Babe Ruth thinking about his swing, Anna Pavlova being concerned with the intracacies of a pirouette, or Dame Myra Hess or Isaac Stern playing a concert mechanically. In fact, the picture is really ridiculous; for these and other artists, performance is characterized by effortless grace and precision. In much the same way, life at the higher level of well-being is recognized by an ease and smoothness in personal relationships.

In order to clarify this point, perhaps you can recall the first time you danced, played bridge, or engaged in some other similar activity. Probably you were tense, highly self critical, and very much afraid of making a mistake. In fact, the experience altogether may have been almost painful. No doubt that during the intervening period you have gained in confidence to the point now that you engage in such activities freely and naturally, with little concern over whether or not you are making the right move. An awareness of being able to do whatever is necessary with ease and grace may perhaps provide a sensitivity and appreciation for the majesty of living at a higher level of well-being. The pure joy that the actualizing person experiences may cause him to feel that something extremely important and valuable is happening. Moreover, he may exhibit the delightful uninhibited naturalness of a child so that he expresses whatever he feels at a particular moment without undue concern over the reactions and judgments that other people place upon his behavior.

Unfortunately, society forces people to live differently, with an emphasis upon conformity, exactness, and punctuality that is onerous. On occasion, it seems as if it is even possible to predict what people will be doing at a certain time and in a particular place. King (1958, pp. 36-37) noticed this tendency in the school systems of France and reported that, "though it is not quite true that every child in a given class in France is being taught the same thing at the same time, anyone examining the minutely regulated school programs might very well think so."

The behavior of the actualizing person, however, may not be anticipated in such a way. He remains dependable, but it is possible to know him very well and still be unable to tell what his behavior will be in a given situation. On relatively inconsequential matters, he has learned to surrender to the inevitable demands for conformity, but, at the same time, he is careful to protect his individuality by distinguishing significant issues upon which he needs to take a stand from busy little trivialities.

In addition to behaving spontaneously, the actualizing person experiences a great deal of impulse freedom in that he learns to trust his feelings and reactions when deciding whether or not behavior is right for him. Sometimes it is believed that when a person is allowed to rely on his own impulses, there is a danger that his lack of inhibition will cause a great deal of destructiveness to take place. Rogers (1961, pp. 105-106) has disagreed and responded by stating that when a person is most fully aware of his impulses, then he is to be trusted and his behavior accordingly is constructive. It may not always be conventional or conforming, but it will be socialized and uniquely characteristic of the person.

The creative living of the actualizing person also bears the unmistakable stamp of his individuality. It may be expressed through keeping house, running an office, or in any number of seemingly routine tasks that the person undertakes. Creative potential is not seen as being limited to persons who are able to produce works of art, music, or inventions, but instead occurs as a result of any behavior which causes the person to go beyond the customary way of looking at life.

Unfortunately, the creativity in many conforming persons is lost and they approach life with a perfunctory fulfillment of their responsibilities and it seems almost unnatural for them to act, speak, or write as individuals, spontaneously and uniquely being themselves. Jarrell (1962, p. 78) has asked the question: "If what you see in *Life* (the magazine) is different from what you see in life, which of the two are you to believe?" Whereas the conformist would choose to emulate *Life*, the actualizing person who is living creatively would prefer to actually experience it.

Rich Interpersonal Relationships

The actualizing person may be recognized most easily of all by the quality of his interpersonal relationships. The ways in which his behavior is clearly distinguishable from that of the over-conforming person are described below:

Actualizing Person

1. Possesses quick understanding, empathy, and insight into what other people are doing and feeling. By utilizing both intuition and direct sensory evidence, he easily becomes aware of the goals of another person.

2. Tends to have a few deep and intimate friendships in which he is willing to lay the mask of everyday living aside and allow himself to be known for what he is as a person.

3. Tends to have friends and acquaintances from widely varied social, occupational, and national groups. He is likely to feel comfortable with both males and females, young and old alike. Among his friends may be found both the religious person and one who cares to have nothing to do with the church. The prohibitionist and the social drinker are also likely to be part of his circle of friends. He is at home in a variety of interpersonal environments and social situations.

Over-Conforming Person

Lacks the ability to be sensitive to other people and gain insight into their behavior.

Prefers to have many casual acquaintances but few really meaningful friendships.

Friends and acquaintances are likely to be limited to a single social, occupational, national, or age group. He is comfortable only in a certain kind of interpersonal environment or social situation.

4. Able to give and receive compliments and gifts gracefully and naturally. Because he loves and respects himself, the expression of other people's feelings do not embarrass him. In turn, he is a lavish giver of praise, gifts, and helpful activities, which are not false attempts to "win friends and influence people," but an honest expression of his admiration of the positive qualities in other people. Such gestures are performed joyously without causing the recipient to feel guilty or indebted.

On hearing a compliment probably he responds by negating or decrying his behavior or by turning the compliment into a joke, perhaps through stating, "I know you; you are after something." Upon receipt of a gift, he is likely to say, "Oh, you really shouldn't have done it." His attitude on giving a present to someone else is liable to convey the feeling that he expects the other person to act the way he wants in return, thus causing his behavior to seem more like a bribe than an expression of friendship.

5. Tends to be positive in his remarks about other people, being sensitively aware that a casual remark of his might greatly influence the life of another person. This attitude is not a Pollyanna type of expression as much as it is the habitual refusal to be destructively critical of the behavior of other people. Frequently he is found to be the only member of a group who is willing to defend an individual who has drawn the group's condemnation upon himself.

Tends to belittle other people and likes to gossip. He seldom thinks that what he says makes any real difference and usually he is "just talking."

6. Likes other people and generally they tend to seek out his company.

Really he does not care for people very much and most persons usually do not voluntarily choose his companionship.

7. He is a good winner as well as a good loser in the sense that both experiences are accepted as inevitable parts of life.

A victory tends to assume the guise of the total destruction of the other person and the defeat the annihilation of himself. Consequently, competition tends to have a vicious life or death element and cooperation becomes half-hearted or next to impossible.

8. Cares what other people think of him but does not allow his concern to dictate his behavior in the important aspects of living.

May claim not to care what other people think of him or he may be worried constantly about their reactions.

9. Can show and express hurt directly. For example, he is not afraid to cry.

Tends to feel that it is necessary to present a stoic exterior that often masks an inexpressible feeling of being hurt.

10. Can react to criticism without rejecting, in turn, the person who offered it. He recognizes the fact that other people may disapprove of him and his ideas and acknowledges their right to do so without feeling that the total relationship will be destroyed.

Finds it impossible to react to the criticism without rejecting the person who is criticizing him. Almost entirely his personal warmth is reserved for those persons who support and sustain him.

11. Often admits that he is wrong. He is seldom a perfectionist for himself and other people and as a result his goals are realistic.

He is never wrong and always has an excuse to explain his limitations or failures. His standards of perfectionism are so unrealistic that neither he nor anyone else can win total approval.

12. Can be openly critical of the ideas and behavior of himself and other people when the circumstances warrant it, by conveying the message that the person has done a disapproved deed and not that he is subject to disapproval. Although his position on controversial matters may change, he is not afraid to take a stand.

Seldom can distinguish between the person and his behavior. As a result, his condemnation is total. Although he is harshly critical of himself and others, his comments are rarely expressed directly and openly. Instead, he "pays off" in slights, sneers, and innuendo, plus, on occasion, a total rejection of the person who has offended him.

13. Can respond when necessary to requests with a firm "no." Knows that he cannot be "all things to all men" and consequently does not try, thereby succeeding in being something to some men. Accepts the fact that not everyone can love him and is ready when necessary to bear another person's hostility for having turned down a date, a dinner invitation, an appointment to a committee or some other activity in which he does not choose to participate.

Feels a compulsion to accede to almost any request made of him. As a result, he is often caught in a round of activities and affairs that he openly or secretly resents.

14. Rather scrupulously avoids platitudes and clichés in his conversation.

Tends to rely on hackneyed phrases and expressions to convey his thoughts and feelings.

15. Avoids teasing and the playing of practical jokes.

He is unaware of the hostility that lies behind his questionable humor.

16. Seldom is jealous or envious. Instead, he is happy and pleased over the achievements and possessions of other people.

Begrudges the sharing of time, talent, money, and ideas, and tends to live with the attitude of "If I can't have it, then you can't either.

17. Successful both as a leader and a follower. He can work alone or in cooperation or competition with other people. He can gracefully give orders as well as receive them.

Tends to be either a good leader or good follower but is seldom capable of being both.

18. Suffers few regrets about past relationships.

Worries about past events, feeling that he has "missed the boat" or "failed other people."

19. When help is needed, he is willing to seek what other persons have to offer. While he can "go it alone" when necessary, he does not perceive himself as "self-made."

Either has difficulty in seeking the assistance of other people or is constantly looking for help from everyone.

20. Tends to be acceptant of different religious and political views.

Frequently adopts positions of fanaticism or of indifference on these matters.

21. Enjoys privacy and often prefers to be alone.

May hate to be alone and believes the emptiness of his life can only be filled by the presence of other people.

22. Capable of intense and tremendously satisfying sexual relations. While he is not preoccupied with sex, it is held to be one of the most fundamental joys of life.

Frequently sexually crippled and inhibited. May look upon sexuality as disgusting or as a necessary evil or duty. Often obsessed with the trappings of sex and may always be telling dirty jokes.

23. Neither overly optimistic nor overly pessimistic. When events justify a limited optimism, he proceeds hopefully and when they warrant somewhat of a pessimism, he accepts the possibility of a negative outcome.

Tends to be at one extreme or another of optimism or pessimism. He may refuse to recognize evil or else see nothing but the unfortunate and seamy side of life.

24. Tends to individualize other persons and responds to their unique characteristics.

Prefers to stereotype other people and treat them accordingly.

25. Enjoys caring for people in terms of what they actually are, as well as for their efficient and ideal qualities.

Appreciates those persons who are efficient by his definition and also the people who meet his ideals. The persons who fail to meet these criteria are discounted or ignored.

26. Prefers to be active and is often enthusiastic over both the small and great experiences that he finds interesting. He has a continuing freshness of appreciation.

Usually is bored and apathetic. Finds life to be the same thing over and over again.

27. Can make worry-free decisions even when they have to be based upon limited knowledge. Knowing that he has done the best that was possible under the circumstances, he is willing to live with the consequences of his behavior.	Suffers not only from frequent and prolonged indecision but tends to worry even after the decision has finally been made.
28. Willing to "let go" when necessary and not force social situations into being what makes him most comfortable.	Tends to probe and dominate social relationships in order to satisfy his personal needs.

SUMMARY

1. The behavior of the actualizing person is characterized by a continual need to experience the type of interpersonal relationships that aid his becoming more integrated, autonomous, and self-directing.

2. People have an excellent chance of reaching the higher level of well-being when primarily they enjoy a wide variety of experiences which are characterized by gratification and acceptance.

3. The continuous growth and development that leads to actualization and an emerging concept of self occurs as a result of the person's willingness to be motivated intrinsically toward establishing a value system that is characterized by a rational morality and an openness to experience.

4. The ability to look at a social situation rationally, particularly in terms of its relationship to the past, present, and future, but, at the same time, to enjoy some degree of spontaneity, is the mark of the integrated, autonomous, and self-directing individual.

5. The interpersonal relationships of the actualizing person are distinguishable from those of the over-conformist on the basis of a genuine appreciation for and acceptance of both himself and other people.

EXERCISE 8

Observing Others' Behavior in Groups

To be fully aware of what is happening around you is intrinsically a satisfying and rewarding experience. Moreover, it has practical value. To deal adequately with situations demands accurate perception. Many human activities are carried out through group efforts. Therefore, one area in which to practice accurate observation is in the dynamics of group behavior.

In groups in which you have participated recently, can you remember seeing anyone . . .

YES   NO

_____ _____ 1. encourage another member to participate?

_____ _____ 2. who was exceptionally agreeable or accepting of others?

_____ _____ 3. propose direction or action for the group to take?

_____ _____ 4. ask for opinions or suggestions?

_____ _____ 5. express praise or appreciation?

_____ _____ 6. freely give his opinion?

_____ _____ 7. overdo giving his opinions?

_____ _____ 8. help keep the group focused on the problems?

_____ _____ 9. comfortably assuming temporary leadership?

_____ _____ 10. being protective of others?

_____ _____ 11. depreciating himself?

_____ _____ 12. helping to clarify the problem?

_____ _____ 13. arbitrating disagreements?

_____ _____ 14. who was able to disagree without appearing to be hostile?

_____ _____ 15. freely giving information?

_____ _____ 16. overdoing giving information?

_____ _____ 17. who was able to draw information from others?

_____ _____ 18. freely express warm emotions?

_____ _____ 19. who seemed cold and emotionless?

_____ _____ 20. trying to oversell himself?

_____ _____ 21. who was able to assert himself comfortably?

_____ _____ 22. being left out?

_____ _____ 23. deliberately calling attention to himself, showing off, etc.?

_____ _____ 24. who kept getting the group off the subject?

_____ _____ 25. who was obviously hostile?

_____ _____ 26. who was overly passive?

_____ _____ 27. who was trying unsuccessfully to be a leader?

_____ _____ 28. who expressed trust in the others?

_____ _____ 29. who was uncomfortable with silence?

_____ _____ 30. being disagreeable?

_____ _____ 31. withdrawing?

_____ _____ 32. addressing his remarks to individual members rather than to the group?

Now go back over the behaviors you have observed and list the five that were the most significant to you. List them in the order of their importance.

1. _____

2. _____

3. _____

4. _____

5. _____

Taking each item separately, see if you can list specific behaviors that were involved. For example, if item 11 (depreciating himself) was one you selected, list everything this person did that contributed to your impression. Do the same for each of the five.

CHAPTER 10

Learning and Thinking

Learning is influenced by what a person is as a human being and the goals that he desires to achieve for his life. The cycle of behavior shown in Figure 8 is repeated over and over again so that, in time, it becomes impossible to separate any of the three categories in a meaningful way. Learning affects being and desire just as they, in turn, influence learning. For the actualizing person who comes to be, then learns, and subsequently desires in terms of that learning, the cycle of behavior is replaced by the one shown in Figure 9. It should be noted, however, that no matter what the cycle of behavior, learning occurs from the beginning of life so that both being and desire are also functions of learning.

Maturation

Not all changes in behavior may be classified as learning phenomena. Some of them result from a process known as maturation which may be defined as an organismic development that brings about behavioral change. As an infant matures, he acquires greater strength and dexterity, along with increased coordination of all parts of the body. In addition to bringing about changes in his motor behavior, maturation leads to a longer attention span and the cortical ability to conceptualize reality in new ways. As a result, maturation and the ability to learn are related directly and, on occasion, the level of a person's maturation is referred to as a learning readiness level.

It is necessary for a child, for instance, to have matured to the appropriate level before he can walk, talk, read, or make any number of even finer physical and motor discriminations. Such processes are ingrained in the physiology of man and in the person's unique variation within the human species. Thus, when a particular child is physiologically ready to walk, which occurs usually at about 14 months, he begins to take the first tottering steps and with practice, of course, his ability begins to improve. It is important to note, moreover, that nothing is accomplished

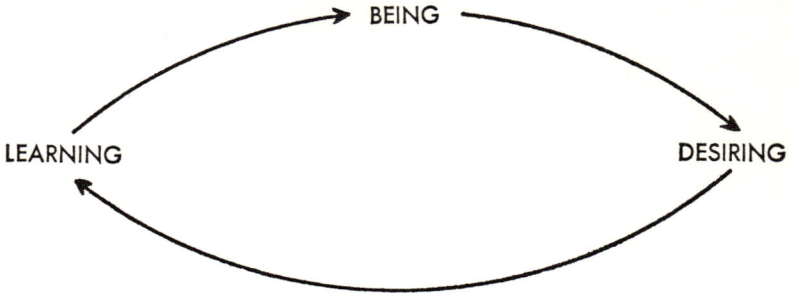

FIGURE 8.   The cycle of being, desiring, and learning.

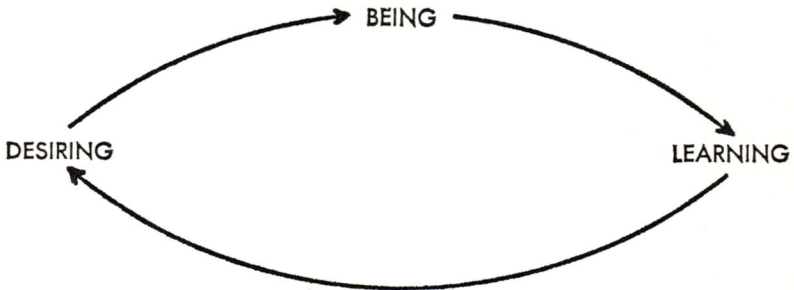

FIGURE 9.   The cycle of being, learning, and desiring.

in terms of speeding up development by making demands for performance that the child cannot meet. He has simply not reached the appropriate level of maturation and any undue pressure for successful accomplishment is liable to hinder more than help his eventual development.

There is considerable evidence in the writings of Hebb (1949), Piaget (1952), and Bruner (1964) to indicate that maturational changes influence the conceptual processes utilized for grouping objects, perceiving relationships, and expressing other mental abilities. These ideas have important ramifications. Generally, parents are not worried about the child of nine months who crawls but does not walk, because it is understood that, once he has passed through this stage in the growth process, he will begin to walk. Similarly, it well may be that the child, who confuses fact and fantasy by exaggerating or by telling stories that obviously are not true, is simply not ready to be making such discriminations accurately. Just as in the case of the nine-month-old child who is still crawling, such failures in behavior need only become a matter of concern when the child has reached a level of maturation that would make it possible for more advanced behavior to take place.

Learning

Learning consists of persistent changes that take place within the person as a result of his exchange with the environment. From birth, and perhaps even before birth, a person's behavior is undergoing constant modification and revision. Responses which at one time were satisfactory to the individual are discarded and new responses are acquired. A person may learn muscular responses and habits, perceptual discriminations, motives and goals, attitudes and evaluative responses, belief and value systems, emotional reactions, language and communicative responses, methods of solving problems, ways of looking at the self and at other people, and, in fact, an endless variety of different kinds of learning.

Internal and environmental stimuli and cues, both singly and in combinations, serve as signs from which people may learn. If perceived correctly, a caution sign on the highway or a heartbeat of a different rhythm may signify the presence of a danger. A pretty girl or a daydream of a pretty girl may serve as an erotic stimulus to a man. Depending upon their orientations, two people may respond very differently to the same stimulus. For one person, a dance hall may mean a place of entertainment and pleasure; for another, it may signify sinful living and the devil's workshop. Thus, perhaps it may be seen that learning involves the tying together of cues and responses in both individually and culturally shared ways.

The Effect of Childhood Learning Upon Adult Learning

One of the major problems in understanding learning concerns the impact of childhood experiences upon a person's subsequent ability to learn. Freud was one of the most influential proponents of the point of view which emphasized that whatever is learned during the first five years of life becomes a relatively permanent influence on the person's learning experiences. Although surface changes in behavior occur, they are seen as being only expressions of the basic childhood pattern of behavior. As a result, new learning is seldom, if ever, free from old experiences and the child is truly "father of the man."

In contrast, Allport (1937) has been the leading exponent of the opposite viewpoint which sees present experience as being a lot more important influence than the dimly remembered events of childhood. He has written extensively concerning a concept, referred to as functional autonomy, in which new learning is held to occur relatively independently of previous learning.

Advocates of both positions have been able to marshal together impressive evidence to support the accuracy of their observations. Figure 10

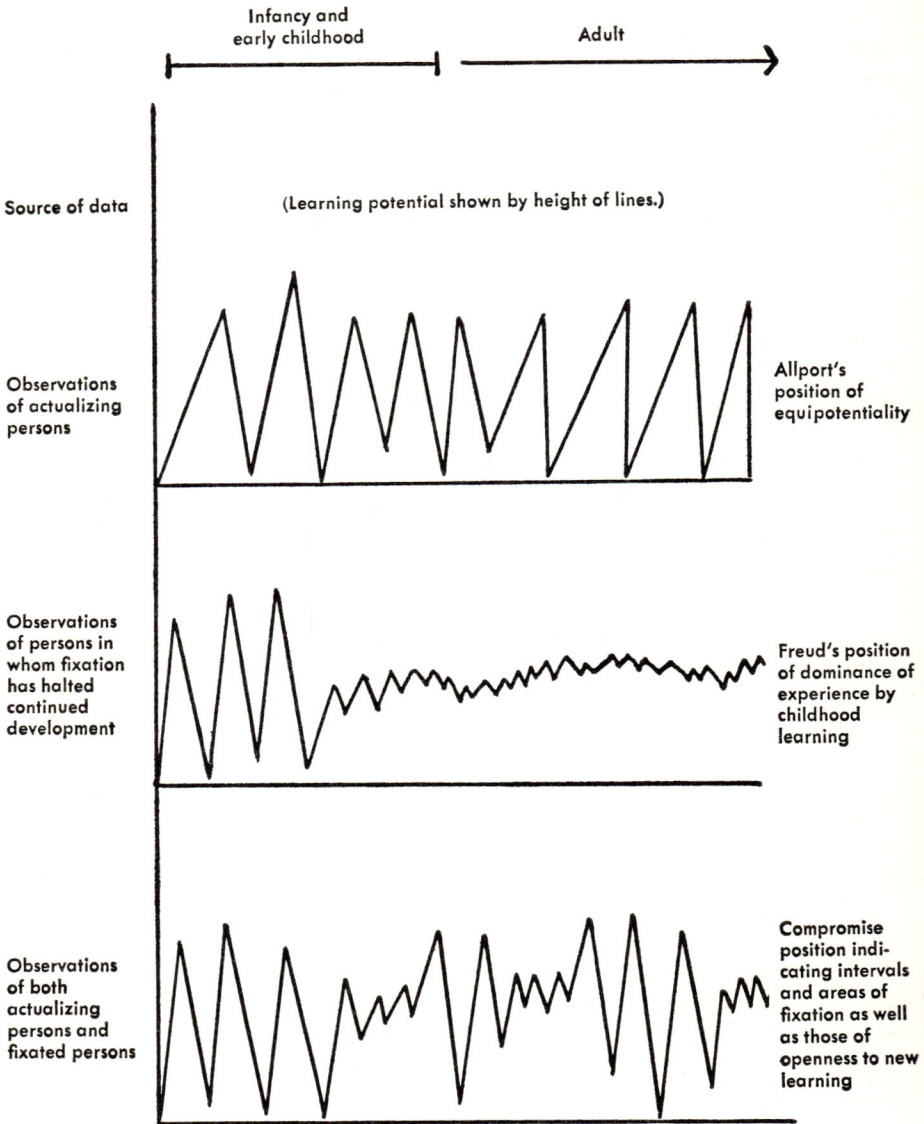

FIGURE 10.   Change potential according to age from three theoretical points
of view.

may be used perhaps to illustrate how they both may be correct. It is
not true that the actualizing person is a captive of his past, for it is obvious
from his behavior that, during some periods of his life at least, he is

capable of experiencing relative autonomy. New goal emergence is likely to be a continuous process throughout his life. Conversely, other people, who lack ego strength and feelings of psychological safety, frequently find that the influence of the early experiences in life remains strong. Because they suffer from such a crippling frustration of their goals, they remain emotionally the same persons they were as children and they become closed to the idea of new learning.

Learning Concepts

In order to understand how learning takes place, it is necessary to appreciate the importance of a number of basic ideas and terms that have been introduced by the different learning theorists. These concepts are described in some detail in the paragraphs that follow.

IMPRINTING

Imprinting is an instantaneous kind of learning that has been observed mainly in animals. Tinbergen (1951, p. 150) described an instance of imprinting in Eskimo dogs in East Greenland:

> The members of a pack defend their group territory against all other dogs. All dogs of an Eskimo settlement have an exact and detailed knowledge of the topography of the territories of other packs; they know where attacks from other packs must be feared. Immature dogs, however, do not defend the territory. Moreover, they often roam through the whole settlement, very often trespassing into other territories, where they are promptly chased. In spite of these frequent attacks, during which they may be severely treated, they do not learn the territories' topography and for the observer their stupidity in this respect is amazing. While the young dogs are growing sexually mature, however, they begin to learn the other territories and within a week their trespassing adventures are over. In two male dogs the first copulation, the first defense of territory, and the first avoidance of strange territory, all occurred within one week.

Relatively little is known about the role of imprinting on human learning. It is quite possible that periods of sensitivity to imprinting are obscured by the complex interaction of the human being and his environment. On occasion, however, it is evident that whereas some learning takes place as a result of repeated exposure to stimuli, other learning occurs with an immediacy that rivals the experiences of the dogs in Tinbergen's example.

CLASSICAL CONDITIONING

Classical conditioning is the kind of learning that was recognized around the beginning of the century by Ivan Pavlov, the great Russian physiologist and Nobel prize winner. Such learning takes place when a new stimulus is combined with an old stimulus so that in time it alone elicits the response that formerly was evoked only by the old stimulus. In this way, for instance, people learn to react to the sight of a red-hot stove as they would if they touched the stove. The new or conditioned stimulus (the sight of the stove) evokes the same response as that elicited by the old or unconditioned stimulus (the burn caused from touching the stove).

In a similar manner, pigs may be conditioned to rush to the feeding trough when food is dumped into it. They may even learn to go to the trough when the squeak of a gate signals the arrival of the truck bearing the offal. Thus, even the lowly hog is capable of making associations concerning "what leads to what."

A conditioned stimulus becomes more or less equivalent to the unconditioned stimulus because of the frequency of the association and the degree of contiguity in time. Learning occurs when the conditioned stimulus precedes the unconditioned stimulus by an interval between 0 and 1.5 seconds, and most readily when this interval is about 0.5 second. In this way, responses, sensations, and objects which occur immediately before the presentation of the unconditioned stimulus are likely to become conditioned stimuli. The smell of food, for instance, which has been associated with food itself, will evoke the response of hunger. Similarly, a person may become hungry at twelve o'clock, not so much because he is physiologically hungry but because he is conditioned to expect to eat at that particular time of the day.

Experiments with human beings and animals in the psychological laboratory have led some observers to the conclusion that classical conditioning represents a rather low level of learning in which in many instances human beings have failed to excel the response of animals. Such a conclusion, however, may be premature. The sensitivity of association of events—new versions of "what leads to what"—may cause a person to order his world in terms of the clues and pictures that he encounters. Thus, his responses are adequate and appropriate to the social situation in which he finds himself and, generally, they contribute in one way or another to the enrichment of his life and an understanding of the world about him.

Operant Conditioning

With operant conditioning, the organism acts in some manner upon its environment without being influenced directly by specific stimuli. In time, it learns to repeat the responses that are rewarded or reinforced. If a rat, for instance, presses three levers and one of these responses brings about the appearance of a pellet of food, it learns to press only the lever producing the food and to ignore the others. Much human behavior is shaped also in such a purposeful and efficient manner. Responses which are emitted by the person tend to be repeated when reinforced while other responses which are not rewarded tend to be ignored. It is important to note, moreover, that whereas in classical conditioning reward or reinforcement occurs irrespective of the person's behavior, in operant conditioning, it is the action of the person himself which brings about the reinforcement.

Skinner (1958, p. 98) has gone so far as to interpret all behavior as a "set of reinforcing contingencies," believing that by planned reinforcement according to certain schedules it is possible to control human behavior completely. While this position is controversial and possibly overly enthusiastic, there is no doubt that the works of Skinner offer impressive evidence indicating that operant conditioning is an important aspect of human learning.

The growth of superstitious behavior is a case in point. Suppose for a moment that a person has a severe cold and on Monday he goes to his physician and receives medication. He stays in bed all of Tuesday but the cold lingers on. Wednesday he tries taking whiskey and honey but that approach does not seem to make very much difference. He has the cold still on Thursday and so, in desperation, he decides nothing can be lost by taking Mother Hubbard's cure-all for colds, arthritis, warts, corns, and other assorted ills and pains. Lo and behold, by Friday the cold is gone. Thereafter, the man becomes a sworn advocate of Mother Hubbard's horrendous brew and urges its use upon the members of his family, friends, and anyone else who will listen to him. Because this quack remedy was the last response to be attempted before the cold disappeared, it is likely to be repeated the next time the condition occurs. The fact that it was actually the medication from the physician and the stay in bed that caused the cold to disappear makes little difference. The person is convinced that he knows what produced the cure and nothing will influence him to change his mind.

Unfortunately, many orientations and pictures of reality are brought about in the same manner. Some hint as to how frequently this situation occurs may be provided by observing the behavior of pigeons after they have been given food. One of them may have happened to have had a wing outstretched when the food appeared. Consequently, he is liable to be spending a great deal of time repeating this behavior. Similarly, other pigeons may be turning their heads, lifting legs, twirling, etc., all going through movements that seemingly cause food to appear. As a result, perhaps it may be seen that the person who controls the system of rewards has a great deal to do with the orientations and the behavior of the people in his particular social situation.

REINFORCEMENT

In his Law of Effect, Thorndike (1932), stated that behavior which is followed by rewarding effects is strengthened and tends to be repeated and behavior which is not followed by rewarding consequences is weakened or, at least, is not strengthened. Despite some question about the research methods Thorndike used to support his position, most psychologists are in agreement that rewards do work and rewarding or reinforcement is perhaps the most important single factor that influences learning.

Although it has been established quite firmly that reinforcement controls behavior, little is actually known about how to reinforce the complexly functioning person. Quite often answers to the question have been sought through the effect of providing simple rewards in simple situations to less complicated organisms. To what extent the results of such studies may be generalized to adult behavior is questionable and problematical and sometimes learning theorists have been guilty of minimizing this limitation.

At least one generalization may be made, however, concerning the reinforcement of human behavior. It is necessary to relate it meaningfully to behavior leading to goal achievement. To a hungry person, the provision of food is an effective method of reinforcement; to a frightened person, anything that causes him to feel safe is successful. Thus, if a person's goals are identified accurately and the person aided in the achievement of these goals, learning and changes in behavior in all probability will follow.

Although this statement seems to be simple and straight-forward, in actuality, putting it into practice is a lot more complicated. Behavior which seems from the external viewpoint as if it should be reinforcing is frequently not reinforcing. Unfortunately, when such a situation occurs, it is assumed quite often that the failure lies with the person who did not respond to the reinforcement that was offered. In actuality, of course, the person who presented the attempted reinforcement was the one who failed because what he did not realize was that another person can be rewarded only in terms of his own particular goals.

In schools and colleges, for example, it is assumed that students are oriented toward gaining enlightenment and, therefore, that the reinforcement of behavior leading to the goal of enlightenment will motivate them to learn. As long as students value this goal, such reinforcement works very well. For students whose goals do not involve enlightenment, however, the approach fails rather miserably, as evidenced by the introduction of punishment devices to stop students from cutting class, the frantic last minute cramming of students, and the high casualty lists of failing students.

Recent research has indicated that even severely retarded persons, who had been considered incapable of learning, under certain conditions have been helped to learn. Masland, Sarason, and Gladwin (1958) pointed out that when strong motivation is present severely retarded subjects are capable of sustaining attention and solving problems in surprisingly good manner. The problem seems to be more one of attention than of the stimuli which are presented. Working with a similar group, McKinney (1962) concluded that purposefulness accounted for the greatest percentage of variance in learning efficiency. In another experiment, McKinney and Keele (1963) found that mothering was related directly to the presence or the absence of purposefulness. Increased learning occurred in a group of children who had adequate mothering. Apparently the children were reinforced in terms of their need for love and psychological safety. Thus, perhaps any person who is frightened may be reinforced only in terms of his need for emotional support and his failure to respond to other reinforcements is not an indication of indifference or retardation but of the fact that while a person is afraid the ordinary methods of reinforcement are ineffective.

Skinner (1958, p. 97) has pointed out that:

> The world in which man lives may be regarded as an extraordinarily complex set of positive and negative reinforcing contingencies. In addition to the physical environment to which he is sensitively attuned and with which he carries on an important interchange, we have (as he has) to contend with social stimuli, social reinforcers, and a network of personal and institutional control and countercontrol—all of amazing intricacy. The contingencies of reinforcement which man has made for man are wonderful to behold.

If a child acts in a way that pleases his parents and they express approval of what he does by reinforcing it with a smile, then the same behavior is liable to reoccur. On the other hand, if the parents punish the child by withdrawing their affection, his behavior is less likely to be repeated. Sometimes the actions of the child, although approved by the parents, are taken for granted. In terms of feelings of belonging ness, the attention gained from receiving punishment is more satisfying than being ignored and, consequently, the child may choose to repeat the behavior that had resulted previously in his being punished.

Generally, people in America are very competent in reinforcing the goals of wealth, skill, power, and even enlightenment, but they fall far short in terms of being aware of the importance of providing respect and in satisfying the needs of other persons for love and belongingness.

The teacher, for instance, who only reinforces the behavior of her students in terms of their attempts to obtain enlightenment probably will accomplish far less positive results than if she is prepared to reinforce behavior associated with attaining the belongingness goals as well. It is not necessary, however, for the teacher to reinforce the behavior of her students every time. Once a pattern of behavior has been established, reinforcements only need occur often enough to make sure that the desired response does not weaken. Thus, the teacher does not have to be concerned if, on occasion, she fails to reinforce the behavior of her students.

Not only does man create reinforcers for other men but he creates them also for himself. Thus, any experience that "fits" the orientational expectancies of a person tends to be reinforcing. If a person feels that "people are not good," then any fact that is in accordance with this belief will be learned and, conversely, any indication that people are loving, considerate, and kind will remain ignored. While it is satisfying to gain support for one's position, it is also meaningful for a person to find out that he has been wrong and, subsequently, for him to grow, enhance, and actualize himself in the direction of greater congruence with reality.

Similarly, while it is often rewarding for a child to let his mother do something for him, it is also satisfying to be able to take care of himself. The wise mother is sensitive to both needs. She reinforces the child's growth toward independence by letting him do things for himself but, at the same time, she satisfies his need for belongingness by allowing him on occasion to be dependent.

Goal achievement, frequently referred to as the concept of level of aspiration, is related also to the problem of reinforcement. A student, for example, who is expecting a B grade or lower in a course will be rewarded by obtaining an A. If he is expecting an A, however, a B will be disappointing. Moreover, if the person looks upon himself as an academically ineffectual person, an A or a B grade may be unrewarding and even upsetting. While to the outsider such a grade looks rewarding, it may force the student to change the image of himself when, in actuality, he would prefer to maintain the one that already exists, thus avoiding the possibility of having to revise his orientation.

In this way, many people go on believing what they wish because it is intrinsically more satisfying to do so. Arguments and exhortations are usually to no avail. Often they only threaten the person and make him all the more determined to hold on to his position.

As may be realized, reinforcement is so complicated that a person has little choice but to act with only a severely limited knowledge of what will be learned from any specific interaction. As Oppenheimer (1956, p. 134) noted, "The physical world is not completely determinate. . . .Physics is predictive, but within limits; its world is ordered, but not completely causal. . . . Every atomic event is individual. It is not, in its essentials, reproducible." Such a statement is even more true of reinforcement and human learning.

EXTINCTION

If a conditioned response remains unrewarded, it will tend to be weakened and eventually in time become extinguished. Suppose, for instance, that a small boy has learned to expect that the sound of the bell on an ice cream cart that daily passes by his house will lead to his having an ice cream cone. Then one day the vendor drives by, but his mother fails to buy the usual ice cream. If this situation continues day after day, the boy's "ice cream" response to the bell will tend to disappear and the association between the sound of the bell and having an ice cream cone will be weakened.

Sometimes it is necessary for established patterns of behavior to be extinguished before new learning may take place. The baseball coach, for example, who succeeds in stopping his players from swinging for the fence on every pitch may have taken a vital first step in preparing them to become more effective hitters.

The relationship between extinction and punishment is especially important. Skinner (1953, pp. 183-184) reported that provided the circumstances surrounding the acquisition of a response are known, in the ordinary process of extinction through the withholding of reinforcement, the number of times an animal will make the response before it disappears may be predicted reasonably well. If the first few responses in the extinction process are punished, however, perhaps with an electric shock, it might be expected that the punishing experience would help to decrease the total number of responses necessary for extinction. In actuality, the punishment succeeds only in reducing momentarily the rate of responding and the frequency increases again as soon as the punishment is discontinued. Even more surprisingly, the same number of responses are made ultimately before extinction is achieved. Skinner (1953, p. 184) concluded that under such circumstances "the effect of punishment was a temporary suppression of the behavior, not a reduction in the total number of responses."

On the surface, such evidence would seem to present a powerful argument against the effectiveness of punishment. There is a danger, nevertheless, of carrying the limitations of punishment to extreme, thereby missing the point that it may be of positive value in changing behavior. The teen-ager, for example, who indulges in destructive behavior may be restrained temporarily probably only by punishment. It is vitally important, however, that during the period in which his behavior is inhibited, he be provided with opportunities for new learning to take place. If this situation does not occur, then although the punishment may be emotionally satisfying to the person administering it, the teen-ager will not have been helped in finding a more acceptable way of achieving his goals. Furthermore, the person providing the punishment runs the additional risk that, instead of eliminating undesirable behavior, he may only cause the transgressor to hate or fear him all the more.

Spontaneous Recovery

Even after extinction seems to be complete, responses that no longer are necessary or appropriate reappear unexpectedly. The person, for instance, who has driven for years a car with a clutch and who later becomes accustomed to driving with an automatic transmission may find himself on occasion releasing a non-existent clutch.

It may be that the experiences of knowing what a person is going to say before he speaks or feeling a sense of familiarity with a place that is being visited for the first time are also expressions of spontaneous recovery. Such experiences, known by the French words, déjà vu, meaning already seen, usually are associated with some incident in the past that has been forgotten. Possibly, as a person approaches a house for the first time, a rosebush, located in approximately the same position as a forgotten one that stood in the yard of his childhood home, may cause the surroundings to seem to be familiar.

Generalization

Through the process of generalization, responses that are made to a certain stimulus tend to be evoked also by other similar stimuli. The Watson (1926) study of Albert and the white rat is a well-known illustration. As described in the chapter on the adjustment mechanisms, Albert's fear of the white rat was generalized to furry objects and finally to a piece of cotton wool. In a similar manner, many of the seemingly irrational fears that people experience may begin to make sense if one is able to understand what the behavior that is causing the difficulty means to the people who are frightened.

The use of generalization is of great value in helping a person relate to his environment. Behavior would be interrupted endlessly if it were necessary to learn to respond anew every time a minutely different stimulus is presented. Instead, learning in one situation is carried over to other similar experiences, thereby allowing the person to make the appropriate responses in the face of minor differences without undergoing new learning. Thus, although one make of car may differ slightly from another, the responses necessary for driving one automobile are by and large appropriate for handling all cars.

DISCRIMINATION

At the heart of learning is the ability to use discrimination when generalizing. The socially sensitive person learns that it is not always appropriate to react toward all stimuli that are similar in terms of a single response that previously has proved to be effective. A student, for example, may be encouraged to express his ideas freely to other people. He does so with the members of his family, his friends, and in fact in any social situation where the opportunity is presented. In Professor Jones' class he is a huge success because this teacher likes his students to challenge his ideas and he encourages the expression of different opinions. In Professor Smith's class, however, the student suffers an unexpected failure in that this teacher has a strongly negative attitude toward students expressing their views in his class. The student has overgeneralized the idea of expressing himself freely and thus failed to realize that behavior valued by Professor Jones is completely inappropriate in Professor Smith's class.

Furthermore, the student may make the even more serious mistake of condemning Professor Smith, thereby denying him the right to conduct a class according to his own educational beliefs. Although the student is free to object to the professor's value system and even to oppose if he so wishes, the power to make the rules under which the class is conducted rests in the professor's hands. The student, however, has the right to break the rules and, if necessary, pay the consequences of such behavior. To fail to make the necessary discrimination, however, and to be surprised at the outcome of such behavior is an expression of foolish insensitivity.

Altogether, inability to recognize such personal characteristics among people and to acknowledge their right to these unique differences is frequently a costly human error and the source of a great deal of misery and unhappiness. Unfortunately, unlike Western movies which solve the problem of discrimination by the simple expedient of having the good guys wear white hats and the bad guys black ones, there is no easy way for the person who wishes to function effectively in society to avoid making an endless number of distinctions and discriminations.

There is some evidence to indicate that not all learning is motivated consciously. Some of it seems to occur accidentally without any specific intention being present. A person, for instance, may be strolling through a city in an apparently aimless manner, seemingly not noticing anything in particular. Later in the day when he becomes hungry and begins to think about finding somewhere to eat, he remembers where he saw an interesting-looking restaurant.

As described in the chapter on Well-Being Level II, such non-motivating learning is characteristic of the actualizing person. He is comfortable enough with himself that the efficiency of his observations is not impaired by living in a casual or non-immediate sense. Occasionally, for instance, he enjoys thoroughly walking just to be walking, reading light and innocuous fiction for the sake of reading, listening to music purely for the emotional satisfaction that it provides, all of which experiences take place without any awareness that the person's behavior has to be geared toward moving in a specific direction.

Cognitive Functioning

In addition to behavior being changed by the learning that occurs as a result of conditioning, a person comes to modify his behavior as well through cognitive functioning, the development of new perceptions and awarenesses, the acquiring of new insights, and the reorganization of his knowledge. Such learning occurs provided an external event can be fitted easily into a person's orientation. If the person is not consciously aware of any relationship, however, then the experience will remain relatively unnoticed, will be forgotten quickly, or will not have the intended effect. Such a situation may occur when an attempt is made to impose a new system of thought upon an established cultural tradition. During World War II, for instance, the American Armed Services on a certain island in the Pacific provided sweat shirts for the bare-breasted native women. As requested, the women started wearing the shirts, but with two holes cut in the material at, on the basis of American standards, the most unfortunately inappropriate places. Obviously the behavior that had been learned was at considerable variance from that which had been intended.

Hebb (1958, pp. 202-203) has noted the following three characteristics which are a part of a person's conscious awareness: (1) the experience of immediate memory; (2) perception of things going on about the person; and (3) the intermittent appearance of purposive and insightful behavior. Thus, the past, present, and future are represented in consciousness in what St. Augustine (Pusey, 1953, p. 266) referred to as "a present of things past, a present of things present, and a present of things future."

In the present of things past, it is not the past itself which affects behavior but the internal representation of the past which is active in the present. Experiences, for instance, may be based upon events that really happened, upon distortions of what took place, or upon purely imaginary occurrences. As a result, in order to understand a person, it is necessary to attend to his version of his past because he is the only person who has access to the present of things past as it exists for him.

Because thought processes tend to move toward coherence, order, and completion, any experience that does not make sense by itself is likely to be re-structured so that it is understood in terms of the person's wishes, desires, and orientational pattern. The influence of the Zeigarnik Effect, a tendency to remember uncompleted tasks better than completed ones, may explain, moreover, why certain events remain in the memory and others do not. Perhaps this experience explains why old, unrequited love lingers on so tenaciously. It may explain as well, in part, why the disturbances that are associated with goal failures are so profound. Whereas success in goal achievement brings about the reduction of tension and forgetting, the failure to obtain satiation may set up a Zeigarnik Effect, causing the memory to continue to persist as a very real part of things past.

In the present of things present, what is occurring to the person is again less crucial to understanding his behavior than knowing his perception of this particular phenomenon. If a person smiles at another individual, but this gesture is interpreted as a threatening grimace, then the behavior is equivalent to the subjective interpretation and not to the objective evidence. Similarly, if thirty people attend the same movie, one person may react to the pathos of the story, another enjoy the humor, still another attend to the technical problems of production, and, altogether, probably all thirty persons will have differing perceptions of what is being shown on the screen.

In addition to an awareness of the past and the present, the human being has the facility to envision future actions and possibilities in an expression of the present in things of the future. Obviously it can not be the actual future that is present but, instead, the person develops a picture of how things might turn out to be. When the present of things future is favorable, it is called hope, the presence of which may make the difference between continued learning, growth, and striving and the person's inability to make any effort toward the achievement of his goals.

Thus, for example, a student may decide to study instead of going to a movie because the hopeful picture of success in the future is preferable to the immediate satisfaction of seeing the movie.

Thinking

Thinking is the process of dealing with objects and ideas that are not physically present. As a person faces a problem situation, for instance, he becomes aware of an array of ideas, hunches, and hypotheses, all of which potentially may lead to the solution of his problem. Some of these concepts are primarily autistic in that they are products of the internal wishes and daydreams of the person. Other possible solutions are more realistic and may be tested in terms of trial and error behavior or implicitly through picturing the results of probable outcomes. Cantril and Bumstead (1960, p. 176) commented that to sustain the world of reality, a person's prognosis of outcome, when tested in action, must bring an anticipated degree of satisfaction. Otherwise his confidence and self-esteem sink to a low level. In order to be fully human, however, a person must be willing to take a chance on some hypotheses which may turn out to be mistaken. To blame oneself too severely for failure freezes one's "assumptive" world and encourages reliance upon autistic thought where perfection is easily if emptily obtained.

To hesitate to act, however, is not necessarily a sign of inability to make a decision. Instead, it may be a cue to the presence of several competing possibilities of choice that may be classified under two general types: (1) knowing the destination or goal but being uncertain of how to reach it and (2) understanding the issues in terms of the values that are involved rather than their usefulness for obtaining a goal.

In the first case, the problem is one of finding the means and assessing progress in terms of movement toward or from a goal. Awareness of the rules of logic is uppermost and the approach to thinking is methodical and non-emotional. Emphasis upon such thinking has led to the placing of great reliance upon rational and systematic thought, the use of measurement devices and techniques, and the preference for data processing machines as providing the most satisfactory means of arriving at decisions.

The second and more difficult type of problem, however, involves the examination of issues in terms of their relative value instead of relative progress. As Cantril and Bumstead (1960, p. 173) pointed out, "Rational inquiry alone cannot give the answers to questions of why and what for, to the question of what the goals of human living should be." Whereas some decisions are rightfully the result of a process that is primarily rational, examination of the more serious social questions of the present time may only be pursued adequately in terms of the person's emotional reactions combined with his intellectual responses.

Insight and Intuitive Thought

Insight refers to the sudden discovery of the solution to a problem. It has been described as the "aha" experience of "seeing the light." Ideas and concepts that previously made no sense at all suddenly fall into place. Often major changes in behavior follow such an experience, permitting activity that at one time had been aimless and random to become purposive and directive. Hutchinson (1949, p. 35) observes that some problems which a person encounters are characterized by the fact that they may be solved "deliberately, progressively, with a minimum of trial and error activity, and with full awareness of the meaning of each step taken." There are also problems, however, which remain unsolved after all these technical, disciplined, and logical methods have been applied to them. In addition, there are still other situations in which the problem is not even formulated or, if it is, it is done so incorrectly. In all of the latter cases, the problem solver remains baffled and his direct efforts to achieve a solution are frustrated. Subsequently, there inevitably occurs a waiting period or a time of standing back from the problem. Apparently all the emotional and intellectual resources of the person are brought to bear upon the problem in an indirect manner. Little is known of these processes except that the ability to develop such insight seems to be restricted to those persons who have known a diversity of experience and, through being open to new ways of looking at life, are able to let go temporarily of logical and systematic approaches to solving problems.

Insight may be considered to be a basic phenomenon to all social understanding. Through the possession of insight, another person may be seen as lonely and afraid whereas before he was considered to be arrogant and domineering. Similarly, a person who has been stereotyped according to his particular class or group may emerge suddenly as an individual whose unique being is recognizable. Matson (1964, p. 255) has pointed out:

> With respect to things human, it is not disinterest that makes knowledge possible but its opposite; without the factor of *interest,* in the primary sense of concern or care, there can be no recognition of the subject matter in its distinctive human character—and hence no real awareness of its situation and no understanding of its behavior.

Hutchinson (1949, pp. 38-40) has described four stages of intuitive thought. The first is concerned with preparation and may entail a lifetime of the acquisition of skill and knowledge. Such learning is not necessarily oriented toward the achievement of a specific goal, and thus, a person may not know where he is going in a specific sense, but only that he is moving in some general direction.

The second stage of the intuitive process is that of frustration. In this period, the problem has emerged, but the traditional solution has either failed or been rejected. The person, for instance, may be searching for a cure of cancer, attempting to understand himself better, or simply wanting to bake a new kind of cake. In any case, frustration is experienced because an acceptable solution is not readily available.

The third stage contains the experience of gaining insight. Its appearance is unpredictable and it may occur when the person is working at something else. On occasion, it is accompanied by a flood of ideas, with several possible solutions coming to mind, but, generally, the person gaining the insight is able to offer little explanation of the processes leading to the emergence of the solution to the problem.

The final stage is that of verification, elaboration, and evaluation. During this period, all the rules of accepted practice are brought into play and the new idea is submitted to objective and reality testing. In the light of day and sober appraisal many seemingly insightful solutions pale. Others stand up. In any case, intuitive thought is just as subject to the demands of the nature of reality as logical and systematic thought.

It should be noted, moreover, that intuitive thought is appropriate to many of the problems that people face in daily living. While a house, for instance, may be furnished and decorated logically and systematically, it is also possible for a person to do it intuitively in terms of the choices that seem "right" to him. Frequently, the difference may be seen in the atmosphere of a coldly efficient house and the warmth and "lived-in" type quality of a home.

In the complete life, both systematic and intuitive thought are necessary and the omission of either factor places some crippling limitations on the learning and thinking experiences of the people who are involved.

SUMMARY

1. A person must have attained the necessary level of maturation before learning may be expected to take place.
2. The more a person has achieved a degree of actualization, the less likelihood there is that his learning will be influenced by childhood experiences.
3. Reinforcement is most effective when it is applied to behavior that leads to goal achievement.
4. When a person combines the use of generalization with discrimination, he increases the possibility of effective learning taking place.
5. Examination of serious social issues of the present time is approached most thoroughly through combining rational inquiry with personal and intuitive thought.

EXERCISE 9

Individual Roles in Groups

The climates of various groups are very different. Try to recall from a group you were in recently whether . . .

YES   NO

_____ _____ 1. the goals of the group were clear.

_____ _____ 2. the methods the group evolved for solving the problem were clear.

_____ _____ 3. the quality of the group's accomplishment was high.

_____ _____ 4. the group would have continued to function well over a long period.

_____ _____ 5. most people in the group were highly involved in what was occurring.

_____ _____ 6. most people in the group contributed to the discussion or solution.

_____ _____ 7. the group was permissive toward its individual members.

_____ _____ 8. the atmosphere within the group was sometimes competitive.

_____ _____ 9. the atmosphere within the group was sometimes cooperative.

_____ _____ 10. the atmosphere within the group was sometimes pretty hostile.

_____ _____ 11. conditions in the group brought out the best in everyone.

_____ _____ 12. this group efficiently used the human resources that were available.

_____ _____ 13. the group had a "togetherness" feeling.

_____ _____ 14. this group could be trusted to find good solutions to important problems.

_____ _____ 15. there was a lot of loyalty generated in this group.

_____ _____ 16. the group morale was high.

_____ _____ 17. the group quickly developed an appropriate structure for its functioning.

If your answers were "yes," some authorities would say yours was a very efficient and worthwhile group. If your answers were "no," it was probably an inefficient and frustrating group to be in. Do you agree?

Two outcomes of groups are of interest to us. First is product. We are interested in what the group produces. Second is process or how things are accomplished. Here the question is "What happened to people while the group functioned?" A person or persons, for example, might emerge from an experience much stronger and more capable of contributing—or, conversely, damaged and less likely to contribute to future group interactions.

Following are some typical roles individuals enact in groups.

Task Roles—Sharing Resources

1. Initiating action or procedure (providing structure-proposing solutions—new attacks on the problem).
2. Giving information and opinion (utilizing group resources).
3. Seeking information and opinion (making sure all of the group's resources are used).
4. Clarifying and elaborating.
5. Summarizing (trying out the practicality and workability of the group's productions).
6. Testing consensus (seeing where everyone is in relation to where the group seems to be going).

Group Maintenance Roles

7. Facilitating self-expression of members (keeping channels of communication open—helping others get in—increasing participation).
8. Establishing group norms (standard-setting and testing).
9. Harmonizing (reconciling solutions that offer a measure of satisfaction to all).
10. Compromising (finding solutions that offer a measure of satisfaction to all).
11. Giving feedback (encouraging—being responsive—showing interest in others' contributions).
12. Commenting on what is happening in the group.

Disruptive Roles

13. Over-aggression (attacking viciously, blaming, etc.).
14. Taking over (going off on personal tangents—arguing blindly, rejecting ideas without consideration).
15. Disrupting (horsing around, attention-seeking, talking too much).

16. Withdrawing (psychologically taking oneself out of the group while physically present).

Take each of the first 12 roles that have been described and write a sample statement a group member might make when he is filling this particular role. For example in No. 7, facilitating self-expression, he might say. "We haven't heard anything from Walter about this." In No. 12, commenting on what is happening, someone might say, "It seems to me the atmosphere we are creating is too hostile and I wonder if everyone right now isn't fighting everyone else." In this manner, make a statement that would fit each of the roles. There will be overlap between some, but do not worry about this.

1. _____

2. _____

3. _____

4. _____

5. _____

6. _____

7. _____

8. _____

9. _____

10. _____

11. _____

12. _____

You might wish to practice utilizing different roles in groups. The versatile person can thus develop the facility to provide those which seem to be lacking in a particular group.

CHAPTER 11

Emotional Behavior

THE INTENSITY OF EMOTIONS

Behavior cannot be understood entirely in terms of a person's attempts to achieve the various goals in the hierarchy but must be considered as well in terms of the degree of intensity of the emotion that accompanies the pursuit of a goal. Depending on the particular situation, there is a great deal of variation in the intensity that is expressed and, as a result, it is possible for every emotion to be placed along a continuum that ranges from very mild to very strong.

At the point of greatest emotional arousal, there occurs a psycho-physical situation in which, as Peckham (1962, p. 42) noted, the autonomic nervous system, which partially governs emotional responses, reacts with such intensity that a person may die from internal stress or from his failure to cope with some environmental danger. An example of the latter may be observed in the driver of an automobile who freezes at the wheel when confronted with a highway situation calling for an immediate response, thereby causing an accident which would have been avoided had he been less emotionally aroused.

Ordinarily, however, the person at the arousal end of the emotional continuum is not so likely to be immobilized as he is to react by turning to flight, fighting, working, playing, or some other active type of response. Occasionally such emotional states are accompanied as well by the inability to sleep, to relax, or to be alone. Continuous exposure to such heavy arousal appears to lead to the blunting of emotions, thus causing the person to become passive and unconcerned.

At the opposite end of the continuum is the emotional state of the person who is involved to only a minimum degree. Because his condition is characterized by torpor and sluggish inactivity, he may fail also to react to threatening situations and, in addition, have very little reason to move toward the achievement of any goals.

The person who successfully attains his goals, however, experiences a pattern of emotional involvement that includes the conditions that are characteristic of both ends of the continuum. Thus, arousal is followed by relaxation which, in turn, is followed again by more arousal.

There are significant individual differences in potential for emotional arousal. A study by Bindra (1959, p. 221) revealed that "skin resistance measured under identical conditions in normal human adults in a resting state may show a range from 5,000 to considerably above 50,000 ohms." Moreover, when the resting state is disturbed by some form of activity, additional changes in the performance of the various bodily organs may take place. One man's heart rate, for instance, may increase whereas, under the same circumstances, the heart of another person may show just the opposite effect.

Contrary to popular opinion, strong emotions are not necessarily bad and mild ones are not necessarily good. Instead, the appropriateness of the intensity of the emotion depends upon the amount of effort demanded by the situation or set of circumstances in which the individual finds himself.

Because the excessive control of emotions may lead to a loss of spontaneity and to the curtailment of energy necessary to cope with the environment, it is desirable for a person to have a number of opportunities for releasing his strong feelings. The most acceptable method of getting rid of excessive emotion is through talking over the problem situation with another person. The expression of humor, which contains the whole gamut of human emotionality from aggression and sexuality to the sustaining communication of love and belongingness, is also helpful. In general, it is considered healthier for emotions to be aired in some way, by talking, laughing, crying, or even swearing, rather than to be contained without being acted or released, and thereby becoming potentially dangerous and explosive.

The Physiological Basis for Emotions

Although for the purpose of this book it is probably not necessary to provide a detailed description of the physiological basis for emotions, the presentation of certain basic facts may help to provide an understanding of the importance of physiological functioning.

The autonomic or involuntary nervous system consists of two parts: the sympathetic nervous system and the parasympathetic system. The sympathetic system is concerned with preparing the organism for action, work, or play, a process which may involve any of the following responses: dilation of the pupil of the eye, increase in heart rate, a rise in blood pressure, re-routing of the blood from the skin and stomach to the muscles of the limbs, inhibition of the digestive processes, drying of the mouth, increased coldness in the hands and feet, increased sweat activity, and erection of the hairs of the skin, generally known as goose flesh or goose pimples. These responses occur when situations are seen as threatening or following extreme changes in temperature, excessive exercise, and pain and bodily injury, and generally, they cannot consciously be controlled. Thus, for example, if suddenly a person is informed during a luncheon that he is expected to give a speech, it is quite probable that he will perceive the situation as a threat and find his hands becoming moist and his appetite disappearing. As much as he may try to control these physiological changes, they are likely to persist, at least until he has started making the speech and the situation has become less bothersome. The function of the parasympathetic nervous system, on the other hand, is concerned primarily with the conservation of energy, the restoration of the organism after exercise or tissue damage, and generally the maintenance of the vegetative processes of food, digestion, and sleep.

Although this presentation has been oversimplified, in that the functions of both systems are controlled by the integrated action of the cerebrospinal nervous system and the hormonal system, working in coordination with the autonomic system, the relationship of the two alternative influences on human goal-directed behavior, nevertheless, is important. After a goal has been obtained, satiation, relaxation, and temporary cessation of activity follow. No matter how fleeting or brief, a sense of peace and fulfillment is experienced before it is inevitably followed by new activity. Thus, arousal and activation of the sympathetic system is followed in the healthy person by the restoration of energy and relaxation which is brought about by parasympathetic domination of the bodily processes.

The Conditions of Emotional Arousal

The three conditions of emotional arousal that influence human behavior are goal arousal, conflict, and environmental stress. Goal arousal occurs as a result of a person's awareness of a need to attain the goals described in the earlier chapters of this book. Conflict and environmental stress, however, are states of emotional arousal that interfere with the successful achievement of goals.

GOAL AROUSAL

Perhaps the difference between goal arousal and the other two conditions may be understood more clearly by imagining that a student has been informed that after a period of three weeks he will be given a test in a course that he is taking. If his emotional state is primarily that of goal arousal and his purpose, for instance, is the achievement of enlightenment, then his subsequent behavior is likely to be consistent with the idea of attaining his acknowledged goal. Because probably he enjoys a fairly high level of well-being, the emotional experience which accompanies his efforts is likely to be just strong enough to allow him to perform at the upper limits of his capability, thus insuring an adequate preparation for the examination.

On the other hand, if the student's emotional state is based upon a conflict in goals or environmental stress, his behavior is liable to be vacillatory in nature. Although he may try to study, it becomes increasingly difficult for him to concentrate on what he needs to know. Instead of settling down to doing the necessary preparation, he spends most of his time sitting with a book in front of him without comprehending what he is reading or watching television and going to movies, the programs of which, incidentally, he has little difficulty in recalling in detail. By the time the day of the test arrives, he is so nervous and tense that, on looking at the questions, his mind goes blank and, of course, he fails to pass. Because of the unpleasantness of the experience, he is likely to try to avoid the necessity of having to study for other tests, thereby lessening the chance of his behavior ever being motivated by goal arousal and the eventual achievement of the goal of enlightenment.

CONFLICT

The influence of conflict upon emotional arousal may be considered in terms of the following four categories: plus-plus; minus-minus, plus-minus, and cognitive dissonance.

Plus-Plus Conflict. The plus-plus conflict results from the simultaneous desire, which may be either conscious or unconscious, to obtain two or more goals. Such a situation may be illustrated in its simplest form by thinking of a child in a candy store who wants equally as much to have an ice cream cone and a bag of jelly beans but who has only enough money to buy one of them. Having one means giving up the other, but the closer the child comes to the point of reaching a decision, the more the severity of the conflict begins to diminish. Thus, as he chooses the jelly beans, watches them being placed in a paper bag, and takes them in his hand, they become increasingly attractive and, correspondingly, the ice cream cone is less and less desirable.

Another example of the plus-plus conflict is seen in the behavior of the co-ed who is asked by two different boys to go to a dance. She enjoys dating both of them and, as a result, she will be rewarded whichever choice she makes. To some extent, she will be frustrated as well, because no matter what she decides, she is going to have to miss being with one of them.

When the resolving of a plus-plus conflict has lifetime implications, however, it becomes a much more serious and final matter. The choice of a mate or of an occupation, where two equally desirable alternatives exist, are cases in point. The man who gives up the possibility of practicing law, for instance, in order to become a dentist may experience a sense of nostalgia throughout his life as a result of the sacrificed element in a plus-plus conflict.

Minus-Minus Conflict. In the minus-minus conflict, a choice must be made between two negative and undesirable situations. The student, for instance, who does not possess the goal of enlightenment may find himself a victim of a minus-minus conflict from which he cannot escape. His parents may not be willing for him to drop out of school, and consequently he has to either do the studying he would prefer to avoid or face the equally unpleasant possibility that he may "flunk out" of college. Neither alternative is acceptable, but because he is afraid that he may jeopardize seriously the opportunity for achieving other goals that are important to him, he begins to study. Much student behavior may be understood as resulting from this type of conflict. Studying is postponed for as long as possible and then is followed by intensive cramming and the burning of the midnight oil right before tests and examinations.

It is in minus-minus conflict situations that the use of punishment appears to work so effectively. When the alternative courses of action are equally attractive or unattractive, quite frequently the person becomes immobilized and it is the added threat of punishment which causes him to move in one direction or another. The student, for instance, who is unable to study because of a minus-minus conflict, after being lectured to by the dean or threatened by his parents, may display a temporary spurt in studying. In actuality, the punishment is a minor part of the dynamics of the total situation, but it is given credit for bringing about some impressive looking results. Unfortunately, the basic problem has not been resolved and there is the danger of new conflicts being added. Because the parents have threatened the student, for example, he may have feelings of hostility toward them which are directly opposite to the love he has known previously. The net result may be that externally he behaves a little better, but internally he suffers from even greater conflict and difficulty.

Some people are continually the victims of minus-minus conflicts in their daily lives. They find, for instance, that if they do not laugh at the jokes told by the boss and agree with him, they endanger their chances of gaining promotions. Other persons face the possibility of either saving money or worrying about their financial security in the future, of accepting an invitation to dinner with the Joneses or standing to lose their friendship, of visiting the dentist or suffering from toothache, of mowing the lawn or having to look at the long grass. The list could be extended indefinitely, and in each case, the conflict tends to be disruptive of ongoing constructive behavior.

Plus-Minus Conflict. The plus-minus conflict is by far the most disturbing because it exists when both reward and punishment have been associated with the same goal, person, or situation. The person experiencing the plus-minus conflict has ambivalent feelings in that he both loves and hates, feels positively and negatively, and is attracted to and repelled by the person, situation, or behavior.

In order to appreciate the strength of the intensity of the plus-minus conflict, perhaps you can imagine a small boy who is eying a jar which contains the cookies he enjoys very much. As he moves closer, he becomes increasingly aware of the spanking he has been promised for taking cookies out of the jar. He turns away but the further he goes, the more attractive the cookies become and less important the punishment seems to be. Again he approaches the jar, only to be held up short by his fear of punishment. He desires the cookies too much to leave the kitchen, but, at the same time, he is too afraid of being punished to go ahead and take them and satisfy his desire. The boy is trapped hopelessly and he finds himself in a conflict situation which causes him to become increasingly more tense.

Suppose also that the boy's parents go out of town. While they are away and there is less threat of punishment, he takes several of the cookies from the jar. His desire is appeased partially, but he feels guilty about what he has done and the expectation that in time he will be punished nullifies his satisfaction. The desire for more cookies returns and he repeats the behavior, thereby aggravating his feelings of guilt and tension.

While a small boy taking cookies from a jar may seem like a minor incident, there are many other more serious situations in which conflict is aroused by the positive and negative connotations associated with behavior. The area of sex is perhaps one of the clearest examples. Young people learn that sex is an important and beautiful part of life but, at the same time, they are exposed to influences which either make it taboo or treat it in the most casual of ways. As a result, feelings of ambivalence and inconsistency are liable to develop concerning the place that sexual behavior should have in their lives.

In a similar manner, it is important for a child to receive consistent discipline and for him to be helped in discriminating as to which behavior is appropriate in a particular social situation. Imagine, for example, a small boy named Little Willie slugs a neighbor's boy. The reaction of Little Willie's parents is that their son is all boy and after all it is a good thing that he knows how to take care of himself. Then Little Willie hauls off and punches his sister and immediately the parents respond by giving him a harsh spanking. The same aggressive behavior has been both rewarded and punished and unless the parents clarify the situation for him so that he learns that it is all right for him to punch boys, but not girls, he is liable to develop some ambivalence over the expression of his aggressive feelings.

Horney (1937, p. 35) has suggested the following five major areas in American life as ones in which plus-minus conflicts are most likely to occur: the giving and receiving of affection, the evaluation of the self, self-assertion and feelings of dependency, aggression, and sexuality. All of them represent a segment of life in which behavior is rewarded sometimes but punished on other occasions.

The following more comprehensive descriptions of conflicts in basic values have been presented by Naegale (1949):

Achievement vs. Passivity	The need to assume responsibility for personal achievement conflicts with the practice of waiting passively for something to happen.
Liberty vs. Conformity	Recognition of the importance of the personal achievement of goals conflicts with the desires of the members of a group.
Equality of Opportunity vs. Uneven Breaks and "Pull"	Belief in the importance of providing all people with opportunities for achieving their goals conflicts with the idea of certain people benefiting from personal contact and influence.
Competitive Success vs. Brotherly Love	The need to achieve successfully one's own goals conflicts with the idea of being concerned with the welfare of other persons.
Spending vs. Saving	The need to possess and display various materialistic indications of success conflicts with the desire to save for the future.
Simplicity and Sincerity vs. Extravagance and "Show"	Living simply and naturally conflicts with the idea of gaining attention and creating a favorable impression.
Stimulation of Needs vs. Possibility of Satisfaction	The stimulation of a person's needs conflicts with his ability to satisfy these needs.
Playing Safe vs. Taking Risks	An emphasis on conservatism conflicts with the excitement of taking a chance and playing for high stakes.

Cognitive Dissonance. Cognitive dissonance, a term developed by Festinger (1959, pp. 65-86), incorporates the plus-plus, minus-minus, and plus-minus conflicts but instead of the difficulty centering around the person and his attempts to deal with his environment, the conflict results from the orientation of the person. A young man, for example, may believe in loving mankind but encounter a contradictory view that expects him to be hostile to Negroes. Cognitive dissonance would be likely to occur from his having to hold such incompatible orientations.

Several alternatives are available to him for easing the conflict. He may choose to try to avoid Negroes and not have any contact with the social issues involved in their existence, thereby protecting his internal inconsistency from being disturbed by any outside stimulation. Even more drastically, he may distort the problem by insisting that Negroes are not really part of mankind, and allowing, consequently, his distorted perception of reality to give credence to his cognitive inconsistence. On the other hand, he may treat Negroes like everyone else, thereby achieving internal cognitive consistence, but, at the same time, creating conflict for himself with those persons in the environment who would urge their orientation upon him. This difficulty may lead, in turn, to further cognitive dissonance over doing what seems to be right and, at the same time, relating to one's friends and associates.

Often the price of internal consistency is external conflict and, conversely, adaptation to the values of the environment may cause the person to experience internal discord. Although nominally he may give up his orientation of loving mankind and conform to the expected pattern of behavior in order to keep the peace with his associates, somewhere within him cognitive dissonance is likely to be at work, motivating his behavior on an unconscious level and perhaps causing unsatiated tension to dominate his experience of living.

One of the most important and pervasive kinds of cognitive dissonance is seen in the discrepancy between the person's actual concept of himself and his ideal self or picture of the type of person that he would like to be. The differences between the self concept and the ideal self for two persons are illustrated in Figure 11. On the top is a man whose high level of well-being is indicated by the largeness of area 1 and the relative smallness of areas 2 and 3. In other words, he likes the sort of person that he sees himself to be and there is not too much in his behavior that he would want to change. The man on the bottom, however, has a low level of well-being, as evidenced by the overlap of the two circles representing his actual and desired behavior. Probably he feels that he has fallen far short of his ideal and there is a lot in his behavior that he would prefer to disown.

PERSON 1

Considerable congruence between
actual and ideal behavior—area
of actualization large

Actual
Behavior

Ideal
Behavior

PERSON 2

Ideal
Behavior

Actual
Behavior

Limited congruence between actual
and ideal behavior—area of
actualization small

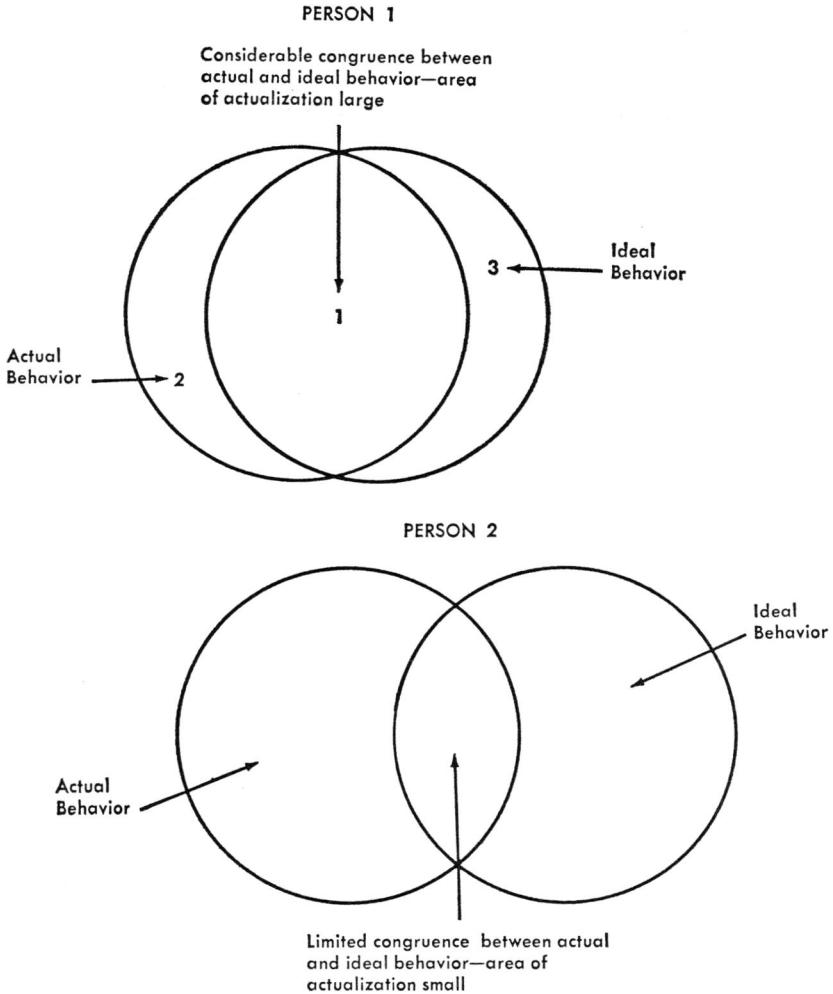

FIGURE 11.   Degree of congruence between actual and ideal behavior.

There are two avenues which such a person may take in order to reduce
this discrepancy. He may realize that his standards for behavior are too
high and inhuman and consequently decide to lower his unrealistic expectations or he may accept the fact that he is capable of achieving more
and attempt to improve his performance level. One of the dangers of a
person altering his behavior too drastically, however, as discussed in the
chapter on physiological goals, is that in attempting to obtain greater
congruence with his ideals, he may lose sight of what his physiological
awareness says is important and right for him.

ENVIRONMENTAL STRESS

A person is not always motivated by the goals he has chosen for himself or by the handling of conflict situations. Some of his behavior is forced upon him by stresses he encounters in the environment. Weaning, toilet training, the development of manners and habits of dress are but a few of the demands for compliance to external expectations that are placed upon the child early in his life. At a later stage in his development, a person may be expected to do well in school and eventually earn his own livelihood. Along with such demands come other frustrating experiences which are caused by delays, deficiencies, losses, failures, and unreasonable demands, all of which have to be handled with a minimum amount of difficulty.

Delays. In the army there is a popular saying, "hurry up and wait," but not only in the army is delay an inevitable part of life. People, opportunities, and events are not always immediately available and learning to wait with some degree of equanimity becomes necessary. No matter how intensively he may apply himself, for example, the person who chooses a physician's career has many years to wait before his goal is realized.

Deficiencies. A person has to learn also to live with various deficiencies in himself and his environment. A child may find, for example, that he does not possess the necessary intelligence or ability to accomplish the career goal that he has chosen for himself. Despite tremendous desire and determination, the ninety-pound weakling simply does not have the physique to become a college fullback. During some years the environment of the farmer lacks sufficient rain while the social experiences of a child may not provide the love and belongingness that is necessary for his development. In fact, there is no end to the deficiencies and shortages that any person is liable to encounter.

Losses. Losses differ from deficiencies in that relationship or ability that once was enjoyed is lost permanently. People who are loved die, while old friendships become less important with the advent of new circumstances. Houses and other possessions are destroyed by fire and storm, and money that has been earned by much diligent work disappears as a result of ill-starred investments. Youth passes and is lost forever while a way of life may become outmoded with the passage of time.

Failures. The place of failure in environmental stress is readily apparent. The only alternative to occasional and even frequent failure is the cessation of activity and the refusal to try anymore. Probably the most important factor is the way that the failure is perceived. For one person it is followed by refusal to try again, but for another individual it is seen as a challenge to renewed effort and eventual growth and new goal emergence.

Unreasonable Demands. In a culture where to a large extent the expectancies of other people determine what a person should be, the stress from unreasonable demands is high. Parents who insist, for example, that their unacademically oriented and intellectually mediocre daughter make straight A's in college are making unreasonable demands upon her. In America today, everyone is expected to be a success and frequently one hears that all that is necessary to succeed is that the person work hard. Nothing could be further from the truth. No matter how hard a person tries, there are many situations in which he will not perform well. The belief that all worthy, hard-working people are successful, moreover, may cause the person who has not been able to reach the top to conclude that he is incompetent and a failure. Thus, for instance, the person, who has every reason to be proud of his ability as a high school biology teacher, may feel that he has failed because he was unable to gain entrance into medical school and become a physician.

Patterns of Emotional Experience

Figures 12, 13, 14, and 15 indicate four general patterns of emotional experience that lead either to growth, development, and new goal emergence or to fixation and even regression. No person ever experiences any of these patterns in their pure forms but, instead, all of them are encountered at one time or another in relationship to some aspect of a person's life. Generally, however, behavior may be characterized primarily by one or another of the different patterns.

EMOTIONAL GROWTH OF THE INFANT

In Figure 12, the ideal conditions for the development of feelings of safety, trust, and security during the first few months of the infant's life are depicted. At first, he is completely helpless and he can only give indications of his state of goal arousal by such activities as general restlessness and crying. Someone outside of himself must see to it that his goals, which are relatively limited in number and complexity, are met.

As the child begins to feel stomach contractions because of hunger, the discomfort causes him to move away from a feeling of relaxation to a state of emotional arousal. He experiences tension which, in turn, leads to generalized activity and eventually to crying. When he is fed, however, the crying stops, his hands begin to unclench as the tension disappears, and he feels gratified. If he is also cuddled, stroked, and given attention by his mother, he becomes even more relaxed. When this pattern of behavior is repeated over and over again, so that the child continually experiences the immediate and total gratification of his needs, his chance

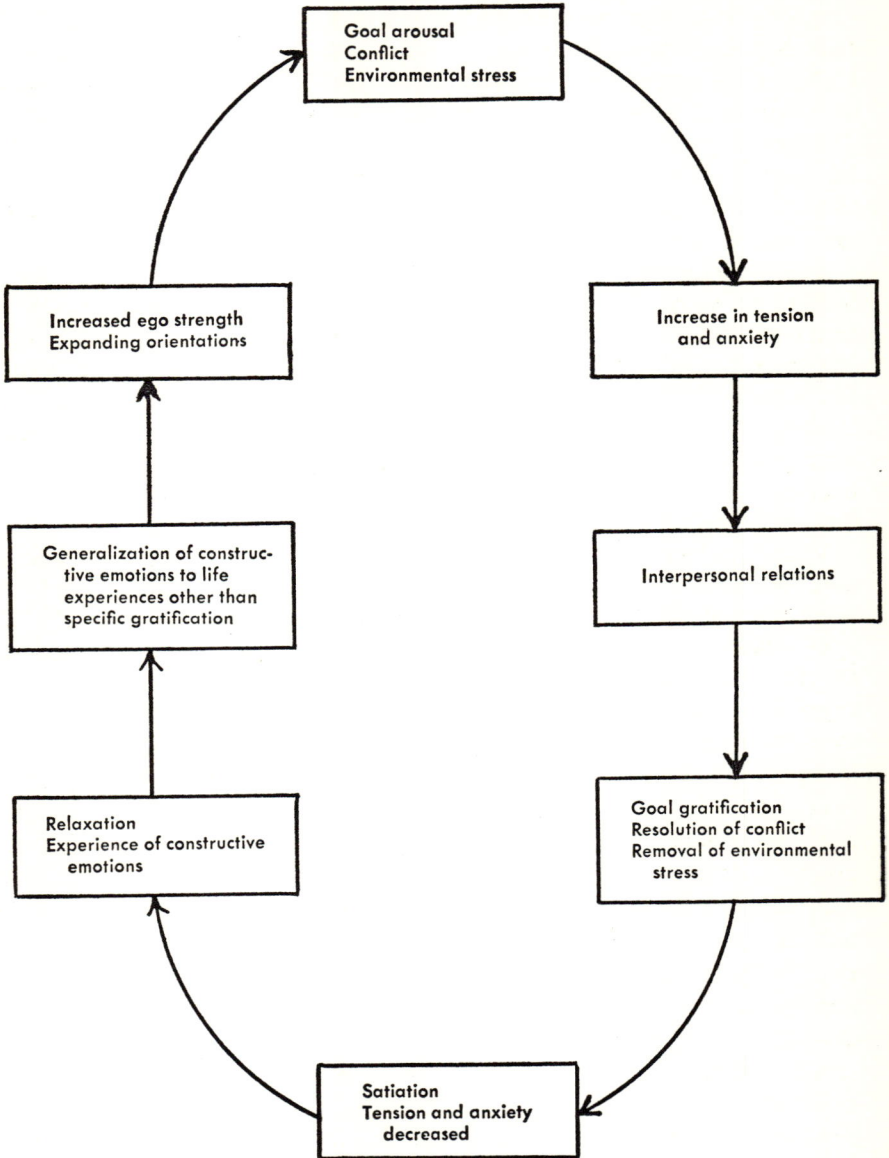

FIGURE 12. Ideal emotional growth of the infant.

of eventually achieving a high level of well-being is off to a very good beginning.

Unfortunately, due to the sometimes harsh attitudes that parents have toward their children and to the events beyond the control of the parents, conditions approaching perfect gratification are seldom attained. A rigid feeding schedule may mean that a hungry infant will experience a high level of tension for many minutes or even hours before the appointed time for his feeding arrives. In fact, only too frequently, the child is deprived of the satisfaction of his needs more than he is gratified and the negative cycle of deprivation shown in Figure 15 takes place. Frustration leads to more frustration and subsequently tension is increased in all areas of experience.

It is believed sometimes that a child needs to "get on schedule" in his feeding as early as possible. This reaction is undoubtedly true, but it seems reasonable to assume that during infancy little tolerance for frustration exists, and that, consequently, the early months of life are hardly likely to be the optimum time for the development in the child of the ability to withstand frustration. Furthermore, at a cost to future development that cannot be measured, the angry parent whose sleep has been interrupted for several nights sometimes adds to the stress that is keeping the child awake by ignoring him or even administering punishment.

When the mother treats the child with coldness, rejection, and harshness, the development of the ability to love and be loved is marred. A number of studies including one by Sears, Maccoby, and Levin (1957) have related rejection of the mother to feeding problems, bed-wetting, etc. On the whole, punishment by the rejecting parent tends to make the child angry and retaliatory and the subsequent emphasis throughout life for the over-frustrated child is likely to be a demand for self-gratification without, in turn, the compensatory growth of the capacity and desire to provide gratification for others. While there is insufficient evidence to prove conclusively a hypothesis supporting the total gratification of the infant's needs, it does stretch the imagination greatly to insist that the opposite approach of deprivation is beneficial to the development of a few-months-old child. Rank has emphasized the trauma involved in moving from the safe and protected environment of the womb, in which every need is met immediately, to the more harsh and demanding world outside (Mullahy, 1948). To insist, therefore, that the newly born infant learn to feed on schedule right away would seem to be inappropriate and quite probably more of an indulgence of the orientational needs of the parent than a contribution to the constructive disciplining of the child. Coleman (1960, p. 99) has stated that if the mother is responsive to the infant when he is hungry or cold or cries, he is influenced in a positive way and his ability to love and be loved has a healthy beginning. The satisfaction of his needs leads in time to feelings of self acceptance, self-confidence, trust, tolerance of failure and disappointment, and the ability to form warm and open relationships with others.

EMOTIONAL GROWTH OF THE CHILD AND THE ADULT

Figure 13 points out the conditions under which optimum development occurs during childhood and the adult years. As the infant grows and develops, he is no longer helplessly dependent upon the people around him. The activities of work and play are added to his behavioral repertoire and it becomes possible to satisfy some of his needs on his own initiative. Whenever his behavior is efficient, he experiences satiation and temporary relaxation from his tensions. Since many people desire experiences and the attainment of goals that are either hard to reach or available only to a limited degree, even effective and appropriate behavior patterns are sometimes met by goal failure, frustration, and disappointment. Such experiences are inevitably a part of life and if a person is to continue to grow and develop, he has to learn to deal with them effectively. One response to such frustration is to turn to using the adjustment mechanisms which are discussed in detail in the next chapter. A more meaningful approach, however, is to rely upon the processes of re-trial and reinterpretation.

Re-trial. In re-trial the person repeats basically the same approach in an attempt to attain his goal. A student, for instance, who has failed a course may decide to take it again, presumably with more determination to do better a second time. While in most cases it is appropriate to try again, nevertheless it is foolish to persist long after there has been sufficient exposure to a situation to indicate that the person cannot compete adequately.

Reinterpretation. With reinterpretation the same student may come to the conclusion that he has selected the wrong major field and that his ability lies in some other area of study. He may decide, therefore, that there is no point in repeating the same mistake and subsequently may transfer to another program. The ability to undertake such mature behavior, however, begins to be developed during the early years of life. If a child, for instance, finds that his ball has rolled behind a chair, it may be good for him to be allowed to experience frustration momentarily. In the process, he may bump his head against the chair and work himself into an emotional uproar. Sooner or later, however, when he is ready to deal with the situation, he will reinterpret it and succeed in going around the chair in order to retrieve the ball.

In such a case, the child has suffered frustration but in the end, by being made to reinterpret the situation, he has gained the crucial experience of obtaining relief from frustration as a result of his own efforts. Experience with frustration that leads ultimately to satiation and the decrease of tension is a necessary and unavoidable part of the growth

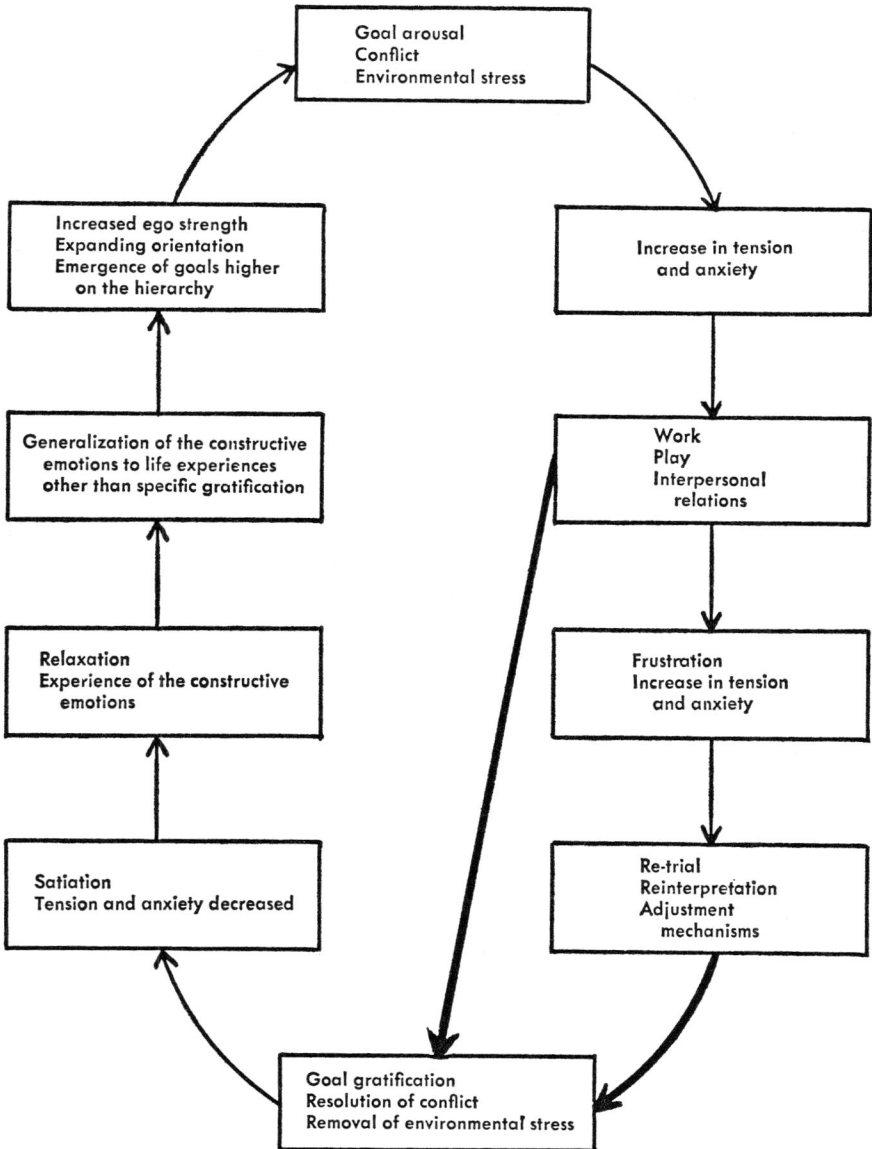

FIGURE 13. Ideal emotional growth of the child and the adult.

process. Frustration, on the other hand, that culminates in more frustration which is not followed eventually by satiation, results almost inevitably in fixation or regression to an earlier stage of development. The child needs to be protected from such barren experiences that fail to provide gratification and satiation. At the same time, he needs also to be spared from the overprotection that denies him the chance to deal with frustrations that he himself is capable of overcoming.

Factors That Influence Frustration Tolerance. Several factors help to determine how much frustration a person may be able to tolerate without becoming overly frustrated and losing his growth potential. With the exception of very old people, it is generally true that the older the person, the greater amount of frustration that he can handle comfortably. In addition, the person who has been given many opportunities for learning to deal constructively with frustration is likely to have more tolerance of distressing situations than the person with a history of overprotection or the person who has been subjected to severe frustration. When the individual is familiar with the experience he is encountering, he is also liable to handle the frustration more positively than the person who faces a strange situation. As a result, it is important that people who move into new and different social situations be given a temporary period of protection from pressure and stress before they be expected to deal with anything but the barest minimum of frustration. The amount of stress that a person can tolerate, and still continue to grow, is an individual matter and, consequently, each person needs to be related to in terms of his readiness and ability to tolerate frustration and not automatically on the basis of an ideal which he is expected to attain.

AMBIVALENT EMOTIONAL GROWTH

Figure 14 indicates the place of ambivalence in the pattern of emotional experience. A person may attain certain achievement goals successfully but, at the same time, fail to secure the love and belongingness that he needs. Although his accomplishments, personally and from society's viewpoint, are both real and consequential, he is seldom deeply satisfied with himself and, as a result, he is constantly searching for new opportunities for gaining satiation. Under such conditions, both negative and positive emotions are generalized to other segments of the pattern of emotional experience and the person's behavior is dominated by his feelings of ambivalence. Such great but unhappy and even tragic figures as Van Gogh, Beethoven, and Dostoevski, as well as a number of titans in industry and the political world, have exemplified lives that alternated sharply between constructive and destructive behavior, both to themselves and to other people.

It seems reasonable to hypothesize that many Americans find themselves living less dramatic versions of the same pattern of behavior. They

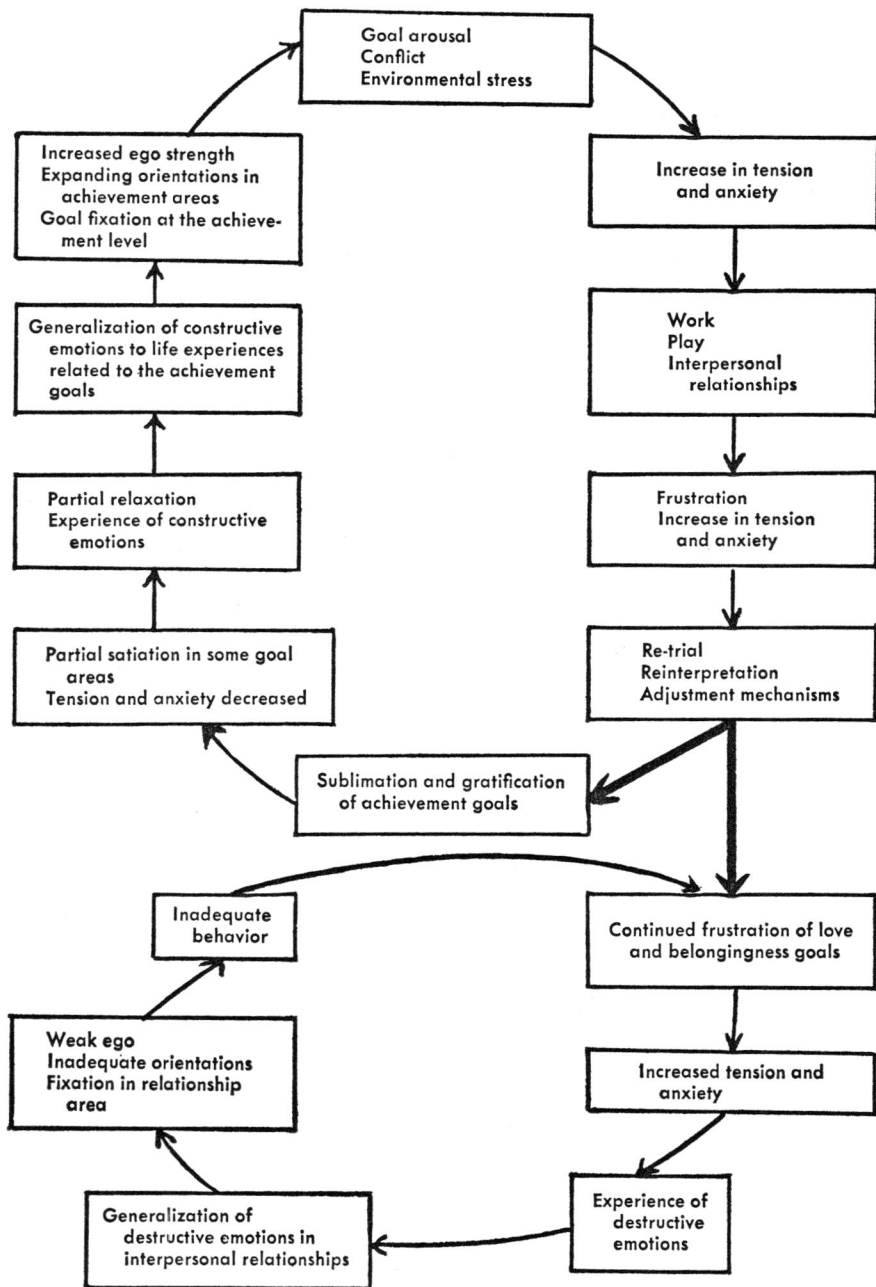

FIGURE 14.   Ambivalent emotional growth.

are frustrated by the difficulty involved in attaining love, belongingness, and psychological safety and, therefore, they turn to living in the future. It is much easier to believe that conditions will improve with time than it is to accept past failures and present shortcomings as a part of the orientational system.

As a consequence, life is seen as promising to be much better once a person has been graduated from college, begun his career, obtained another job or promotion, got married, started his family, bought a new car, paid the mortgage on the house, vacationed in Europe and, in fact, in any way that may be seen as part of a glorious and nebulous future. But somehow the anticipated improvement in living and increase in satisfaction never comes to very many people. It beckons, but when reached, already it has dissipated. From the outside, the lives of such people look full and rich. They are envied and their manner of living dreamed about by other less successful people caught in the same cycle of events. From the inside, however, their lives are often ones of tension and quiet desperation. The shock that comes when such unfortunate people end their lives by suicide is even greater than when the same act is performed by a person who obviously has very little.

DESTRUCTIVE EMOTIONAL INFLUENCES

Figure 15 illustrates the emotional experiences that occur when goal deprivation and non-satiation are intense, continuous, and of long duration. Frustration builds upon frustration and tension upon tension. In time, the person begins to exhibit some of the following symptoms: vacillation and indecision, discouragement, unwillingness to accept compromise, boredom, apathy and indifference, inability to concentrate, lowered aspirations, attention-getting behavior, anti-social behavior of all kinds, negativism, defiance of authority, and destructiveness toward the self and others.

The negative emotions which are experienced in one form or another tend to be generalized to other aspects of experience and to people other than the ones specifically responsible for bringing about the negative reaction. As reliance on the use of the negative aspects of adjustment mechanisms increases, there tends to be a greater distortion of reality, causing the person's efforts to be even more futile. He is forced to exist with less and less gratification and satiation and as the cycle of behavior is repeated over and over again, the tension is increased to an unbearable level.

If the tension persists for too long, it may easily turn into anxiety. Perhaps you can imagine what it would be like to live every moment with the feeling that occurs when you know that you have to make an im-

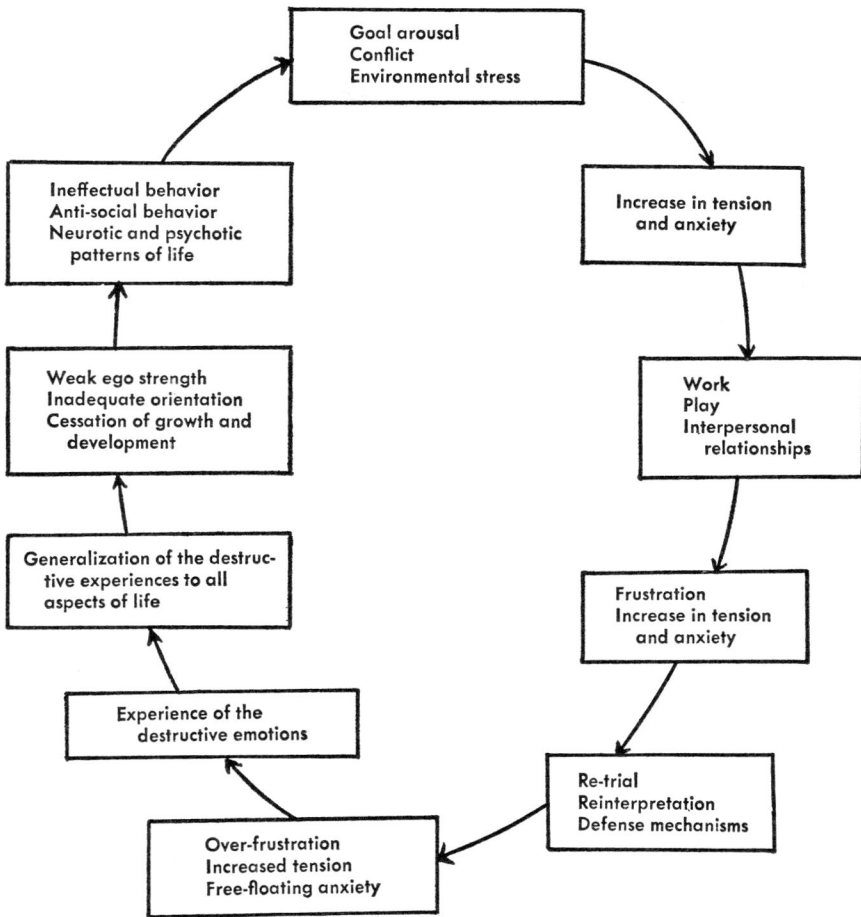

FIGURE 15. Destructive emotional influence.

portant speech in five minutes. If so, then you have some conception of the tension experienced by the person suffering from generalized or what has been called free-floating anxiety.

At a less intense level is the mild form of anxiety which occurs when the person feels that something is wrong, that he has failed in some way, that he has a forgotten task that he was expected to do. May (1958, pp. 50-51) has commented on this type of anxiety stating that:

> The anxiety a person feels when someone he respects passes him on the street without speaking, for example, is not as intense as the fear he experiences when the dentist seizes the drill to attack a sensitive tooth. But the gnawing threat of the slight on the street may hound him all day

long and torment his dreams at night, whereas the feeling of fear, though it was quantitatively greater, is gone forever as soon as he steps out of the dentist's chair. The difference is that the anxiety strikes at the center core of his self-esteem and his sense of value as a self, which is one important aspect of his experience of himself as a being. Fear, in contrast, is a threat to the periphery of his existence; it can be objectivated and the person can stand outside and look at it.

Existential anxiety is another type which May (1958, p. 52) described "as an experience of threat which carries both anguish and dread, indeed the most painful and basic threat which any being can suffer, for it is the threat of loss of existence itself." May (1961, p. 19) made reference to his own experience of trying to understand the meaning of anxiety when he faced the possibility of death for a year and a half while in bed in a tuberculosis sanatorium. It would seem that the experiencing of existential anxiety and the facing of vital questions raised by the prospect of death and destruction, and even the experiencing of other crises in daily living, may cause a person on occasion to examine carefully his goals and quite possibly modify them so that, like the individual living at the second level of well-being, he is more likely to become what he is capable of being.

In its more excessive form, however, anxiety forces the person to search for any action or behavioral pattern that, irrespective of whether or not it is appropriate or logical, gives an indication of helping to ease or alleviate the tension. He feels he must do something to escape from the anxiety but, because of the vagueness and ambiguity of his situation, he has difficulty deciding specifically in which direction he should move. As a result, his potential for living is seriously crippled and he may find himself being driven to the company of small groups of lonely and unfortunate persons, perhaps experiencing through such associations sufficient gratification to lead him into adopting their defiant behavioral patterns, and thus easing the tension under which he is living.

The psychotic suffers even more damage and regresses to the point that even the basic orientation necessary for just marginal existence is destroyed. Alienation from life may finally become so severe that the person is driven to suicide, thus bringing an end to his non-satiated existence.

The Generalization of Love and Hate

There is a tendency for a person to generalize his emotional reactions toward specific people, experiences, and situations to other aspects of his life. Thus, for example, the person who has received gratification may carry the positive emotions that he has known into his work, play, and interpersonal relationships; to periods of re-trial and reinterpretation; and, in short, to all the experiences of the mature life. Furthermore, his feelings of love may be extended successfully from the parent-child relationship to other family members, to friends and neighbors, to members of other similar cultural groups, to one's mate, to one's own children, to strangers, and to a broad love of all mankind.

Conversely, with the increased tension that follows continued deprivation, the person experiences the entire range of destructive emotions. His positive feelings are limited by and large to people who provide specific gratification. Thus, the child who flees a non-gratifying home environment will prefer the company of neighbors, the street corner gang, or any group that offers a potential for satiation. In such a case, however, the search is for new gratification as a replacement for what has not been received in the home. Similarly, the criminal, who has generalized destructive emotions to most aspects of society, may give loyalty and even affection to the leader who offers him a means of finding gratification.

The Love and Hate Continuum

Love and hate responses may be seen as existing on a continuum in the way shown in Figure 16. In the direction of A, emotions of approval and liking, for example, are felt for the dog that wags his tail and licks a person's hand, but in the direction of B, emotions of dislike and disapproval are felt for the mongrel that barks, growls, bares his fangs, and attempts to bite.

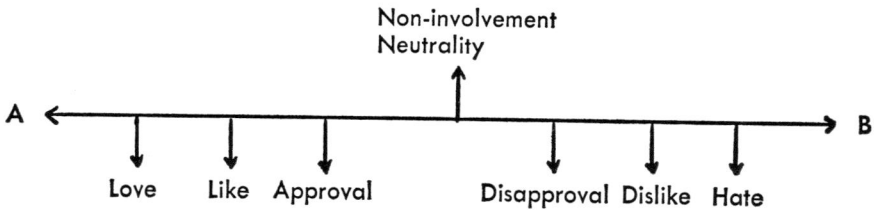

FIGURE 16. The love-hate continuum.

On a more complex level, America feels A-direction emotions toward England, West Germany, and other countries that aid in the achievement of the United States' foreign policy and material goals. In contrast, B-direction emotions are expressed toward the U.S.S.R., Red China, and those countries that threaten America's position in the world. During World War II, the Germans and Japanese were hated violently because they were seen as a direct threat to the United States. The Soviet Union was an ally, but soon after the end of World War II, the positions were reversed. It would seem that, on the international level, love turns to hate and vice versa with bewildering rapidity, depending primarily on whether or not a nation is seen as providing gratification of goals and needs.

Similarly, the love a child has for his mother is a response to the gratification that he receives over a long period of time. During the early years, his relationship with the parent is intensely personal. As he grows older, even under ideal conditions, the purity of the early emotional feelings is corrupted by the deprivation and frustration he attributes to the parent and by the increase in gratification potential of other people in his environment. He will begin to experience negative emotions in the B-direction, and he may go so far as to express directly his feelings with the open statement, "I hate you." Since the expression of such negative feelings toward parents is generally unacceptable, the feelings are more often repressed, to be expressed unconsciously through neglect, lack of concern, non-initiation of contact, and generally the shortcomings of omission.

If you ask a typical college student whether he loves his mother, the quick and outraged reply is likely to be that of course he does. If you ask about the attention he pays her, the responses are likely to be more subdued. Examination of his behavior reveals that friends, dating, sports events, hobbies, reading, music, etc., all have become more gratifying than the company of his parents. However, when the student is relieved of the necessity of pretending to feel a perfect love for them, then he becomes capable of displaying a reasonable amount of concern and affectionate behavior.

The Ambivalence of Emotions

Ideally emotions are either positive and characterized by love and constructive attitudes or they are negative and contain certain destructive elements. In actuality, however, this view is highly artificial because love is never pure and uncontaminated in that ambivalence, as shown in Figure 17, may occur at any point along the love-hate continuum. People experience loving and hating, not in clear, undiluted forms but in dynamic ever-changing combinations. Even the most positive of emotions tends to decrease in intensity during the course of time. Thus, elation may

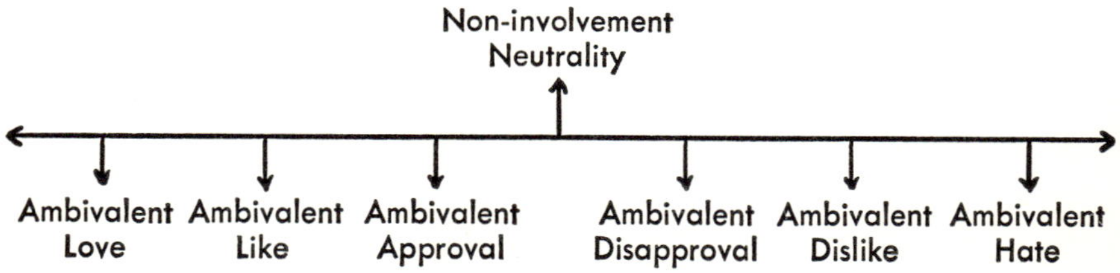

FIGURE 17. The love-hate ambivalence continuum.

change to happiness to contentment to neutrality to boredom to discomfort. In contrast to the Hollywood version of life, every story does not end with an outstanding success. Life goes on, and to avoid boredom and discontent following upon success, new goals must emerge which encourage the person to seek development in other more challenging aspects of life.

The Dynamics of Changing Emotions

In the manner of Lewin (1935, pp. 88-94), Figure 18 depicts boy A who dates two girls, B and C. Girl B for reasons of her own, laughs at the boy's appearance, argues with all of his opinions, openly flirts with other boys, and even refuses him a goodnight kiss. During their date one way or another she deprives him of achieving his goals of love, belongingness, and psychological safety, respect, skill, and power. These experiences

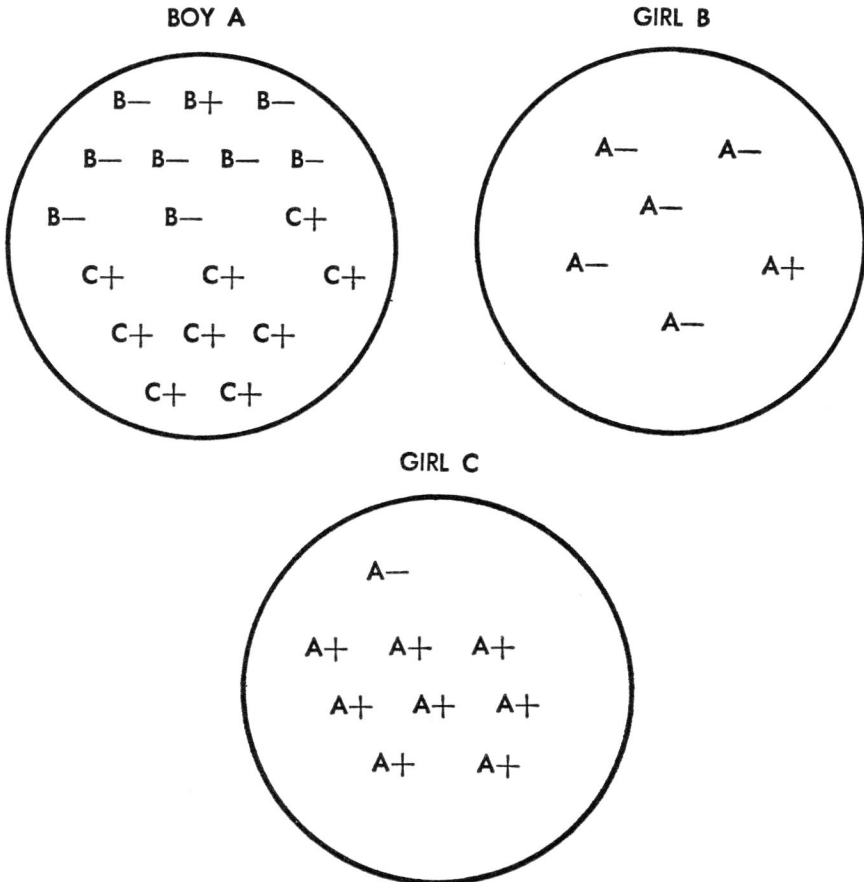

FIGURE 18. The dynamics of changing emotions.

are shown as B minuses within A's circle of experience, while the fact that he still sees her as pretty accounts for the single B plus. Girl C, again for her own reasons and consistent with her orientation, indicates during the course of the date that she thinks the boy is good-looking and intelligent. She gives him all of her attention and responds to his advances with a reasonable amount of affection. She gratifies many of his goals and thus C pluses are created within his experiential field. Since the boy has satisfied many of her needs also, A pluses are indicated in her own experiential field. Unless he is a damaged person, who finds the punishment meted out by girl B to be gratifying, or an adventurer who sees her refusal as a challenge, it is more likely that he will date girl C a second time in preference to girl B.

The hypothetical relationship of boy A and girl C may be followed further. As they continue to date, they find they have much in common and that they gratify one another in a number of different ways. The increasing strength of their relationship is depicted in Figure 19. The pluses increase, but so do the minuses. The girl has an orientation that it is time to fall in love and despite such noticeable shortcomings as that he dresses a little too sloppily, smokes too much, tends to be a braggart on occasion, and has different ideas on politics and religion, he does provide her with more gratification than deprivation. The situation is approximately the same for the boy and his ambivalent feelings for the girl are located far toward the positive or A end of the love-hate ambivalence continuum. As these conditions continue to prevail, the romance deepens

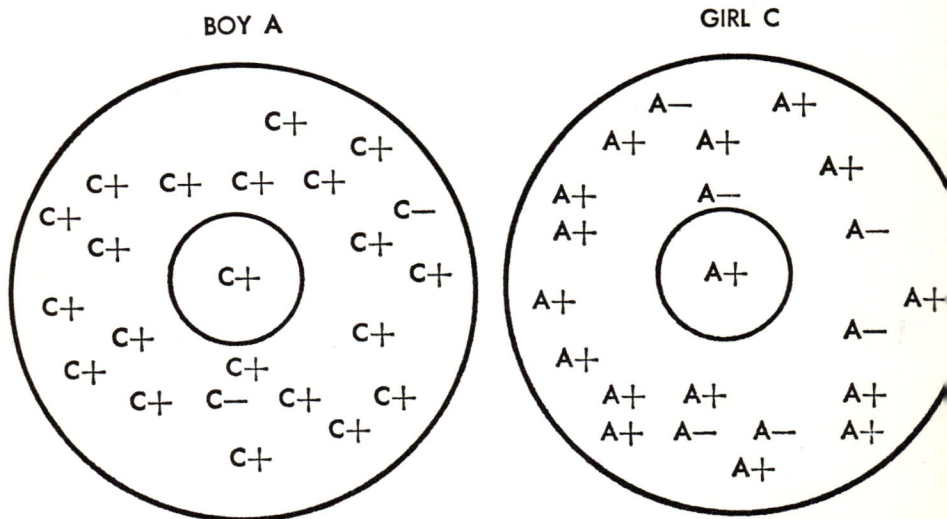

FIGURE 19.   Emotional conditions leading to close personal relationships.

speedily. Not to be minimized as well is the potential erotic gratification, signified as A plus and C plus, that these two persons hold for one another. In fact, this influence may be so strong that it causes both the boy and girl to distort each other's traits and characteristics.

As the relationship continues, the pluses come to exceed the minuses to such an extent that marriage ensues. With the passage of time, erotic gratification takes place sufficiently enough for the influence of this factor to have diminished, and the couple's perceptions of each other have altered considerably. The boy begins to see the girl as selfish, rigid, immaculate, and conforming and willing to marry anyone who came along in order to escape from a home environment that she found intolerable. In turn, he is seen as a stingy, arrogant, and domineering person. Under the strain of everyday living, the relationship deteriorates. Positive emotions give way to destructive ones, and soon the couple is filing for divorce. The number of pluses decreases while the minuses increase; Figure 20 indicates the new internal conditions of love and hate.

Thus, perhaps it may be seen that the concept of a perfect and constant love is purely fictional. Instead, love is a mixture and balance of gratification of self and of the other person which is constantly changing. Under optimum conditions, love is expressed by gratifying the other person as well as oneself. Persons differ immensely in the immediacy and the quality of the satisfaction or gratification they must have. The tragedy is that all too often the more starved a person is for love, the less capable he is of either giving or receiving it, and consequently the less able he is to engage in the constructive behavior that is likely to win him the love that he so desperately seeks.

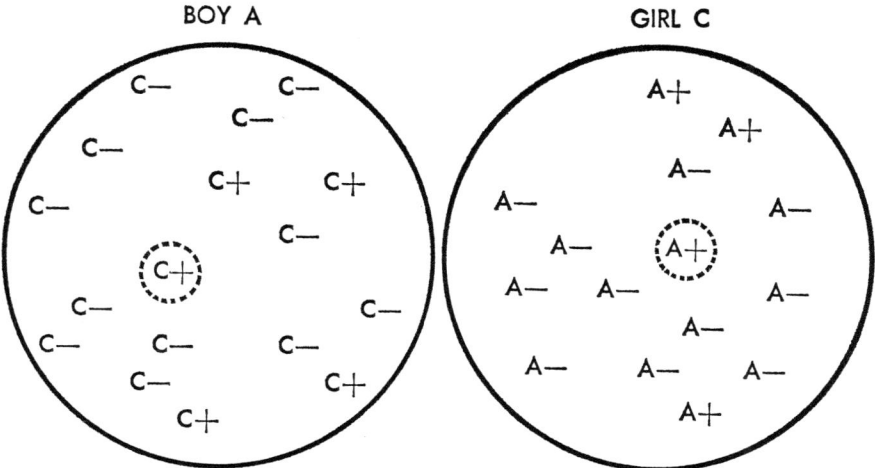

FIGURE 20. Emotional conditions leading to the severing of relationships.

Other Positive Emotions

The most important positive or constructive emotion, of course, is that of love but some of the other more positive emotions are joy, sympathy, wonder, satisfaction, purpose, admiration and friendship, hope, and surprise. They have been described in detail by Krech and Crutchfield (1958, pp. 230-264) and are discussed in relationship to the context of this book in the paragraphs that follow.

Joy. Joy is the emotion that is felt when, under conditions which involve the very strong possibility of failure, a goal is achieved successfully. A student may apply, for example, for a position which he wants very much to obtain. He has a chance of succeeding, but he knows at the same time that the competition is strong and there is every likelihood that he will not be chosen. Obtaining the position under these circumstances leads to the emotional experience of joy or even triumph. Triumph, however, tends to be the more competitive emotion that is enjoyed at the expense of another's failure.

Sympathy. When another suffers, the person who feels the emotion of sympathy experiences pain and grief as well. Generally, sympathy is expressed between people who see themselves as equals. When it occurs with a person who is seen as being inferior it is more likely that it is the emotion of pity that is expressed.

According to Russell (Egner and Denonn, 1961, p. 643), many different attitudes may be taken toward human suffering: the sadist finds pleasure in it; the sentimentalist insists that it is not as bad as it seems; the person who relies on rationalization is detached and generally ignores it, tending to think that the victim brought it on himself; but the compassionate or sympathetic person attempts to understand the nature of the experience in order that he may do whatever is in his power to alleviate it.

Wonder. Wonder is the emotion that is associated with experiences that are seen as being overwhelming, astonishing, inexplicable, and generally little subject to natural appraisal and understanding. When the circumstances that accompany such experiences are threatening or when the person is helpless in the face of these happenings, the emotion is liable to become one of dread.

Satisfaction. Satisfaction is the feeling that accompanies realistic goal achievement and is likely to be experienced when the level of aspiration coincides with the skill and ability level.

Purpose. Purpose is associated with the intention to achieve a recognized goal by a particular means that is satisfying. Without it, the person wanders aimlessly through life, never knowing quite what he wants nor how to go about finding it.

Admiration and Friendship. A person shows admiration for another individual when he recognizes characteristics and attributes which he would like to have but does not possess. Friendship, on the other hand, tends to be based on the sharing of similar attitudes and traits. When a person does not care for what he sees in himself, he may dislike the person who is similar to him and choose his friends from people who are very different. When a person respects himself, however, he is unlikely to be drawn close to those people who have attitudes which are dissimilar to those he values.

Hope. Hope represents the orientation toward future goal success. The joys associated with hope may sustain a person for a time, but he cannot survive indefinitely the repeated disillusionments of failure. Instead, he needs to feel that his efforts are not futile. Thus, the wise person, in order to avoid being discouraged, provides a series of sub-goals along the path toward a distant or far-off goal. The level of aspiration must be realistic as well for, according to Durkheim (1960, p. 451), to pursue a goal that is unattainable is to condemn oneself to a perpetual state of discontent.

Surprise. Surprise is the emotion that is associated with an experience that is rather sharply different from what is expected in a given situation. Perhaps you will imagine that a person is walking down the Champs Élysées in Paris and not expecting to see a familiar face when suddenly he spies old Joe Brown who lives just down the block in his home town. Seeing Joe at home would have occasioned no surprise and he might have been ignored. Seeing him in Paris does provide a surprise and the two may act like long-lost brothers.

Negative Emotions

Some of the negative emotions are those of hate, indecision, boredom, disappointment, jealousy, envy, greed, shame and remorse, scorn, resentment, apathy, and fear.

Hate. Hate is the emotion of deprivation and is expressed through one kind of destructive behavior or another. Fromm (1960, p. 523) has stated that if a person cannot create life, he can affirm his identity by destroying it. According to Kelley (1961, p. 14), when Hitler came into power he found a people who were "frustrated by defeat, hungry, wearied by inflation." During World War II hate reached the highest level of all time when thousands and thousands of people in Europe were killed in a blood bath of destruction. When carried to such an extreme point, the dynamics of hate are very real and if not understood may easily endanger the future of civilization and mankind.

Disappointment. Disappointment is the emotion that follows goal failure when success was expected. It may occur also when the achievement is less than that anticipated. A student, for instance, who expects an A in a course, will be disappointed with the B he receives. In fact, any anticipated success that does not materialize or is subject to delay will result in feelings of disappointment. The person who constantly sets his goals too high in terms of his capabilities can thus create for himself a lifetime of disappointment and frustration. High school students who, in competition with people of all abilities in their age group, made straight A's sometimes doom themselves to disappointment when they expect to make A's in college in competition with the more talented segment of their peers. Grief is a stronger form of disappointment, but it tends to be related more to the loss of someone or something than to failure to obtain a certain degree of achievement.

Jealousy. Jealousy is engendered when love and belongingness are threatened. It may be felt toward a loved one when he is attracted to another person or it may be experienced by a young child when a baby comes into the family. Even animals are capable of this feeling apparently, for frequently they display symptoms of jealousy when another pet or a new child arrives on the scene. Feelings of jealousy may be realistic when there is a serious danger of loss, but more often they are unrealistic, in which case the person's reaction is disproportionate to the actual experience. Frequently, such a person will create a threat which has no basis of reality in order that he can feel jealous. Since he has not experienced the love of others, he does not feel worthy of being loved and with such an attitude, ordinary behavior of a loved one will be interpreted as a threat, no matter what the loved one does or does not do.

Since children are almost insatiable in their need for love, it is impossible for parents to avoid some of the frustrations which lead to the creation of jealousy. Almost every child has felt at one time or another that his parents preferred each other or a brother or sister to himself. To some extent everyone feels some unrealistic jealousy. Whereas the immature adult, like a child, continues to have these feelings and to want all the love that can be had, the more mature adult learns to live with a restricted diet of love, confining his feelings of jealousy to situations which realistically justify them.

Envy. Envy is related closely to jealousy, except that it concerns characteristics and possessions of other people instead of the loss of a specific love object. The single person, for example, may envy a happily married couple the love they possess. He may envy the man with a brand-new car or a big house or the man who can run the hundred-yard dash in under ten seconds. One woman may envy another her figure or her poise and ease in social situations. The essence of the feeling is the wish for something that is lacking that other people are seen enjoying.

Greed. Greed is the emotion of insatiability and is accompanied by goal confusion. Because a person's basic needs are not satisfied he turns, as a substitute, to greater and greater achievement of a conscious goal in a rather hopeless effort to satiate the basic and unconscious goal. Tragically for such a person nothing is ever enough and his life situation is made worse by modern advertising which aids and abets the process by emphasizing an unrealistic goal attainment that exists nowhere outside the imagination.

Shame and Remorse. Shame is the emotion of self-disapproval which occurs when behavior is found to be incongruent with the feeling of what it should have been. The emotions felt by Floyd Patterson, for example, on suffering first-round knockouts in two heavyweight championship fights were those of shame (Talese, 1964). In addition, quite frequently, society expects behavior of a person to be different from what he wants for himself and the perception of this disparity results in feelings of shame.

Remorse is related to shame but has more of a connotation with the past. It concerns behavior that a person feels that he should not have done or the omission of deeds that he feels he should have performed. Remorse is experienced frequently at funerals, for example, when it is too late to amend the mistakes of the past.

Scorn. Scorn is a negative emotion which is felt toward those persons who are considered to be inferior. Some element of threat and goal frustration, whether real or potential, is involved. When scorn is felt, for instance, for "lazy inferiors," there is always the possibility that the person would like to be lazier than his own orientation to life will allow him to be or the person feels he is in reality lazier than he should be.

Resentment. Resentment is the negative emotion that is felt toward those persons who are seen as being superior. The person who is able to take an afternoon off from work in order to play golf may bring forth feelings of resentment in those workers who do not feel free to do so.

Apathy. Apathy is a mildly negative emotion that is perhaps best described as a lack of concern or sympathy. It shows a lack of emotional involvement that may change to a much stronger reaction under slightly different circumstances. The announcement that 100,000 chickens were slaughtered in a poultry plant produces only mild disturbance, if any at all. Were 100,000 dogs slaughtered, however, a much stronger response is likely to be forthcoming, as may be evidenced by the hue and cry that went up by dog-lovers across the nation over President Lyndon B. Johnson's lifting some beagles by their ears.

Fear.   Fear occurs when a person is unable to cope with a threatening situation. Basically there are two types of fear: a realistic and healthy reaction to a dangerous situation and an irrational or neurotic response that is not justified in terms of objective reality. On occasion, both types of fear are present at the same time inasmuch as a person may over-react to a somewhat dangerous and fear-arousing situation. Aggression is related closely to the developing of fear. When attacked, for instance, a person may flee while feeling very fearful or he may attack in order to cover up his fear and subsequently remain fearful over the possibility of reprisal. The extreme expression of fear is panic which occurs when a person is unable to mobilize his resources in order to respond in any way to a threatening situation.

SUMMARY

1. During the course of the pursuit of his goals, a person experiences emotional arousal that is replaced in time by a feeling of relaxation which is followed, in turn, by another period of emotional involvement.

2. Whereas goal arousal stems from a desire to attain goals, conflict and environmental stress interfere with attempts to gain successful goal achievement.

3. The discrepancy between actual behavior and a person's ideal concept of himself becomes less destructive when the person is willing either to modify his unrealistic expectations or to improve his actual level of performance.

4. Particularly during the first few months of life, it is important for an infant's needs to be gratified at the earliest opportunity.

5. If a person is to grow and develop, it is essential that he not encounter more frustration than he is capable of handling.

6. The inability of a person to attain goal satisfaction over a long period of time leads to his experiencing excessive tension and anxiety.

7. People tend to generalize specific emotional reactions to other aspects of their lives.

8. An individual's emotions undergo a great deal of variation during the course of a highly personal relationship with another person.

EXERCISE 10

Observing Non-verbal Behavior

Frequently, we express how we feel not with words, but in a variety of non-verbal ways. We believe it will help you achieve your goals and become a more sensitive person if you develop skills for attending to these subtle messages, which may be quite different from our words.

Think of groups you have been in recently. Do you recall noticing anyone . . .

YES   No

_____ _____ 1. moving backward or forward in his chair?

_____ _____ 2. smile or sneer on the side (not toward the speaker but to someone else)?

_____ _____ 3. look at his watch, the ceiling, or out the window?

_____ _____ 4. laugh at inopportune moments?

_____ _____ 5. wrinkle his forehead?

_____ _____ 6. shrug his shoulders?

_____ _____ 7. sweat?

_____ _____ 8. wring his hands?

_____ _____ 9. blush?

_____ _____ 10. fidget?

_____ _____ 11. raise his voice?

_____ _____ 12. experience a voice break while speaking?

_____ _____ 13. show almost no facial expression?

_____ _____ 14. really look at the speaker?

_____ _____ 15. laugh excessively?

_____ _____ 16. smoke more than usual?

_____ _____ 17. whose hands were trembling?

_____ _____ 18. listen alertly (body posture, expression, etc.)?

_____ _____ 19. who seemed to be up-tight with tension?

_____ _____ 20. scratch?

In the next group with which you participate, make a list of the non-verbal, expressive behaviors you observe. Enter them in the following space.

_____

_____

_____

Select five non-verbal behaviors from your list. After each, write the message you think the person who exhibited them was communicating. In general, was this the same or a different message from the one the person gave verbally?

Non-verbal Behavior	Possible Meaning
1. _____	_____
2. _____	_____
3. _____	_____
4. _____	_____
5. _____	_____

Try to evaluate the importance to yourself of sensitivity to these and other non-verbal behaviors for understanding others, or for dealing with persons with whom you interact. If the effort seems worthwhile, you might want to repeat the above exercise until noticing these things becomes automatic and part of your social self.

CHAPTER 12

The Adjustment Mechanisms

In the previous chapter, the adjustment mechanisms, together with re-trial and reinterpretation, were described as being the behavioral responses to the tension that accompanies need for activity, goal arousal, conflict, and environmental stress. Adjustment mechanisms are seen as being positive in function when they lead to the satiation of a person's goals but negative when they serve ultimately only to increase tension. According to Lehner and Kube (1955, pp. 136-137), mechanisms are negative and cease to be adjustive when reliance upon them becomes excessive and leads to other difficulties, when they obscure the real nature of the problem confronting the person and the source of his conflicts, and when they stop him from making an objective appraisal of his situation and cause him to fail to see the alternative courses of action of re-trial and reinter-pretation.

Peckham (1962, p. 82) has noted that if tensions cannot be discharged by comprehending a situation and behaving effectively, a person will use adjustment mechanisms or ascribe value to anything that is able to relieve the tension. Menninger (1963, p. 157) has coined the term "dysorgan-ization" to describe the state of the organism while it is using adjustment mechanisms. He sees it as being inefficient, expensive emotionally, some-what uncomfortable, and altogether a lesser state of organization than that used by the efficiently functioning person. At the same time, there is greater organization than is the case with the person who is experiencing a complete breakdown of function and pathological disorder. Perhaps the situation may be compared to the physical state of the fortified and walled city described by Mumford (1961, p. 358). The fortification is a necessary plan for defense against the threat of attack but, as a conse-quence, the city is limited in its growth and, thus, it must fit into a strait-jacket imposed by the external limits of the walls. In a similar manner, the person who relies excessively on the use of adjustment mechanisms as a means of protecting himself against attack places himself also in a strait-jacket that restricts his growth and development.

The primary precipitating factor in the use of adjustment mechanisms is the frustration brought about by failure to obtain goal achievement and the subsequent need to defend the concept of the self. A person enters every social situation with a picture of himself as he likes to see himself and when he does not behave in a way that is consistent with his image, then he has two courses of action: he may change the picture of himself, which is very demanding and difficult, or he may distort the experience by turning to the use of adjustment mechanisms, which is very easy to do.

Suppression

Suppression and repression, two of the most prominent adjustment mechanisms, are assumed to underlie the use of all adjustment mechanisms. Suppression may be defined as the conscious determination and effort not to recognize a certain aspect of experience. Sometimes a person will decide quite deliberately, for example, to not think about an unpleasant experience or to postpone considering the solution of a problem until a later date.

Repression

Repression, on the other hand, represents the complete banishing of thoughts, wishes, and experiences from conscious awareness. Thus, a person may even feel an attraction for objects, situations, or persons that make him feel secure and comfortable with no awareness that he is frightened or threatened. Similarly, he may desire and obtain certain objects or goals without ever experiencing any conscious awareness of why he wanted them. If a person cannot believe that he would behave in a particular way, the process of repression enables him to avoid facing the knowledge that actually he did act in such a manner. Thus, as stated by Sappenfield (1954, p. 195), "the 'unthinkable' becomes truly *unthinkable*." The experience has not been destroyed, however, but only banished from conscious awareness. In the same way that a clock which is wound and placed in a closet keeps ticking and recording time, regardless of whether or not it is heard, repressed experiences continue to influence behavior, despite the person's unawareness of their existence. Perhaps an event in the life of one of the authors may be used as an example. While a student in graduate school, he saw one of Marlon Brando's earliest movies in which there was a scene of a paraplegic crying for his mother. All of a sudden the author felt his hands becoming moist and himself growing so faint that he had to be helped out of the theater. Soon afterwards the source of the difficulty became apparent. During World War II the author served on a British destroyer that was hit as a result of a dive-bombing attack by a Japanese airplane. A number of people were killed and one eighteen-year-old boy died in his arms while crying for his mother. The highly charged emotional aspect of the experience caused it to be repressed, but the similarity to the scene in the movie produced a physical reaction which indicated that the attempt to forget it had only been partially successful.

Freud and subsequently many psychologists and psychiatrists have emphasized the repression of sex, aggression, and fear and in doing so they have ignored or minimized the fact that such positive emotions as love may be repressed as well. It is relatively easy to understand how the girl who has known feelings of sexual attraction while wrestling with her brother would repress the experience as too terrible to contemplate. It is more difficult to understand that the same dynamics are at work when the "tough guy" or "hard-nosed" realist finds his tender impulses threatening the image of himself. If man may be assumed to have both constructive and destructive impulses and there is no question about the fact that the latter ones are subject to repression, then it would seem logical to believe that the same situation would hold true for the positive emotions.

DREAMS

Freud (1914) described extensively the way repressed material may break through a person's behavior pattern and show itself in the form of slips of tongue, lapses in memory, forgetting, wit and humor, and most of all may show itself symbolically in dreams. A recent study has substantiated Freud's position and clarified the function of dreams. Scientists are able to record the brain wave pattern for sleep by attaching electrodes to the scalp and tracing the pattern through a stylus connected with a recording drum in such a way that the onset of the dream can be identified by changes in the brain waves of the sleeper. Dement (1960) devised an experiment in which people who were sleeping were awakened as soon as they began to dream. Later they were aroused from their sleep when they were not dreaming. It was found that no ill effects occurred as long as the subjects of the experiment were allowed to dream, but if they were not permitted to dream, they suffered from such relatively severe behavioral disturbances as anxiety, irritability, and difficulty in concentrating. It would seem, therefore, that dreaming is an important condition of normal behavior.

FORGETTING

Forgetting is also a form of repression. In addition to forgetting innumerable relatively unimportant experiences during the passage of time, people tend to forget the unpleasant aspects of life. Consequently, they tend to recall only the good old days and frequently at Homecoming celebrations, for example, one may observe alumni recalling their college days with aggressive fervor. For other people, memory may work in the opposite direction in that they forget and repress the pleasant experiences and recall and enlarge upon the upsetting ones.

Perhaps the following example may make the relationship of forgetting and repression clearer. A child may experience real feelings of hostility toward his younger brother who has just broken his model airplane and he expresses his emotion and frustration by punching and pounding the brother. The parents are outraged and they indicate in no uncertain terms that nice boys don't punch their younger brothers and that he is never to do it again. Since the boy wants to be safe and keep the love of his parents, he controls his rage and perhaps apologizes as well. If this pattern of behavior continues every time the child experiences hostility, the suppression will turn to repression and he will never be able to allow himself to express rage or other aggressively strong feelings. He may grow up to be a person who has forgotten and, therefore, repressed his earlier experiences and who proudly states with firm conviction that he does not bear hostility toward anyone. However, some frustration and hostility are inevitably part of life and the person who denies these experiences in himself is liable to behave in a damaging way to himself and other people. For example, he may even "kill his friends with kindness" so that even the most neutral observer would consider his behavior to be hostile.

Recognition of Adjustment Mechanisms

In the discussion of specific adjustment mechanisms that follows it is inevitable that you will find some aspect of your own behavior being described. By being able to recognize and accept such behavior in yourself, however, it is unlikely that you will need to rely upon using adjustment mechanisms to an extent that would be detrimental to the achievement of the important goals in your life. Moreover, if you are able to recognize the use of adjustment mechanisms by the people with whom you come in contact, probably you will not be unduly threatened by their behavior, and you may be able to help reduce the untold number of interpersonal conflicts which occur because the people involved are unable to recognize the presence of adjustment mechanisms.

No really satisfactory system for classifying the adjustment mechanisms can be established because none of them is as distinct or discrete as the description would imply. In fact, all of them tend to contain aspects of the others and they are separated only for the purpose of examining their influence on behavior. As a result, they are grouped somewhat artificially into the four divisions that are shown in the accompanying chart and they will be discussed accordingly in turn.

The Adjustment Mechanisms

I. Adjustment mechanisms used in alternative methods of gaining satiation
   A. Compensation and sublimation
   B. Nomadism and hyperactivity
   C. Fantasy and daydreaming
   D. Alcoholism and drug addiction

II. Adjustment mechanisms used in incompatible methods of gaining satiation
   A. Projection
   B. Rationalization
   C. Logic tight compartments, reaction formation, and perceptual rigidity
   D. Displaced hostility and scapegoating, phobias, obsessions, and compulsive behavior

III. Adjustment mechanisms to avoid or decrease the need for satiation
   A. Shyness
   B. Regression
   C. Depression
   D. Impotency and frigidity

IV. Adjustment mechanisms for destroying or punishing the non-satiated self
   A. Over-conformity
   B. Psychosomatic symptoms
   C. Accident proneness
   D. Self-defeating behavior and suicide

Adjustment Mechanisms Used in Alternative Methods of Gaining Satiation

COMPENSATION AND SUBLIMATION

When a person fails to obtain an important goal in his life, he turns to compensation and sublimation as a means of handling his feelings of disappointment and inadequacy. The failure may be due to the fact that his goal was physically inaccessible or it may result from the fact that the achievement of the goal was too demanding, painful, or guilt-provoking.

In either case the person turns toward obtaining a substitute goal as a means of gaining satiation. With sublimation the new goal is invariably more socially acceptable than the original one, but with compensation the second goal is not necessarily preferable to the first one.

Compensation and sublimation may be found in the behavior of groups of people as well as individual persons. Mumford (1961, p. 221), for example, has described how in ancient Rome people in the lower classes, who were undergoing daily indignities and terrors which brutalized their lives, demanded an outlet for their frustration and deprivation that led eventually to carnivals of death and destruction. Thus, they were able to compensate for their own suffering by gloating over people who were forced to endure even more severe misfortunes and degradation.

Compensation may be observed in a number of more individualized aspects of life. For example, it may be seen in the behavior of weak students who become skilled athletes or social charmers and in the actions of frustrated athletes who become excellent students, scholars, and intellectuals. Overly possessive and dominant parents, moreover, frequently attempt to compensate for their own lack of achievement by demanding high standards of their children.

A man who feels dissatisfied with his home and family life may compensate by devoting an excessive amount of time to his job and career. He cannot refuse any imposition that is placed upon his personal life and thus he accedes to any demand that is made of him. The extra hours of working are seen as an honest attempt to provide for his wife and children and any suggestion that he may be moving away from the members of his family instead of toward them is rejected as being "unthinkable."

Compensation may be seen also in the behavior of the mother whose children grow up and leave home to attend college. She may feel unneeded and unloved and find it necessary to fill this void in her life by joining numerous clubs, obtaining a job, having an affair, or becoming a busybody and the unwanted mother of all the children in the neighborhood.

The boy who is unsure of his masculinity may compensate by swearing, bullying, fighting, suppressing tender feelings, driving a car recklessly, and generally behaving like a hellion. He claims a hatred of poetry, art, and symphonic music and vehemently expresses his disapproval at every opportunity. If he were really so strongly opposed to the socially sensitive and aesthetic aspects of life, he would simply choose to ignore them.

Adler (1917) emphasized the importance of what he referred to as organ inferiority, which included unattractiveness, obesity, small stature, in addition to specific structural deviations, as one of the factors which may cause a person to feel inadequate and consequently need to compensate for his feelings of inferiority. Many prominent authoritarian leaders have been of small stature and Napoleon, Hitler, and Stalin are names that come to mind immediately. Shakespeare noted this expression of compensation most poignantly in his play, *Richard III,* when he had the Duke of Gloucester exclaim:

But I, that am not shaped for sportive tricks,
Nor made to court an amorous looking-glass;
I, that am rudely stampt, and want love's majesty
To strut before a wanton ambling nymph;
I, that am curtail'd of this fair proportion,
Cheated of feature by dissembling nature,
Deform'd, unfinisht, sent before my time
Into this breathing world, scarce half made up,
And that so lamely and unfashionable
That dogs bark at me as I halt by them;—
Why, I, in this weak piping time of peace,
Have no delight to pass away the time,
Unless to spy my shadow in the sun,
And descant on mine own deformity;
And therefore, since I cannot prove a lover,
To entertain these fair well-spoken days,
I am determined to prove a villain,
And hate the idle pleasures of these days.

Not all compensation for physical handicap, however, leads to aggressive behavior. Glen Cunningham, the great mile and distance runner, once had his legs paralyzed and in compensating for what must have been a distressing illness, he became an outstanding athlete and an inspiration for a countless number of other persons.

In addition, athletic games offer opportunities for the sublimation of strong feelings. Restrained from the direct expression of hostility, a person may do so more acceptably by blocking and tackling, sliding on the basepaths, etc. Such highly competitive games as bridge, monopoly, chess, etc., provide occasion for a similar release of strong feelings. Frequently, for example, the hostility that may become part of playing bridge is demonstrated by husbands and wives who prefer to play against rather than with one another. As opponents their hostility may be expressed in a sublimated manner in the course of the game whereas when they play as partners, by necessity it can be expressed only directly.

Sublimation may be seen also in the behavior of the person who takes undue interest in the affairs of other people. If he is astute enough, he may even make a career from his activities and qualify as a syndicated columnist, writing at length about very personal events in the lives of other people. With sufficient sublimation, the hostile person may become a movie, drama, or music critic, attacking quite viciously, on occasion, the work of his more creative victims.

The dynamics behind the use of sublimation in everyday life may be illustrated more clearly possibly by the following anecdote concerning one of the authors. Recently he was forced to listen several times during the same day to a campus visitor whose general attitude may be described best of all by his statement that he could determine more about an individual's personality after one interview than most psychologists and psychiatrists could tell after six months of study. The author, whether from personal defensive reasons or realistic outrage, experienced strong feelings of hostility. The man, however, was a guest and, because well-socialized citizens do not insult their guests, the hostility which was felt had to be suppressed. That night the author cut down a dead tree that had needed to be removed from outside his house for a long time, and the next day, because he had found a way of sublimating his hostile feelings, he felt considerably better.

Perhaps society needs to provide opportunities for compensation and sublimation for all its members. In writing about the problems of disturbed and alienated youth, Havighurst and Stiles (1961) point out that:

> These boys want the same things in life that are achieved by boys who are growing up successfully. They would like to have money, a job and as they grow older they want the use of an automobile. They want girl friends, and eventually desire to have a wife and children. Unlike the majority of boys, however, they do not have the combination of family assistance, the intelligence, the social skills, and the good study and work habits necessary to achieve their goal legitimately.

Thwarted in the normal channels of expression, they seek illegitimate means of attaining success and recognition. What they need, of course, instead of the traditional opportunities presented by the school, are alternative pathways which lead to the satisfactory development of adult competencies.

Nomadism and Hyperactivity

Nomadism involves wandering from place to place and the frequent change of jobs, homes, friends, wives, or husbands, and, in fact, any aspect of the person's life situation. Usually the person who is making the change is seeking to achieve the same goal in a different situation. When the failure to obtain the goal and gain satiation is due to the absence of some necessary condition, then moving to a new environment may prove to be successful. When the failure is due, however, to the inability of the person himself to make the appropriate adjustment, which is usually the case with nomadism, then the transfer fails to be helpful and invariably it will be followed by yet another move to a new location.

A young girl, for example, who is teaching school in a small rural town and who wishes to be married, will find probably that there is almost a complete absence of eligible men in her life. By moving to a larger town she will increase her chances of becoming married, but whether she is successful in reaching her goal will depend almost entirely upon her personal traits and characteristics. If she continues to move every year or so, then her behavior will come to take on more and more the characteristics of nomadism.

With hyperactivity the person plunges into a wide variety of different behavior patterns in order to escape his inability to find satiation of a particular goal. The girl who finds herself growing older and in greater danger of becoming an "old maid," for example, may undertake more hobbies, duties, and activities than she could possibly expect to sustain over any extended period of time. She is literally too busy to think about herself and she may escape temporarily, therefore, from her real frustration and concern over being alone and unoccupied. Unfortunately, much of the frantic pace of modern life is an implementation of this adjustment mechanism. The United States has been referred to often as a nation of people on wheels who often travel without awareness of their destinations and who live in fear of what would be encountered if they were to stop.

FANTASY AND DAYDREAMING

A cardinal rule for self-study might include an examination of the content of a person's daydreams, for invariably they reveal the goals that are important but which are not being met in real life. The football player who spends most of the time during a game sitting on the bench, for example, may dream of scoring a last minute winning touchdown before thousands of admiring fans. In the course of daydreams great books are written and fortunes are made and spent. Individual fantasies of escape to Tahiti may be related to visions of a tropical climate and brown-skinned, bare-breasted maidens. Girls who without hesitation say "no" in actual life say "yes" in the world of men's dreams. Harsh reality rarely intrudes and thus everyone can truly become "Queen for a Day."

Green (1922, pp. 42-43) has classified daydreams into the following categories:

1. The display daydream in which the dreamer gains social recognition for some act of ability or daring.

2. The saving daydream in which the dreamer pictures himself performing some brave deed and thus gaining the affection and appreciation of the person rescued.
3. The grandeur daydream in which the dreamer imagines himself to be a great person such as a king or some highly honored personage.
4. The homage daydream in which the dreamer performs a service for the person that he loves.

A current aspect of American society that is the concern of many observers is the commercial practice of the mass media of utilizing the rewarding fantasy found in the dream worlds of many frustrated persons. The fantasy thus becomes a replacement for actual participation in the experiences of life and, for some persons, it is not even necessary to go to the trouble of creating their own dream worlds because with a flick of a button the dreams are available ready-made. The theme, for example, of the Beverly Hillbillies, a popular television show, highlights the gaining of easy money and then, subsequently, the obtaining of equally easy acceptance. According to this myopic view of life, the good things come without effort. Thus, a person never has to change or grow up, because the world fits itself to his pattern of behavior and everybody loves him. For many people, it is just like a dream come true.

Miss America contests are made-to-order daydreams for many women and the early afternoon television soap operas present an expression of unrestrained emotionality that satisfies in part the needs of the persons who relentlessly view such programs every day. The appeal, however, would seem to be chiefly for those persons who are somewhat frustrated emotionally. Although there is a very real danger in relying on such unrestrained devotion to fantasy, to restrict such an opportunity for fantasy and daydreaming would be equally harmful.

Wild West stories serve the same purpose for men, for a fellow may not be much of a man taking orders at the office all day but at least he can be free to "ride the range" at night. Unfortunately, there is a possibility that the youngsters who view the television westerns may obtain the idea that a horse, sagebrush, laconic inanity, immunity to bullets, and the ability to whip everyone in sight at the slightest provocation are the ingredients of masculinity. Needless to say, the world of television can hardly sustain these dreams to the point of their being realized.

Hayakawa (1958, p. 394) has stressed the seriousness of creating such unrealistic and false expectations. Modern songs, he pointed out, tend to create impossible love ideals and young people are taught to seek "dream-girls" and "dream-men" who simply do not exist. With such an indoctrination, the probable course of action is to attribute the quality of imaginary perfection to someone the person meets for the first time. Although the love-at-first-sight fantasy is more exciting, the high divorce rate indicates that young people might be better advised to take a long, judicious look before leaping into marriage. As Hayakawa (1958, p. 400) has stated, "If our symbolic representations give a false or misleading impression of what life is likely to be, we are worse prepared for life than we would have been had we not been exposed to them at all."

Whereas adults are wont to conceal the fact that they are day-dreaming, preferring to describe themselves as "deep in thought," children act out their daydreams quite often. They are, openly and unashamedly, airplane pilots, firemen, mountain climbers, doctors, nurses, fathers, or mothers. For them, daydreaming is a means of trying out some of the various adult roles that perhaps they sense they will never understand without imaginative trial. In this sense, daydreams have a very definite positive function. Moreover, a person may daydream of a certain state of affairs and find this situation so superior to his present condition that he is led into a deeper involvement with life that makes it possible for his dream to become a reality.

ALCOHOLISM AND DRUG ADDICTION

According to Coleman (1964, p. 421), there are 70 million users of alcohol in the United States, of whom five million or roughly six percent of the adult population may be classified as alcoholics. Although alcohol is actually a depressant and not a stimulant, as generally supposed, its influence does cause a person to have fewer inhibitions and to act in a way which is not characteristically part of his behavior pattern.

The use of alcohol may help a person to relax pleasantly in a social situation or it may serve as a situational crutch by means of which a person finds interacting with a number of people at a party less threatening. Alcohol may be used also in an attempt to forget an unpleasant experience so that the young man, for example, who has been jilted by his girl friend tries to "drown his troubles" in drink.

The excessive drinker, on the other hand, uses alcohol regularly as a means of escaping from his problem, but unfortunately his behavior results only in his situation becoming worse. In an even more severe dependency upon alcohol, the alcoholic has lost control of his drinking to the point that he becomes very upset if he cannot obtain the alcohol that he feels he must have. Moreover, the pattern of constant reliance on alcohol makes achievement of most of the important goals of life impossible.

Coleman (1964, p. 438) has stated that it is estimated that there are sixty thousand or more people in the United States who are addicted to drugs. Only around five percent of these people become addicted accidentally; the remainder are adolescents and adults who turn to the use of opium, cocaine, and marijuana as a result of a need to experience a thrill, conform to peer group expectancies, and generally rebel against society.

Less dangerous but perhaps ultimately a more serious problem for society is the widespread use of tranquilizers, energizing pills, aspirin tablets, and other medicines having physiological effects on the body. If used under unusual stress situations they are of unquestionable value, but when relied upon continuously, they become a crutch which causes the person to avoid facing up to his life situation. Thus, he never knows the experience of working his way through a problem successfully, and consequently, does not gain the confidence which would help him become more capable of dealing with future difficulties.

Adjustment Mechanisms Used in Incompatible Methods of Gaining Satiation

The adjustment mechanisms that are included below allow the person using them "to have his cake and eat it too." By means of a process best described as masking, the person is able to avoid an awareness of the inconsistency between his behavior and his value system. Thus, it is possible for him to think well of himself and to obtain the goals that are important to him, no matter of what effect his behavior has upon other people. A person, for example, who wishes to obtain power, may have difficulty seeking this goal directly because of the conflict with his particular orientation. By relying upon the adjustment mechanisms in this category, however, he may be able to persuade himself that he is doing only what is necessary for the person's own good and that, in reality, he is a very democratic individual who hates the fact that other people are so weak that they expect him always to decide upon the course of action to be followed.

PROJECTION

Projection involves the repression of an undesirable trait in one's own behavior and the perception of its existence in the actions of other people. As a result, one may attack and condemn the behavior of another person that is feared and despised most in oneself. The person who declares that "everybody is out for whatever they can get" may be saying, for example, that although this attitude may be true of him, he refuses to allow it to be associated with his behavior in any way.

It is possible, however, to perceive correctly undesirable traits in the behavior of other people. When very different aspects of behavior are observed in different persons it is much more likely that the person is accurate in his perceptions than when he assigns the same motives to the behavior of almost all people. The girl, for example, who feels that "boys are all alike and just after one thing" is missing the very important point that although some boys act in the way she implies, there are many others who do not insist that every relationship with a girl have some kind of physical expression. It may be conjectured that the girl's own sexual desires are disturbing and unwanted and that by means of projection she can perceive herself as being innocent of possessing them.

Similarly, the boy who states that "all girls are alike, for all they want is to have a good time and take you for your money," is probably projecting his real feelings, which may be more correctly represented by his belief that "it is just as easy to fall in love with a rich girl as it is with a poor one."

Another example of the projection that is found in the behavior of the person who cannot trust other people may be seen in the mother who requires her daughter to give a detailed account of how she spent her time on a date, despite the complete absence of any indication of misbehavior. The mother is saying perhaps more than she realizes about her own behavior when she was young and about what her present behavior would be if she were given the opportunity to date again.

The person who crusades constantly against the evils of gambling, alcohol, and pornographic literature is indicating that he is projecting by the excessiveness of his campaign and his steadfast refusal to recognize such other social problems as poverty, care of the sick and aged, mental illness, and so forth. Nevertheless, it is possible, for people to become active in the defense of what they believe without projecting. The difference lies, of course, in their willingness to fight many evils instead of only one or two.

Projection may be seen as well in the stereotypes that are used by some people to describe the behavior of members of minority groups. Jews, for instance, are seen as greedy money-chasers; Negroes are considered to be lazy and sexually promiscuous; Latin-Americans and Mexicans are expected to carry knives and invariably attack other people at the slightest provocation. The person who is doing the projection, of course, has none of these traits.

Nations as well as individuals use projection. Muller (1963, p. 363) has observed that the often described savagery of the American Indian was exaggerated greatly because the colonists had to justify their own tactics of chicanery and brutality. Brophy (1962, pp. 34-35), in turn, has emphasized another and more subtle aspect of projection in her analysis of psychological compacts between men and nations. She felt it was the bloodthirstiness of the followers that allowed a tyrannical leader to assume position of power. Thus, the people themselves elevated to high office the man who would take them in the direction that they were determined to go. To what extent the rise to power of Adolph Hitler in Nazi Germany was influenced by such projection may only be conjectured.

RATIONALIZATION

Rationalization consists of giving false but acceptable reasons for one's behavior. As Dunham (1964, p. 299) has stated, "There is no disorder so common, nor indeed so natural, as for men, when once they are engaged in error or sunk in vice, to invent excuses for their errors and apologies for their crimes." With the help of rationalization, professors rarely do a poor job of teaching. It is much more likely, instead, that they find themselves facing a crop of very inferior students. Students, in turn, invariably have trouble studying because of the noise in the dormitory or the library and they are liable to attribute their poor grades in courses primarily to the lack of intellectual stimulation in the classroom.

There are two main types of rationalization: "sour grapes" and "sweet lemon." The "sour grapes" form, named from Aesop's fable of the fox who called the grapes he could not reach sour, insists that whatever a person cannot obtain, he does not want anyway. By using this method, the student who fails to gain admission to Harvard University may rationalize his failure by declaring that a large "Ivy-League" university is not at all suitable for him.

The "sweet lemon" type of rationalization asserts quite simply that the conditions under which a person is living are by far the best. Thus, the student who was not admitted to Harvard may declare that no college could be better than the one that he is attending. After all, it has an excellent academic reputation and due to the small size of the classes, the students enjoy numerous opportunities for discussion with the professors. There is a wide variety of social experiences available and where else could he find a campus with a warmer, friendlier atmosphere?

In many cases, children are taught directly to rationalize. A child may be asked, for example, why he acted in a certain way and when he gives his real reason, he is punished. Very quickly he learns to give acceptable reasons and therefore to avoid punishment. It is only a short step from protecting the self from other people to protecting the self from the self and soon rationalization may be used to help the child see reality as he desires for it to be and not as it may be observed objectively. Thus, in time, he may join such groups as the Young Communist League, the Ku Klux Klan, or the John Birch Society, which permit him to express destructive behavior under the guise of social concern or patriotism in a way that makes it possible to avoid examining the structure of these organizations.

LOGIC TIGHT COMPARTMENTS

The adjustment mechanism of logic tight compartments also allows a person to maintain inconsistency of behavior or ideas. The man who is actively religious in church on Sundays may become an unscrupulously hard business man during the rest of the week. Through the use of logic tight compartments his life is separated into completely isolated segments and thus he is able to ascribe to contradictory values and, at the same time avoid the conflict that would be aroused by viewing his business practices in the light of Christian beliefs. Further examples may be seen in the behavior of the parent who spanks his child while saying, "This will teach you not to hit your brother," and the Christian who, while worshipping a God of Love, sings "Onward Christian Soldiers, Onward as to War."

REACTION FORMATION

Reaction formation causes a person to adopt behavior patterns that are so exaggerated and overdone that they are probably the exact opposite of his real but unacceptable desires and needs. Thus, the person who is using this adjustment mechanism often is so cloyingly nice and polite that no one can stand him. A prime example may be seen in the behavior that is referred to as "smother love." A woman may have wanted a career very badly but instead found herself married and pregnant. She may resent the child unconsciously and even blame the loss of her career upon him. Such feelings are unacceptable and so she literally loves the child to death. She loves him so much that she won't let him play ball with other children because he might catch a disease or get hurt. To the outside observer the element of hostility is but thinly disguised. Although the overprotection looks like loving behavior, in actuality it is highly destructive. In a similar manner, the person who is constantly overconcerned about the welfare of a loved one and fears that he has been hurt in an accident, when the circumstances do not justify the emotion, also may be displaying the underlying hostility that is indicative of reaction formation.

Much of the posturing and posing of misfortune is also an expression of reaction formation. Many of the Nazis, for example, utilized this adjustment mechanism when they emphasized the horrible experiences they had to watch in pursuance of their duties instead of acknowledging the hideous deeds that they performed themselves (Arendt, 1963, p. 93).

Reaction formation may be seen as well in the behavior of the person who seems to be saying that he is weak, ineffective, and quite harmless, but who, in actuality, is fully capable of hurting everyone close to him and exerting tremendous control over the lives of the people upon whose sympathies he plays. Thus, for him, "see how you make me suffer" becomes a silk thread of restraint that is even more effective than the use of more direct and forceful methods.

PERCEPTUAL RIGIDITY

Perceptual rigidity consists of the inability of the person to change his orientation or outlook on life. Consequently, all persons and situations, regardless of whether or not they are different, are treated as if they are the same. A person might perceive his father to be a punishing figure, for example, and therefore treat every older man as an authority figure and a threat to his well-being.

Rokeach (1960, p. 267) carried out an experiment in which he played unfamiliar music to a "closed" group of people who were known to rely upon perceptual rigidity and also to another group of people who were "open" to new experiences. He found that the "closed" group did not like the unfamiliar music and, moreover, they liked it even less after repeated exposure to it. The "open" group, in contrast, did not care for the music at first but grew to appreciate it after listening to it for a number of times. As may be expected, the people in the "closed" group found it difficult to change when exposed to a new experience, for their energies were devoted to maintaining familiar perceptions instead of coping with and adjusting to the changing situation around them.

One of the characteristics of the perceptually rigid person is his need to explain away or dismiss concepts which are different from his in terms of the shortcomings of the person offering the new idea or information. According to Arendt (1963, p. 105), the Jews under Hitler's control who volunteered for deportation from Theresienstadt to Auschwitz convinced themselves they were escaping domination and denounced as not being sane those people who tried to tell them what proved to be the truth, namely, that they were to be slaughtered.

Even nations are guilty of relying on perceptual rigidity. For many people in the United States anything that is associated with socialism is considered to be dangerous and for many years such an attitude prevailed in the face of changing social conditions. According to statistics presented by Mumford (1961, pp. 467-468), the mortality of infants in New York City in 1810 was 120 to 145 per thousand live births; in 1850, the figure was 180 per thousand; in 1860, 220 per thousand; and in 1870, 240 per thousand. Obviously, if the trend was to be averted, the inflexible attitude of the people in New York toward socialized services had to be changed. As Mumford (1961, p. 476) pointed out, "Neither a pure water supply, nor the collective disposal of garbage, waste, and sewage, could be left to the private conscience or attended to only if they could be provided for at a profit." Today, of course, the community socialization of these functions is an accepted fact.

Perceptual rigidity then is often another way of allowing a person's inner wish to dominate his perception of external reality. Such an attitude leads to bigotry and, according to Rokeach (1960, p. 162), to the development of a person "who, due to his overall motivational structure, finds it necessary to reject others on the simple criterion that they agree or disagree with him, regardless of the content of what he happens to believe."

DISPLACED HOSTILITY AND SCAPEGOATING

Displaced hostility consists of directing aggression against an innocent person or animal or against some inanimate object. Usually the victim cannot retaliate or is less capable of defending himself than the person who aroused the hostility. Thus, the man whose ego has suffered at the hands of his boss may restrain himself and swallow his anger, only to attack his wife or children for some minor misdeed at a later time. In other circumstances, the dominated man who is angry with his wife may take out his hostility on the employees working under him at the office.

An interesting but tragic example of displaced hostility is to be found in the "witchhunting" that took place in early American history. In *The Crucible,* Miller (1959) wrote of the experiences of the Reverend Samuel Parris, a very hostile man, whose daughter and niece displaced the hostility they felt toward him by pretending to be attacked by witches and thereby causing a number of the women who were accused of being witches to die on the gallows.

Scapegoating may be traced to the ancient custom of sacrificing a goat to expiate the sins of a group of people. Thus, by projecting their sins upon the animal and destroying it, the people could expect their lives to be safe and guiltless. Today, there is still very much alive a tendency to pick some individual or a particular group of people, blame all troubles on the continued existence of this person or persons, and justify, accordingly, the release of aggressive feelings against them. In the Old South there was a direct relationship between the price of cotton and the number of Negroes who were lynched so that as the economic conditions became worse, the aggression against the Negro increased.

Rokeach (1960, p. 145) has presented research findings which indicate that the greater a person's rejection of Negroes, the more he rejects white people as well. Apparently, people tend to hate all persons, irrespective of whether they are black or white and, similarly, love all people regardless of the color of their skin. In other words, their hatred is generalized from specific frustrating persons to mankind in general and the more obvious expression of scapegoating against members of minority groups is only a symptom of the more generalized release of hostility.

Unfortunately, it would appear that almost everywhere, among nearly all people, some minority group is doomed to fulfill the function of being a scapegoat. Perhaps the best known scapegoat of all was Jesus Christ who, although innocent of any sin, had to suffer and die to alleviate the sins of all men in one supreme atonement.

PHOBIAS

Phobias are unreasonable fears of external objects or situations. They may occur in a wide variety of situations. Included below are the phobias which are found most frequently:

Acrophobia, fear of high places
Agoraphobia, fear of open places
Claustrophobia, fear of closed places
Monophobia, fear of being alone
Zoophobia, fear of animals

Nearly always, an unreasonably strong phobic fear is really a fear of something else that has to be repressed. One of the authors, for example, had a client with a phobic fear of basements. Acting under the advice of one of her friends, she tried to go into the basement of a large department store via the escalator, the friend's theory being that since this method was different from using the customary ones of the stairs or the elevator, she would have a much better chance of being successful and losing her fear. Unfortunately, the suggestion didn't work, for after moving half the way down, she turned and "ran back up the escalator as hard as she could go." During therapy it turned out that basements had come to symbolize the genitals which her parents had taught her were fearful parts of her body. Thus, her conflict was acted out symbolically through the fear of basements.

Horney (1937, pp. 73-74) has provided the following helpful classification of the dynamics of phobic fears:

A. The danger is felt to come from one's own impulses (I am afraid of what I might do if I lost control) and is directed against the self. The resulting phobia might be a fear of high places.

B. The danger is felt to come from one's own impulses and is directed against others. The resulting phobia might be a fear of knives, guns, and other potentially dangerous instruments.

C. The danger is felt to come from the environment with the self as a victim. The resulting phobia might be a fear of thunder-storms, persons, groups, germs, etc.

D. The danger is felt to come from the environment with others as victims. The resulting phobia might be an unreasonable fear of accidents occurring to loved ones.

A phobia may be developed by means of a conditioned response to an upsetting experience in early childhood. Watson's (1926) case of Albert and the white rat may be used as an illustration. Little Albert was placed in a room and every time a white rat was put along with him, a loud noise was sounded. Soon afterwards the child had only to see the rat before he would break into tears and display symptoms of disturbance. Later the startle response was generalized to a piece of cotton wool and little Albert might be described as having a phobic fear of cotton wool. Without awareness of the foregoing events, Albert's fear would seem quite strange and weird, but knowing, however, that he had been frightened by a loud noise that had become associated with the white rat and then generalized to a piece of cotton wool makes the phobia more understandable. Probably many phobias are formed through similar sequence of human responses.

OBSESSIONS

An obsession is an idea or thought that keeps recurring at inappropriate times. The typical example is that of a tune that keeps running through the mind. An obsession cannot be banished voluntarily and when serious, it can dominate the thought processes to such an extent that concentration upon anything else is impossible. Usually the obsessive thought is a symbolic representation of a tempting idea or act which cannot be expressed but which keeps pressing for recognition. Obsessions accompany quite often the compulsive behavior described below.

COMPULSIVE BEHAVIOR

Compulsive behavior involves an irresistible urge to do something in an orderly fashion or according to a set pattern. Usually the behavior accomplishes no rational end and yet it is enacted over and over again. It may vary in seriousness from being quite mild and socially acceptable, as in the case of a person checking several times to make sure a door is locked, to the handicapping urge of having to wash one's hands continuously, to the more deleterious act of compulsive drinking.

Frequently, compulsive behavior is seen as a device for increasing feelings of safety so that it serves to provide a kind of magic spell to protect the person. Smoking is a common compulsive act and the smoker can measure his anxiety level usually by the number of cigarettes that are consumed at a particular time. Many people find that when all is going well they smoke a pack of cigarettes a day but when they are under strain, their consumption rises promptly to two or even three packs per day.

Even animals show evidence of compulsive behavior. The bull in the latter stages of a bull fight has been observed in a certain part of the ring from which to make his last stand. Within this selected area he will charge but he cannot be lured away from the familiar spot.

Adjustment Mechanisms to Avoid or Decrease
the Need for Satiation

The adjustment mechanisms in this section are used when goals are not successfully achieved and the person attempts to reduce frustration by denying the need for goal satiation.

SHYNESS

Shyness is a common form of withdrawal in which the person gives up some part of his striving in order to avoid drawing attention to himself. As a result, relationships with others are curtailed and interaction with the environment is reduced to the barest minimum. It is almost as if the person finds it too painful to achieve his goals and therefore he tries to exist without them.

A child, for example, at one time may have reached out eagerly to participate in the vital experience of living only to have every effort censored, disapproved, or punished. Each activity he initiates is scoffed at and belittled by his parents. He makes up a story and it is dismissed as being foolish. He tells a joke but no one thinks it is funny. He has a plan for carrying out a pet project but his father knows a better way of doing it. In time the child learns to stop making suggestions, telling stories and jokes, offering opinions, or even talking. He no longer acts but only reacts. Because he has learned to expect that everyone will think badly of him, he becomes shy and self-conscious. He is not able to realize that although certain persons, most likely his parents, have laughed at him, the verdict of the rest of the world is not yet in.

Many college students, who describe themselves as shy, report that they are afraid to speak in class for fear of receiving a negative evaluation by the teacher or other students. Silence, passivity, and shyness seem to offer security but, at the same time, because they want to receive the respect of others and to gain the same goals as those about them, frequently they leave the classroom disappointed and frustrated with themselves for having failed to raise a question or make a contribution to class discussion.

If he really wants to change his behavior, the shy person may find it possible to do so by pure determination to participate in class activities. As he gains experience in expressing his views, speaking before other people becomes increasingly easier and, with the help of a sensitive and supportive teacher, he gains in confidence and becomes less concerned about the impression he is making on the people around him.

For some students, however, the shyness is so severe that it is impossible to start talking in class. In this case, it is better to seek the services of a competent and qualified psychologist or psychiatrist and thus gain some help in relieving the fear that is blighting the person's life.

To try to take part in class discussion and fail is frustrating and although it may seem worse, it is not nearly as harmful as the destructiveness brought about by the person's complete inability to share his ideas with other people.

REGRESSION

Regression is the attempt to return to a situation or pattern of behavior with which the person is more comfortable. The student who finds the demands of college life too severe, for example, may choose to return to the more supportive atmosphere provided by his parents and the familiar surroundings of his home town.

In another context, old grads and ex-students have been known to regress to boyish behavior during homecoming weekends while conventions provide opportunities for many men to behave in a way that indicates they have found a temporary escape from adult responsibility.

To a certain extent, all attempts to equate the present with the past are expressions of regression. Unquestionably, Jefferson, Lincoln, and Washington were wise and great men, but an attempt to utilize their ideas as "pat" answers to present day difficulties would indicate probably a need to escape from the task of finding more appropriate solutions to the problems of living in a nuclear age.

Depression

Almost everyone experiences disappointment and subsequent feelings of depression when he encounters the loss of a beloved person in his life or falls short of the goals he has set for himself. These experiences are inevitable and consequently the sense of disappointment and depression that follows is not to be unexpected or considered unusual. Invariably the person regains his characteristic mood within a relatively short period of time.

When the person has impossibly high expectations and levels of aspiration, however, the depression is accompanied frequently by feelings of guilt and unworthiness. If continual failure is encountered so that the guilt feelings begin to dominate the person's experience, his behavior is liable to become characterized more and more by a state of depression and feelings of deep and lasting sadness.

Impotency and Frigidity

Impotence is the inability of the male to achieve sexual gratification. It may be caused by shyness and embarrassment over sexual relations or it may be due to a fear of women or hostility toward them. Most men are impotent occasionally due to fatigue and worry but, according to Coleman (1964, p. 384), prolonged or permanent impotence before the age of 55 is rather rare and invariably the result of psychological conflict.

The counterpart to impotence for the female is frigidity. The majority of women have episodes of frigidity which occur particularly in the early years of marriage. Among the causes are embarrassment, fear of men, fear of pregnancy, and generalized emotional conflicts concerning sexual relations.

Probably the frequency with which both impotence and frigidity occur can be reduced greatly by more effective education before marriage concerning relationships between men and women, child rearing practices, and the role of the family in developing greater emotional well-being and positive mental health.

Adjustment Mechanisms for Destroying or Punishing the Non-Satiated Self

Over-Conformity

In order to live in any society the person must conform to some of the expectancies of that society. If he conforms too little he becomes a destructive element, but, as discussed in Chapter 8, if he conforms too much he gives up his own unique individuality and becomes an automaton.

Like Riesman's (1961) other directed person, he goes through life with his conformity antenna alert continuously, thereby destroying a little part of himself every day. As the poet, T. S. Eliot, said in *The Hollow Men,* "this is the way the world ends. Not with a bang but a whimper," and much of his meaning may embrace the corrosive destructiveness of over-conformity.

An experiment by Asch (1955) may be used to illustrate overly conforming behavior. Groups of students were assembled for what the subjects of the experiment thought were tests of visual judgment. They were asked to choose which one of three lines on a card was the same length as a single line on another card. The answers were announced so that the subjects could hear them. All the students except one, the person who was the actual experimental subject, received instructions prior to the experiment, concerning which answers to give. During the first and second trials they chose the correct line, but for the next several trials they gave incorrect answers. Thereafter correct answers were interspersed occasionally with the incorrect ones. Thus, the experimental subject had two choices: he could act independently, trusting his own judgment, or he could be influenced by the answers of the other people who were numerically in the majority.

In 36.8 percent of the selections, the experimental subjects agreed with the incorrect choices of the other people and, in extreme cases, they agreed every time, even when the difference between the two lines was as much as seven inches. Approximately one quarter of the experimental subjects were completely independent and never did agree with the errors made by the majority of the people in the experiment; among this group were persons whose disagreement became so enthusiastic that they even disagreed when the majority was correct. If conformity to majority opinion can distort judgment in such a simple, concrete situation, it can be imagined readily how significant it may be in such intangible areas as attitudes, values, and opinions concerning the affairs of mankind.

In the every day social situations that produce conflicts, all people face the constant temptation of the conforming response. Suppose, for example, that a freshman college student has grown up in a teetotal atmosphere in which drinking a beer is considered to be a serious sin. He has internalized these values so that his views on drinking are quite firm and he has no conflict over the matter. Then one evening he finds himself socializing with his new college friends in a situation where everyone is drinking a beer and he is forced to choose whether to accept or refuse the drink. If he takes the beer, knowing that for him it is wrong, he solves the conflict by conforming blindly to the other students' behavior, but in avoiding the possibility of censure by the social group for being different, he has done violence to the integrity of his own orientation.

This illustration of over-conformity, however, is much too simple. As time goes by, the student continues to meet people who accept the drinking of beer as a matter of course and through his reading he discovers that alcoholic beverages have been used in the majority of civilizations throughout history. He sees that the extreme and excessive disapproval of the drinking of beer is a local custom which may be unnecessarily harsh. Again he is faced with making a choice. He may conform to the teachings of his home community, forego the drinking of beer, and thereby act in conflict with his changing orientation, or he may try drinking beer and decide for himself whether or not he plans to engage in this type of social activity.

To some extent young people need to conform to the habits of dress and play interests of their peer group. Not to be allowed to wear loafers and slacks when everyone in the social group is doing so may be a traumatic experience for the youngster who is learning to feel safe with other people. Moreover, the teen-ager who is not allowed to date until three years after his peers have done so is quite likely to find his "imposed" difference to be a difficult barrier to overcome in the later expression of his unique individual differences. Only the person who feels he belongs can feel safe and only the person who is psychologically safe can dare to be really different.

Jung noted that the feeling of security is increased and the feeling of responsibility decreased when one is part of a group. The presence of the group strengthens the ego so that the individual by his membership may be more courageous, impertinent and assertive, fresher and less cautious than he would be on his own (Illing, 1963). In some cases, groups may continue to exist because the members have the opportunity to act out impulses that they would not dare or care to engage in without the support of the group. Thus, excessive conformity to the standards of a group may become a way for "not being yourself" and, as such, it represents a mild form of self-destruction.

PSYCHOSOMATIC SYMPTOMS

Some physiological illnesses and physical symptoms are produced by emotional and psychological conflicts. For example, if an off-color joke is told to a person who finds it embarrassing, he is liable to blush and turn red. The mental reaction to the joke has led to physical changes in the body and probably no one finds this reaction miraculous or difficult to understand. Nothing more mysterious is involved in the development of psychosomatic symptoms.

According to Simeons (1961, pp. 43-46), during the process of evolution, man's cerebral cortex, which controls the higher mental processes of the brain, grew with astonishing speed whereas the diencephalon, which controls the internal emotional functioning of the body, remained almost unaltered. In the course of history, artifacts were developed that radically changed man's environment so that, although still only emotionally equipped to live in the jungle, man found himself, within a relatively short period of time, having to react to the pressures and strains of urban life. The diencephalon, however, continued to function as though the newly developed artifacts were non-existent and, consequently, in a number of instances, man's emotional behavior was inappropriate for the new environment that he had created for himself. Many of the ancient dangers that had been rendered harmless continued to set off strong emotional reactions without man being consciously aware of them because he tended to respond consciously to what his culture told him he was supposed to feel, irrespective at times of his physiological processes.

Perhaps an adaptation of Simeons' discussion will help to clarify the situation. Suppose that an African native were to pay a visit to the New York zoo and suddenly, as he arrives at the lions' cage, a beast bares its fangs and rushes in his direction with a blood curdling roar. The African's unconscious emotions take over and he feels terror. His body is prepared for flight and before he can control these unnecessary responses, he may have begun to run. The New Yorker accompanying him, however, who is accustomed to seeing only caged lions would probably not respond so violently to the incident. The primitive fright would be there, but it would not break through into consciousness so easily.

In much the same way, many emotional responses to modern life are denied awareness. The man who is being teased about his lack of height may feel rage below the level of consciousness, but since he is a civilized member of society he does not know he is experiencing the emotion. His responses, however, are affecting his behavior in that they may influence his perception of reality, causing distortions by means of the adjustment mechanisms previously discussed or by directing them inwardly, thereby causing a variety of physical symptoms.

Wolberg (1947) reported a hypnotic experiment illustrating the relationship between conflict and physical symptoms. While hypnotized his subject was told that when he awakened from a deep trance he would find a bar of chocolate next to him and that he would have an intense craving to eat it, but if he did, he would feel guilty because the chocolate was not his. Brought out of the trance the subject avoided looking at the candy and complained of dizziness and faintness. He could scarcely walk, his pulse was rapid, his face pale, and he perspired profusely. The subject was re-hypnotized, of course, and the conflict was removed.

Among the forms that psychosomatic symptoms take are ulcerative colitis, hypertension, bronchial asthma, hyperthyroidism, rheumatoid arthritis, coronary disease, peptic ulcers, and skin disturbances. Coleman (1946, p. 250) has summarized the typical psychosomatic disorders which are shown on the chart below:

Typical Psychosomatic Disorders

Asthma (Occurrence: About three times more common among males). In children appears to involve an appeal for maternal help and protection. In later life may be activated by overdependency and guilt-arousing hostility toward loved ones or by environmental and/or inner conflicts which make the individual feel oppressed and restrict his freedom of living. Constitutional predisposition a key factor, whether resulting from heredity, allergies, or respiratory infections.

Stomach Ulcer (Occurrence: Three to four times more common among males). Ambitious, driving individuals with underlying dependency problems; overemphasis on independence and tendency to react to obstacles with anxiety and sustained hostility. Often a history of severe stress involving chronic insecurity. Much more common among "career women" than other women.

Colitis (Occurrence: Four to five times more common among females). Preponderantly thin, pale persons with marked muscular tension. Often obsessive trends, hypersensitivity, a tendency to be intropunitive in handling hostility, and depressive trends. Constitutional predisposition a key factor in ulcerative colitis in children. Often anxious and hostile, following lack of needed maternal care.

Neurodermatitis (Occurrence: Two or more times more common among males). Strong conflicts involving authority figures toward whom the patient feels both hostile and dependent. Often a feeling of being unfairly treated with helplessness to do anything about it. May be precipitated by relatively diverse anxiety-arousing stress situations. Frequent family history of skin disease. Eczema most prevalent during childhood and again after 35.

Migraine (Occurrence: Found almost exclusively among females). Meticulous, obsessional, scrupulous, perfectionistic, rigid, intelligent with strong conscience development. Headaches usually precipitated by emotional tension stemming from problems relating to financial or social position and by unacceptable hostilities generated in frustrating interpersonal relationships. History of convulsive seizures more common than in general population.

Hypertension (Occurrence: Slightly more common among females). Person tends to feel continual threat and need to be on guard. Stress may involve chronic hostility and/or anxiety stemming from dependency needs and feelings of insecurity. In many instances appears to result from sustained striving toward high goals with unbalanced life activities that do not permit a 'change of pace.' Incidence rises rapidly with age, especially between 34 and 64.

Rheumatoid Arthritis (Occurrence: About twice as common among females as males). Chronic inhibited hostility, resentment, and smoldering discontent, often allayed to some extent by self-sacrifice and serving of others. Strong dependency needs and further hostility when such activities thwarted. Often obsessive tidiness, overconscientiousness, and adherence to routine.

Obesity (Occurrence: Sex ratio about equal in childhood but about twice as common among females in adulthood). Lifelong overeating, which seems to provide compensatory pleasures for frustrations and relief from unbearable tensions. May also serve as a defense; for example, individual too fat to have dates and face problem of marriage, about which he feels inadequate. Also may stem from cultural patterns, metabolic disorders, hereditary tendencies, or brain damage. Obesity appears directly proportional to age.

From examination of the chart it may be seen that the negative emotions that accompany frustration and non-satiation are a source of violent internal disruptive responses which take the form of psychosomatic symptoms and self-destruction. Quite literally the person may be saying, "I no longer wish to live in this non-satiating world and, since I cannot destroy myself directly, I will become ill." In this way the person may achieve the love and belongingness goals that he cannot attain in any other manner and he may be free also of any expectation that he should attempt to achieve the higher goals in the hierarchy because, after all, little can be demanded of a person who is sick.

Generally, there exists a tendency to believe that physical symptoms of illness have either a psychological or a physiological origin. Since the organism is an indivisible whole, however, it seems more reasonable to expect that both may be present. Ruch (1958, p. 155) supported this view by stating that about 50 percent of the patients visiting the family practitioner's office had illnesses that had some psychological connection. It would seem, therefore, that if treatment could be thought of in terms of taking care simultaneously of both the psychological and the physiological aspects of the symptom, a more effective alleviation of illnesses would occur.

ACCIDENT PRONENESS

As indicated by a number of studies, accidents are not always purely coincidental. In a study of thousands of industrial and non-industrial accidents, Schulzinger (1956, p. 182) concluded that fifteen or less percent of all accidents are due to pure chance.

A study in Canada, reported by Hepner (1957, p. 387), of two groups of one hundred automobile drivers indicated that sixty percent of the group of people with four or more accidents had encountered such various situations as being unable to pay their debts, having court records exclusive of traffic violations, being included on social service agency lists, and having utilized public health clinic facilities; only nine percent of the accident free group experienced these situations. Consequently, there is some evidence to indicate that accident proneness is one index of inability to obtain goal satiation and it seems logical to conclude that by suffering an "accident," the non-satiated person allows himself to escape from the barren circumstances of his life and perhaps bring about the punishment he needs to alleviate his guilt.

SELF-DEFEATING BEHAVIOR AND SUICIDE

According to Coleman (1964, p. 333), a suicide takes place somewhere in the United States about 25,000 times a year. In addition there are probably over 200,000 attempts every year.

Many more persons impair parts of their lives in what seems to be self-destructive behavior. The capable student, for example, may behave in just this way when his failure to study leads to his dismissal from college and the end of his fondest dreams for making an outstanding academic record. The jealous person may behave toward the loved one in a manner which is best calculated to drive that person away and yet he seems powerless to control his behavior. A highly intelligent female homosexual client of one of the authors twice left letters from her "lover" in places where her parents could not help but find them; while another married client kept a diary of a former love affair for years that eventually was discovered by her husband, and led to the breakup of her marriage which meant consciously more to her than anything else in the world. It would seem, therefore, that many people need to act in a way that brings upon themselves the punishment they feel has been deserved for a long time.

SUMMARY

1. Adjustment mechanisms are beneficial as long as they do not create so much tension for a person that he is unable to achieve his goals.
2. Frequently the use of adjustment mechanisms allows a person to avoid facing the fact that he has not behaved in a way that is consistent with his self concept.
3. Such adjustment mechanisms as compensation and sublimation are of value in that they provide some degree of satisfaction for a person who is unable to experience it fully and directly.
4. Reliance upon projection, rationalization, etc., causes a person to ignore the inconsistency between his behavior and his value system.
5. For some people, it is easier to deny the importance of obtaining a goal than to take the chance of being frustrated over the failure to achieve it.
6. Some people choose to become sick and punish themselves in order to avoid the necessity of growing, developing, and moving toward the achievement of the higher goals in the hierarchy.

EXERCISE 11

Observing the Effects of Winning or Losing

The effects upon individual members of participation in winning or losing groups are sometimes quite different. Since competition—whether between teams, industries, departments, schools, or whatever—implies the creating of winners and losers, these dynamics have important implications. Many groups continue to work together after suffering in defeat or winning a victory. Cognizance of some of the feelings that have been aroused may enable group leaders or members to act in ways to neutralize or counteract currents of feeling that they feel are detrimental to the group's future. Perhaps one of the best ways for dealing with these emotional by-products of victory or defeat is to allow individuals in the group the opportunity to verbalize their feelings.

Try to remember victorious groups in which you have participated. What did you observe in your group after the results were announced? Check the following in terms of these observations. Did the group members . . .

YES   NO

—— —— 1. become more positive toward one another?

—— —— 2. take on a "fat cat" expansiveness?

—— —— 3. tend to see only the positive aspects of the group?

—— —— 4. close ranks against outsiders?

—— —— 5. become more tolerant of non-conformity of individual members?

—— —— 6. idolize their leaders?

—— —— 7. engage in triumphant play?

—— —— 8. verbalize about who has contributed most to the victory?

—— —— 9. interpret it as a triumph of a few individuals?

—— —— 10. interpret it as a group triumph?

—— —— 11. draw closer together?

—— —— 12. form stereotypes for who can contribute what?

—— —— 13. exhibit a kind of superiority complex?

—— —— 14. act somewhat complacent?

—— —— 15. quarrel over the spoils of the victory?

—— —— 16. become very protective of one another?

—— —— 17. really jump on anyone who didn't go along with the general elation?

_____ _____ 18. become less rigid?

_____ _____ 19. become more honest with one another?

_____ _____ 20. create an atmosphere of "sweetness and light"?

Now try to remember losing groups in which you have participated. Did the members of the groups . . .

YES   No

_____ _____ 1. begin to quarrel and blame one another?

_____ _____ 2. attack the judges or referees?

_____ _____ 3. attack the circumstances of the competition?

_____ _____ 4. seek to analyze what went wrong?

_____ _____ 5. make up reasons for the defeat that would allow them to go on thinking well of themselves?

_____ _____ 6. display a lean and hungry feeling—one of wanting to try again?

_____ _____ 7. show increased hostility toward one another?

_____ _____ 8. blame those who did not contribute much?

_____ _____ 9. blame the leaders?

_____ _____ 10. learn anything from the experience?

_____ _____ 11. lose the group feeling?

_____ _____ 12. see the other group, the judge, etc., as "the enemy"?

_____ _____ 13. see only the worst in themselves?

_____ _____ 14. close ranks in adversity?

_____ _____ 15. withdraw from one another?

_____ _____ 16. change roles within the group?

_____ _____ 17. become more honest with one another?

_____ _____ 18. resolve to "beat hell" out of them next time?

_____ _____ 19. take the position that "it's only a game"?

_____ _____ 20. successfully handle their disappointment?

Try to generalize these effects in terms of individual behavior within nations, minority groups, and other groups you have opportunities to observe. Try to make it a habit to notice the behaviors which occur following defeat or victory. What could you do to minimize effects which you feel might be detrimental?

CHAPTER 13

Institutions

Goal Accessibility

Lasswell (1961) has defined the social process as "man seeking values through institutions using resources." The words "man seeking values" refer to every human creature, regardless of his place or condition, who attempts to attain the goals that are the main subject matter of this book. The rich man and the poor one, for instance, both need love, belonging-ness, and psychological safety. The adult and the child look for respect, the employer and the employee desire power, and the member of a minority group, the cripple, and the retarded person all wish to grow and develop to the point that they are able to enjoy a high level of well-being.

The remaining words in Lasswell's statement are concerned with the institutions or patterns of activities and the resources that are available to people as they pursue their goals. More specifically, the institutions are the practices, laws, customs, and mores by which goals are made accessible to the members of society. Institutions may be formal, as in the case of written law, or informal as with generally accepted practices involving "the thing to do." Altogether it may be said that institutions that lead to a wide sharing of values for all men and which provide access to goals on the basis of merit are desirable in a democratic society. Conversely, institutions that restrict the sharing of values, thereby pro-viding goal accessibility to only a limited number of people, are less conducive to the development of a democratic society.

Institutions are invariably in the process of being changed and, as a result, one which for a period of time restricts goal accessibility to a particular group of people may be modified steadily so that after a while it provides opportunities for all persons to achieve their goals. Similarly, another institution, which originally offered free and equal accessibility to goals on the basis of merit, may come to be changed in the opposite way in order to satisfy the special interests of a particular group of people.

With some exception due to racial and religious differences, young people in America today are generally a lot more free to date and marry anyone whom they may choose than their predecessors of the 1930's. Prior to World War II, most college students were single but today approximately 40 to 60 percent of a typical college student body is married. Much of the community disapproval that was expressed formerly against married college students is directed now toward the growing trend for teen-agers to begin marital life while they are still in high school.

In order to clarify the impact such changes in their extreme form may have upon the members of society, perhaps you would allow the imagination to run wild and suppose that in order to curtail the number of teen-age marriages, society decided to restrict marriage to redheaded persons who could afford to pay a $10,000 fee for the license. Quite obviously, the number of marriages would be reduced immediately and access to the goal of love and belongingness would be limited to the specially favored group of people. It could be expected that the non-wealthy and non-redheaded persons would be most unhappy with this arrangement. In fact, married life might mean so much to a number of them that being denied this right would cause them perhaps to turn to common law marriage as a substitute. Their behavior would be looked upon by wealthy, redheaded persons, subsequently, as an indication that undoubtedly they lacked character and possessed few moral standards. In actuality, of course, what they would not have would be the opportunity to gain the feeling of love and belongingness that causes people to behave in a morally acceptable way.

Education is also an institution that controls the accessibility of goals in that the goal of enlightenment may be limited to those persons who can afford to pay for the privilege of attending college. At present, for instance, tuition fees at most state supported colleges and universities are relatively low. It is possible, therefore, for a student to attend college and only be expected to pay for a small percentage of the cost of his education. In some colleges, the taxpayers of the state bear all of the financial burden, thus ensuring that no student is denied the opportunity of obtaining an education, simply because he lacks the necessary resources. Figure 21 illustrates the relationship between tuition costs and accessibility of a college education.

Some taxpayers, particularly those who do not have children, feel that free or low cost tuition is unjust and, periodically, cries are raised that fees be introduced or be raised. If this policy were ever once carried out, however, it would probably result in further demands for increases in the tuition rate. Inevitably, of course, more and more students would

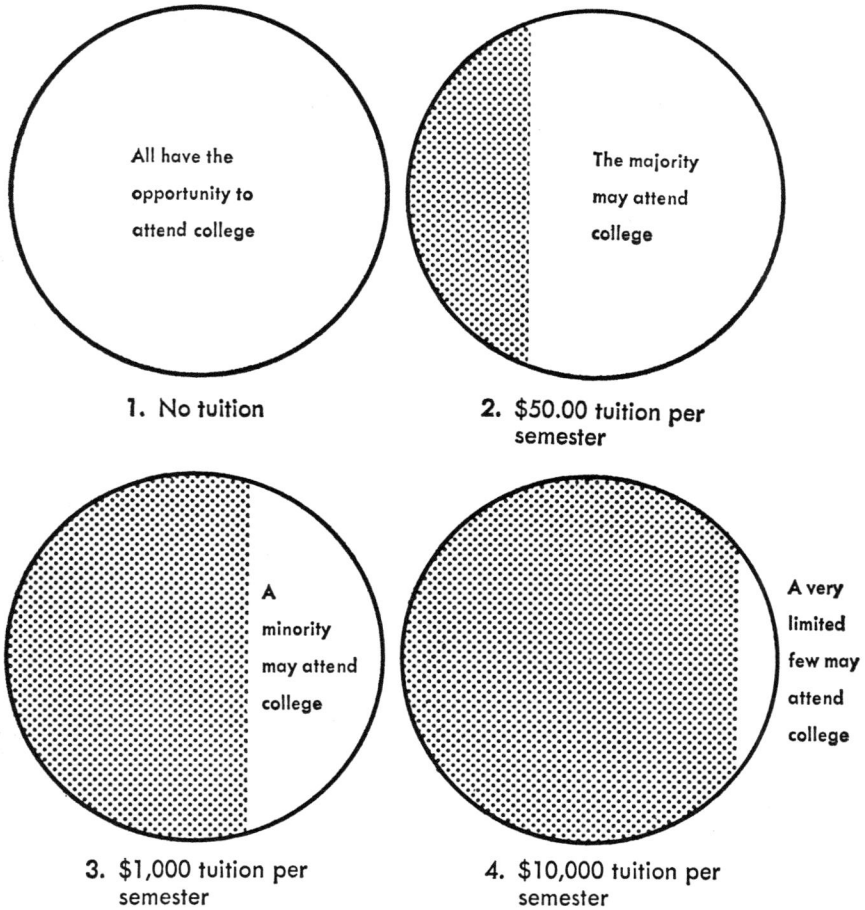

FIGURE 21. The relationship between tuition cost and college attendance.

be denied admission to college or forced to withdraw, purely on the basis of the lack of necessary financial resources.

It is important to note, moreover, that every change in an institution and every proposal for a new institution affects the distribution of values. There are some persons, the ideal citizens in a democratic society, who are able to support practices that are good for everyone. The issues are always complex and a precise and clear-cut answer can never be found. Generally, however, the attainment of such rational morality demands that decisions concerning policy have to be made in terms of the widest distribution of values. Persons who are capable of thinking on this level realize, furthermore, that whatever is beneficial for all people is in the long run going to strengthen both society and their own individual lives.

For the people who are unwilling to support practices that lead to a wider sharing of values, the alternative is to place their faith in the good will of special interest groups or, in fact, anyone who is prepared to advance himself as a candidate for dictating the picture of reality that should prevail. To replace the representation of the views of many people with the judgment of a few persons would seem to be an indication of political and social regression, because no matter how subtly it may be stated, the case for the superiority of a minority group is always a plea for the advancement of some special interest or cause.

Probably democracy will never be achieved in its pure and ideal form. Russell pointed out, however, that if it is to succeed, it must have (1) self reliant people; (2) political propaganda in opposite directions in which many people take part; (3) willingness of the people and the political parties to submit to the decision of the majority when it goes against them; and (4) a population free from hatred and fear (Egner and Denonn, 1961, p. 676).

Position, Role, and Status

Sir Leonard Woolley (Hawkes and Woolley, 1963, p. 414) suggested that civilization begins when the character of the soil and the climate makes surplus production possible and easy, thus allowing the energy of man that hitherto has been invested in problems of survival to be released for creating new institutions. He noted later that:

> What had been an agglomeration of clans or families each more or less self-sufficing and morally and socially independent coalesces into an organized society wherein each citizen has his specialized role and must play his part as a member of a community, profiting by the cooperation of his fellows and bound with them by a common law (Hawkes and Woolley, 1963, p. 466).

In order to sustain interrelationships among people in the group and thus provide continuity from generation to generation, incoming members are taught, more or less dutifully, the various positions and roles that have to be filled if the group is to function effectively. Some of the positions are prized highly and the persons holding them are afforded a great deal of status and acclaim. Such recognition may be given because the person fulfills effectively the role that is assigned to his position or it may be ascribed automatically on the basis of birth and class membership.

Perhaps the significance of such a social system may be made clear by making reference to the positions on a football team. Each one of them requires a particular pattern of behavior, regardless of which member of the team is playing in the game. Although the players may perform with varying degrees of efficiency, by and large they are expected to follow the role that is associated with the position they are playing. Thus, the quarterback takes the ball from the center, the guard pulls out of the line and leads the interference, the end catches a pass, etc., each player attempting to fulfill his role to the best of his ability in the expected and prescribed manner. Furthermore, the various positions on the team hold differing amounts of status. Generally, for instance, the quarterback, largely irrespective of how well he performs on the field, receives more acclaim than the fullback and the fullback, in turn, usually receives more recognition than the guard or tackle.

The person who wants to relate effectively to the people in his social group learns inevitably that there are certain roles that are expected of a person living in society. As these roles become increasingly clearly defined, he realizes that some patterns of behavior are appropriate at times and on other occasions they are out of place. He does not relate to the president of the company for which he works, for example, with the casual familiarity that he shows toward his neighbor down the street. On occasion, however, the person finds himself exposed to conflicting orientations from the members of his social group and he is forced to make a choice which of necessity will be in disagreement with the expectations of some of the people with whom he is relating.

Gross, McEachern, and Mason (1958) examined the different ways that people cope with the same situation. A hundred and five school superintendents in Massachusetts were asked to respond in terms of how they would handle the making of decisions concerning the following four conflict-arousing areas of administrative policy: (1) the hiring and promotion of teachers; (2) the superintendent's allocation of his after-office hours; (3) salary increases for teachers; and (4) the priority the superintendent gives financial or educational needs in drawing up the school budget.

It was found that the superintendents reacted toward the expectations of their staff members basically in three different ways. The first way was characterized by a willingness to recognize the legitimate right of other people to hold their own expectations, with little need to give consideration to the rewards or punishments that would be applied for not conforming to these views. The behavior of the superintendents in this category, who were referred to as "moralists," may be compared to the rational morality of the actualizing person described in Chapter 9. The superintendents with the second orientation were seen as being "expedients" in that their decisions were made on the basis of minimizing the negative sanctions that would be brought to bear by their not conforming to the expectations of the staff members. The persons in the third group, known as the "moral-expedients," were prepared to take into consideration both the legitimacy of the views of the staff members and the amount of pressure that would be placed upon them and make their decisions after balancing the relative effects of both of these factors.

As a result of becoming familiar with the different ways that roles are played in society, a person begins to develop an awareness of the behavior that generally he may expect from the people in his social situation. As long as the behavior remains dependently consistent, he is able to anticipate correctly and life moves along relatively smoothly. On the occasions that his expectations prove to be wrong, however, the effect may be quite startling and even unsettling. Thus, for instance, the behavior of the demure little school teacher who suddenly bursts forth with a stream of profanity is liable to be quite disconcerting to the people around her and cause them to have difficulty in knowing what to say and how to handle their feelings of embarrassment.

The Use of Resources and Potential Abilities

In the past, royalty, dictatorships, the aristocracy, the clergy, etc., all have taken advantage of the opportunity to shape institutions in ways that would make sure that their particular goals were achieved. Under such conditions, the average person knew precisely where he stood in society, but at the same time, no matter what his abilities were, he was limited in the opportunities that were available to him. As a result, he was forced to struggle in order to protect his rights and to change his social situation. Through the abolishment of such practices as slavery, differential justice, religious persecution, censorship, denial of voting rights, and so forth, vast improvements were brought about in the life situations of millions of people.

Muller (1963, p. 299) pointed out that the Levellers in England were among the first to demand equal suffrage and equal justice before the law. One of their adherents stated the case beautifully in words that are both simple and fraught with meaning, "the poorest he that is in England hath a life to live as the greatest he." Although man has succeeded a great deal in improving his institutions, there is still more progress that needs to be accomplished. As Muller (1963, p. 101) noted:

> Democracy requires a faith in ordinary human nature, the sufficient good sense and good will of common men. Freedom of thought, speech, and conscience logically requires at least a tacit admission of uncertainty about the eternal verities, a tacit rejection of all claims to finality, an open agreement upon the right to disagree peaceably on the first and last questions, and a flat denial of absolute authority to any sect or school of thought.

Unfortunately, such attitudes are not always in evidence. Rokeach (1960, p. 68) has suggested that threats to the existence of an institution lead to the narrowing of perception and the maintenance of dogmatic attitudes in much the same manner as occurs when individual members of the group are threatened. According to Muller (1963, p. 183), the long struggle by Spain to drive out the infidel Moors led to that country's tradition of fanaticism. Similarly, in America today, a number of people perceive the threat of Communism and the fear of atomic destruction as dangerous conditions that are giving rise to a variety of social ills, among which is the need to hold on to outmoded institutions.

Such a practice is most noticeably prevalent in the employment policies that are used in hiring women. It is generally true that while in college women compile superior records to men. In fact, if it were possible to select individuals applying for jobs on the basis of academic record alone, many men would be unsuccessful candidates. Despite their inferior performances, however, present policies favor giving the important jobs to men, leaving women with no alternative but to take the less desirable positions. In contrast, the Soviet Union utilizes feminine resources much more effectively than the United States, as evidenced by the fact that less than ten percent of American physicians are women but that females make up over seventy percent of the Russian medical profession. The question may be raised as to how long the United States can stand to allow this outdated practice to continue.

Gemeinschaft and Gesellschaft Societies

The German sociologist, Toennies (1957), divided societies into two general types: the Gemeinschaft and the Gesellschaft. In the Gemeinschaft society, institutions are valued only inasmuch as they provide services for the individual. Despite the fact that the person may be living purely in terms of his own satisfaction, happiness, and well-being and, consequently, not be making contribution to the purposes of the society, his needs still are given primary recognition and consideration.

In contrast, the basic orientation of the Gesellschaft society is concerned with achieving the society's goals of productivity, unity, and harmony. Under such a social system, the evaluation of the worth of a person tends to be made in terms of his productive efficiency and his behavior is viewed favorably as long as it fits into the prevailing middle class orientation. If he should fail to maintain his effective performance level, however, he is liable to be dismissed and another person quickly found to take his place.

As a result of such pressure, people tend to "run scared," an attitude which may be seen in the words of the baseball pitcher, Satchel Paige, who is reported to have said, "Don't look back. Something may be gaining on you." Unfortunately, even when a person is performing effectively, there is always the question as to how long in the future he will be able to continue doing so. Perhaps, at one time or another, almost every worker in America has lived with the fear that sometime he "will be found wanting."

The heavy stress on efficiency and the maintenance of production schedules has produced in American business and industry the bureaucratic type of organization that is most prevalent in the Gesellschaft society. Bell (1961, pp. 319-326) has identified the following characteristics as being essential to the effective functioning of a bureaucracy: (1) division of labor and responsibility; (2) downgrading of the individual; (3) rational decision-making; (4) secrecy; (5) submission to authority; and (6) security for members.

DIVISION OF LABOR AND RESPONSIBILITY

In the modern organization, the "job" has been broken down into many small parts. The individual's contribution consists of repetitious and sometimes meaningless small acts that are related vaguely to the total end product. Such an arrangement not only provides for tremendous efficiency in mass production but also makes the system relatively more independent of the skill of the individual worker. As a result, not only may employees be trained quickly to fill jobs, but also they are more expendable.

DOWNGRADING OF THE INDIVIDUAL

The position or job is described in terms of the necessary skills and qualifications so that any person who possesses the appropriate requirements may be woven into the organization. Thus, no worker ever is considered to be indispensable.

RATIONAL DECISION-MAKING

Decisions in bureaucratic organizations are made objectively and rationally on the basis of the facts gathered by specialists who make only a minimum reference to the human element. Because information and knowledge cannot be carried around in one person's head, it must be placed on file and, consequently, paper work increases at an astonishing rate. In this way, another person may go to the same documents and, on the basis of following the prescribed rules, arrive at the same conclusion.

SECRECY

All professional people attempt to reserve certain areas of decision making exclusively to their profession, thereby maintaining an aura of secrecy. The bureaucratic organization attempts also to maintain the superiority of the personnel who are informed by keeping knowledge of plans and future intentions from most of the employees.

SUBMISSION TO AUTHORITY

The person in a bureaucracy is required to be subordinate to those persons in higher authority. When he is willing to submit to their expectations, his behavior is referred to as "following the party line."

SECURITY FOR MEMBERS

The employee of the private or governmental bureaucracy has a salary that is fixed and can be depended upon, at least as long as the worker is a "good team member." In addition, the concept of tenure for life, which was developed in the bureaucracy, is a direct attempt to solve the problem of too much threat to the individual. The economic security represented by this orientation is augmented by pension plans, sick leaves, vacation pay, insurance programs, etc. Thus, services which were once the function of the family have been taken over by the organization.

In the modern corporation, the danger of being dismissed for personal reasons has been minimized by the attempt to eliminate the emotional and the subjective elements in relationships among persons. Policies have been established to stop decisions being made capriciously and actualizing persons, working in positions of leadership, have been able to help bring about the wedding of the two systems in a way that has improved the lives of millions of people.

If you choose to evaluate the bureaucracy in a somewhat negative manner you may want to pause and contemplate living without an automobile and the other conveniences of modern life. Today it is possible for the person with a fairly low level of income to buy goods that were not available to him a few years ago. Probably one of the most noticeable characteristics of life in Britain at the present time is the number of articles of superior quality that are within the purchasing power of most of the British public. Prior to World War II, most working class people could afford to buy only second rate articles of inferior design and quality that were manufactured specifically for their consumption. Today, however, because of bureaucratic effectiveness in improving productivity and the overall improvement in social conditions, the television set, appliance, etc., that the working man buys is comparable to the ones found in the middle and upper class homes.

The Impersonality of Gesellschaft Institutions

Unfortunately, many American colleges and universities have become Gesellschaft institutions and they operate with much of the impersonality of the bureaucratic organization. As long as the student ascribes to the purposes of the institution, he is evaluated positively, rewarded accordingly, and encouraged to continue his studies. If, indeed, he challenges the policies of the administration or refuses to go along with the rather arbitrary regulations concerning academic expectations in his classes, he is likely to be asked to withdraw from the university. On every campus, there are a certain number of places to be filled, and very frequently it matters very little to the administration whether a student stays, transfers to another institution, or drops out from college. Thousands of high school graduates are ready to enter college and teaching goes on, irrespective of whether Susie, Sally, Bill, John, or someone else is a member of the student body.

The consequences of such an impersonal attitude may result in the increase in American society of delinquency, criminality, and the so-called hate groups. Suppose, for instance, that a student, for any one of a variety of reasons, does not feel a part of the junior or senior high school or college that he is attending. There is a chance that he will decide that he is wasting time, and, as a result, probably he will drop out of school. Without adequate skill and enlightenment, his chances of finding employment are small and he may begin to feel that he is not wanted by anyone. It is still necessary, however, for him to find some place outside his home where he can feel important, and the delinquent gang, the young Communists, the John Birch Society, the Black Muslims, and the Ku Klux Klan are all groups that are liable to beckon. Because these organizations are concerned primarily with gaining numerical support, the student is invited to join and at last he is able to find a place where he belongs. By an exceedingly strange paradox, it is in the group whose behavior is characterized primarily by hate that he finds some degree of meaningful relationship. He is not accepted really for himself, but his relative lack of effectiveness is tolerated a lot more completely than is the case with most social groups. If he cannot perform as well as other people, at least he can gain satisfaction from carrying on a hate campaign, fighting, slashing tires, throwing rocks, etc. On writing about juvenile delinquency, Salisbury (1958, pp. 37-38) commented pertinently on this point:

> In the gang the street boy feels himself important. Nowhere else does he seem to matter. Not at home (if he has what can be called a home). Not at school, where he can barely read, where there is nothing he can do well enough to give him a faint glow of achievement. Not on the job, where the boss makes him feel inadequate and inferior.

But with his comrades in his gang he is important. He is needed. He is wanted. He has a place. His gang is his life. As it grows in rep (reputation), so he grows in rep. He stands taller on the streets. He shows his heart with more reckless abandon. He becomes a Big Man.

Later Salisbury (1958, p. 209) went on to note that:

In the conduct of the gang boy and the conduct of the drug user we see with shocking clarity that the source of the rebellion in each case lies within the social situation itself. It can be no accident that the most vigorous and vicious revolt and most spectacular of its manifestations are found precisely in those strata of the population where conflict abounds, where insecurity is rife, where uncertainty is commonplace and where the ordinary pillars of humanity, the family and the social community, are debased or shattered. The rebellion occurs where neither a youngster's family nor the social forces impinging on his life are prepared or able to give him the support and aid which he needs in adjusting to the complex problems of the contemporary age and the eternal turbulence of adolescence . . .

Their (the juvenile delinquents') objective is unconscious, anarchistic protest against the world as they perceive it. They have not the wit nor the means to offer any alternative. But by combining their youthful energy, their brute vigor and their young ruthlessness they are writing with their knives, their rumbles and their japping a bloody and terrible indictment of their times.

Unquestionably, the impersonality and the pressures to perform continuously at someone else's expected level of effectiveness have helped to produce many of the ills in society. When respect for the individual diminishes, there is a tendency for this degradation of man to be sentimentalized as the inescapable result of circumstances. The pronouncements of institutionalized business, science, and religion are presented as justification for a way of life that is actually very destructive to man. One solution to the problem might be found in returning to the Gemeinschaft society. While this approach would be desirable sentimentally, it is really not practical because, as mentioned previously, very few people would care to do without the practical advantages of living in a modern society. Another possible solution would involve providing the personal benefits of the Gemeinschaft society while at the same time, maintaining the Gesellschaft type of efficiency. Actually, if man is to continue to grow and develop, there is no alternative but to attempt to find a solution through this approach.

During the past, cultural change has taken place relatively slowly and always there has been time for new patterns of behavior to be assimilated. Recently, however, the rate of change has undergone so much acceleration that innovation has been piling upon innovation. Supposedly, the engineer of today has a saying, "If it works, it is obsolete," which illustrates very pertinently the conditions under which man is living.

There is a very real danger, moreover, that man may become so threatened by the rate in which changes are taking place that he will come to resist the very characteristic that makes him human, namely the continual need for change and for the self to emerge into the full expression of its potential. Whereas in the past, man's contacts with the conflicting ideas of diverse cultures and even different segments of his own culture were very limited, today such differences are speeded quickly to individuals in every corner of the earth. Millions of people, living in societies that previously were characterized by fixation and stagnation, are now finding it possible for new goals to emerge in their lives. Thus, a society, which originally was concerned only for its own welfare, is being faced with the alternative of changing its institutional practices so that it may embrace people in other parts of the world as well as its own members. Probably at no other time is William Lloyd Garrison's inscription at the top of *The Liberator*, "our country is the world; our countrymen are mankind," more significantly a part of the future destiny of history.

SUMMARY

1. Institutions that lead to a wide sharing of values are desirable in a democratic society.
2. In order for a society to function effectively, it is necessary for incoming members to be instructed in filling the various positions and roles in society.
3. The fact that the characteristics of a Gesellschaft society may be recognized clearly in American higher education raises some serious questions about the educational experiences that students are receiving.
4. Although there can be no question but what the emphasis on efficiency in America has brought about a vast improvement in standards of living, at the same time the impersonality of the system has been an extremely destructive influence on the individual member of society.
5. There is a very real danger that man will become so threatened by the rapid rate of change in the world that he will give up his desire for continual growth and development.

EXERCISE 12

Effective Interpersonal Behavior

Effective interpersonal behavior is a matter of subtlety and complexity. The same act may be positive or negative, depending, for example, upon timing or upon the total context within which it occurs. Despite these difficulties, more positive behaviors can be discriminated from negative in a general way. While the following list is greatly oversimplified, try to check it in terms of the frequency with which you use each behavior. If often, check "yes." If rarely, check "no."

Do you . . .

YES   NO

_____   _____   1. remember and use other people's names?

_____   _____   2. remember something personal about people with whom you work and ask or comment about these things?

_____   _____   3. make people feel good about themselves by expressing something positive about them?

_____   _____   4. respond in a sensitive way to the moods of others and try to adjust your behavior to fit their moods?

_____   _____   5. try to avoid unnecessary arguments?

_____   _____   6. try to see how it looks from the other's point of view?

_____   _____   7. listen carefully to what the other person is saying?

_____   _____   8. try to accept others who may be different from you in a variety of ways?

_____   _____   9. try to bring out the best in people through showing appreciation and giving praise?

_____   _____ 10. pass along complimentary remarks you have heard a third party make?

_____   _____ 11. keep others' confidences to yourself (refrain from gossip)?

_____   _____ 12. give help to others, where help is wanted?

_____   _____ 13. accept help from others who are willing to help out?

_____   _____ 14. keep a good balance between irritability and cheerfulness in your own moods?

_____   _____ 15. let people know where you stand?

_____ _____ 16. manage to be reasonably dependable?

_____ _____ 17. keep a good balance between humor directed at yourself and at others?

_____ _____ 18. try to avoid being overly critical?

_____ _____ 19. frequently make others feel important?

_____ _____ 20. give others positive expectations for them to live up to?

_____ _____ 21. accept compliments gracefully?

_____ _____ 22. give compliments gracefully?

_____ _____ 23. let people know enough about yourself so they can experience your humanness?

_____ _____ 24. really respect other human beings?

_____ _____ 25. really believe in individual differences?

Some experts believe that "yes" answers indicate that you should be having effective human relationships both on the job and in your social life.

If you do not agree with them, in the following spaces make a list of effective behaviors that you do consider to be essential for good warm relationships. Satisfy yourself. If, in general, you agree with the list as given, add a few more that are your own.

_____

_____

_____

_____

_____

Choose any five of the preceding items that you would like to experiment with in your daily life. List them below in the order that will be easiest for you to implement.

1. _____

2. _____

3. _____

4. _____

5. _____

Make a pact with yourself to do these things as often as you feel comfortable doing them.

CHAPTER 14

Interpersonal Relationships

One of the characteristics of modern life is the tendency for the person to rely upon numerous highly impersonal groups for the expression of his social life. Particularly in the cities, where size seems to inhibit really knowing other people, the person finds himself both alone and lonely. Many people wear masks behind which no one is allowed to penetrate. Thus, although the surface contacts a person makes are endless, the intimate encounters are extremely rare and, to a large extent, each person tends to pursue his own individual goals with limited regard for the goal achievement of his fellows.

Man is a social creature, however, who must relate to other people in order to attain many of his most meaningful goals. According to Muller (1958, p. 115), the Greeks were the first persons to maintain the importance of public interest together with private interest and this realization caused the individual to interpret his experience, not only in terms of his own goal strivings, but in consideration of the goals of other people as well. Similarly, any person in today's society, who desires to continue to grow and develop, must make his own needs predominant on some occasions and, at other times, recognize and fulfill the social demands and expectations of people around him. This ability to balance the needs of the self with the needs of others is a crucial aspect of relating to the people and it is through such relationships that separate and discrete individuals come to be united in a way that satisfies their needs for love, belongingness, and respect. As Dunham (1964, p. 67) said of the early Christians:

> . . . the great thing was the fact of fellowship, the sweet unspeakable communion which went by the name of *agape*. You might have a gift of tongues or of prophecy, you might understand mysteries and sciences, you might impoverish yourself to feed the poor or martyr yourself to save the brotherhood, but everyone knew that if you had not also *agape* (love, charity, comradeliness), and if *agape* were not the motive of all these other wonders, then you were in fact nothing and of no profit.

Both in times past and in the present, it has become clear that one of life's imperatives is man's need for other men and the intimate joy that comes from these associations. The ideal of society becomes then a sense of relatedness without any loss of individuality. The imagery of Scherich (1960), in which he distinguishes between the split pea soup society and the pebble society, makes clear the essence of this democratic ideal. In the first case, the peas which are thrown into a pan of boiling water lose quickly their separateness and become part of the soup of togetherness and commonalty. In the other society, however, the pebbles which are placed in the pan of boiling water retain their unique characteristics despite their common and shared environment. Thus individuality and togetherness coexist. The imagery is valid partially at least for the present time in that society may demand that every person become very much like its other members or it may maintain and enhance the individuality of its members, expecting only that they relate to one another.

The knowledge and acceptance of the responsibilities men have toward one another complement the privileges they are able to enjoy through relating to one another. Neither is possible without the other. Too often, however, a person acts in the manner of a carpenter who possesses only one tool which he has to use for every task and his behavior, consequently, is limited in its effectiveness. Just as the skilled carpenter uses hammers, saws, and a whole variety of tools, each for its specific purpose, so the sophisticated person in human relationships relates to his fellow men in a whole range of different ways. He would no more consider responding to people always in the same manner than the carpenter would think of relying on only one tool.

Seldom, if ever, has the ability to relate to other people been presented as a skill to be learned. Instead, it seems that people are expected to gain competence in human relationships, perhaps by a process of osmosis or even by chance alone. As a result, an exploratory attempt is presented in the following paragraphs with the hope that it will provide the basis for a usable understanding of the problems involved in human relationships.

Bion (1952) has described the following valences of human behavior that are used in interpersonal relationships:

1. Pairing—movement toward intimacy
2. Counterpairing—movement toward isolation
3. Dependency—reliance on external authority
4. Counterdependency—rejection of external authority
5. Fight—attacking others in the face of stress or frustration
6. Flight—fleeing from others in the face of stress or frustration

To these six valences may be added a seventh one, namely adaption, which is the conciliation and compromise with other persons in the face of stress and frustration.

Whenever counterpairing, dependency, counterdependency, fight, and flight are most prominent, human relationships may easily become a source of conflict and even severe emotional disturbance. When characterized by pairing and adaption, however, the people involved in the relationships are able to grow and develop so that eventually it is possible for them to enjoy a high degree of emotional well-being. In every human relationship, a person creates experiences for other people and, in so doing, he helps in part to determine the particular orientations toward life of the people with whom he comes in contact. As John Donne said in his *Devotions,* no man is an island and, in that sense, each person is responsible to some extent for what happens to the people around him.

Particularly when an adult is interacting with a child, part of what the child is to become is being created. Although probably to a lesser degree, the effect is the same with adult relationships. The way you behave to a friend or a roommate, for example, in part will determine the sort of person he will become. If you are sensitive and considerate, he will experience your kindness and probably see himself as worthy of receiving such thoughtful regard. On the other hand, if you are hostile and choose to inflict suffering, he is more likely to perceive himself as a suitable target for your cruelty. Thus, to some extent inevitably you are responsible for your friends' experiences during the course of their interaction with you.

Most human relationships consist of a combination of expressive, manipulative, and altruistic patterns of behavior, with people shifting from one approach to another as the social situation would seem to make it appropriate.

Expressive Relationships

In the expressive mode of behavior, associations with other people are not personal in nature because the individual is quite unconcerned with achieving goals by means of his social relationships. For example, a person may find that at breakfast his toast is burned and the morning newspaper that he likes to read is not delivered. He breaks a shoe string while tying his shoes and when he starts to drive to work, he finds that his car has a flat tire. The bus that he is forced to ride is crowded and he is jostled roughly while standing during the half-hour journey to the office. As a result of this chain of circumstances, he arrives seething with anger and at a focal point of seeking an outlet for his feelings. In such a mood, any chance remark or action by some fellow office worker is capable of accidentally triggering off the release of the feelings of hostility. In fact, this reaction is almost inevitable, for any excuse for giving vent to the person's feelings is going to be seized upon readily. Thus, although the fellow worker becomes the target for the release of aggression, the expressive behavior that occurs is not directed toward him in a personal sense.

At the opposite extreme is the individual who is happy for a number of physiological and psychological reasons. As he encounters different people, he is likely to express his joy largely independently of their behavior or moods and irrespective of what effect his behavior has upon them. In such a case, the person is expressing inner feelings and does not expect his social interaction with other people to cause either himself or them to achieve any particular goal.

The essence of expressive behavior may be captured in some of the responses of a man whose car will not start on a cold morning. He may curse the offending machine and even take a kick at it. None of his behavior aids him in any way in reaching his destination, nor does it change at all the situation with which he is faced. It does, however, provide him with a necessary form of expressive behavior which, although it does not point purposefully toward the achievement of a goal in the external sense, causes some internal changes in the feelings of the man to take place.

Allport (1961, p. 460) has warned that in studying expressive behavior, the usual preoccupation with content and with the purposive goal-directed aspects of behavior must be put aside temporarily in favor of observing "how" the person reacts. The way a person reaches his goal may be almost as revealing as the goal itself. The highest expressive level is attained probably by the dancer, the musician, and the artist. At the more ordinary levels are the bodily changes and movements that are associated generally with behavior. Some of the expressive signs of resistance and negativism, for example, are tardiness, absence, daydreaming, working at something else, restlessness, sleepiness, yawning, looking at one's watch, leaving early, and going out of the room for something. Signs of hostility may be seen in clenching fists, gritting teeth, chip-on-the-shoulder mannerisms, and disdainful behavior. The appeasing person may display a cover-up smile whereas the self-effacing person may be colorless in attire and constricted in bodily movement.

Perhaps the following description of expressive behavior by Halpin (1960) will help to point out just how much can be learned about a person by observing what he does:

You meet John Anderson for the first time in his office by appointment. You arrive on time; his secretary says that he is busy but will see you in a few minutes. He is alone in his office, and, as you wait in the outer office, you note that no lights are glowing on the receptionist's switchboard. Anderson is not on the phone. Yet you wait fifteen minutes until he buzzes his secretary to have her usher you into the inner office.

He is seated behind a large mahogany desk and across the desk directly opposite him is a visitor's chair. He reaches across the desk to shake hands with you, declares that he is happy to meet you, and asks, 'What can I do for you, Mr. X?' In shaking your hand, his handclasp is firm enough, but you feel that his forearm is locked at the elbow. At the same time that he is saying how pleased he is to meet you his hand and his arm are almost pushing you away from him and subtly reminding you that he wants you to keep your distance. This maneuver is emphasized by the obvious status symbol: the impressive mahogany desk. He uses this symbol physically as a barrier which he keeps interposed between you and himself.

You begin to realize more fully the significance of the fifteen-minute wait in the outer office. You recall that, instead of coming to the door himself, he buzzed his secretary to bring you in. The omission of any apology for keeping you waiting fits into the rest of the picture.

Here is a man infatuated by the sense of his own importance, a man who insists on keeping status lines clear and sees to it that you know your place. His voice is hearty, he says all the proper things, he assures you of his co-operation. Yet at least twice during your short conversation he interrupts before you have finished your sentence. During the twenty-minute visit his phone rings three times. He excuses himself on each occasion with a deprecatory gesture, as if trying to say, 'You know how these things are.' But, because his expression shows no concern for you, the intended apology in his gesture does not come through. What comes through instead is a different message: 'See what a busy, important man I am. You should be grateful to me for even seeing you, for letting you nibble at the crumbs of my time which I'm throwing to you.'

When your conversation is finished, Anderson stands—but still behind his barricade—smiles at you, perhaps a bit too unctuously, and tells you, 'Feel free to drop in any time at all. I'm always glad to help. . . .' You notice his stealthy glance at his watch and the slight tightening of the corners of his mouth. These barely detectable movements betray his impatience and fear lest you commit the blunder of prolonging the interview after he has decided to terminate it.

The dichotomy between such expressive behavior and goal-directed behavior which is manipulative and altruistic is somewhat artificial in that both types of behavior are present in every action. Allport (1961, p. 463), however, has observed the following differences between expressive behavior and manipulative and altruistic behavior which he refers to as coping behavior:

A. Manipulative and altruistic behavior is purposive and expressive behavior is not.

B. Manipulative and altruistic behavior is determined more by the needs of the moment and by the situation.

C. Manipulative and altruistic behavior is more easily controlled and more rational, unemotional, and conscious than expressive behavior. The latter is harder to alter or change because it tends to be uncontrollable and below the level of awareness.

D. Manipulative and altruistic behavior is directed to changing either persons or things in the environment whereas expressive behavior aims at changing nothing, unless it is the person using it. The effect upon the environment is incidental although, on occasion, the recipient of expressive behavior may be affected profoundly by his experience but such influences are unplanned in that the results are never expected or anticipated.

Manipulative Relationships

In manipulative relationships the person tries to influence or control the behavior of other people so that his own particular goals are the ones that are achieved. Although manipulation has a negative connotation, these goals do not necessarily have to be undesirable in terms of social value, for they may provide a helpful and constructive influence. The mother, for example, who stops her son from playing in a busy thoroughfare is satisfying her need to protect his safety by insisting on controlling his behavior. When she tries to dissuade him from driving a car until he is twenty-one, however, her behavior is less justifiable although, again, she is probably still concerned with his safety.

Spiegel (1960) stressed the concept of manipulative relatedness and found that the techniques of coercion, coaxing, evaluating, masking, and postponing are the ones that are used primarily. The following discussion of these techniques is based partially upon his ideas.

Coercion

Coercion is the most universal and primitive method of manipulation and essentially it involves the use of the threat of punishment to make another person do what is desired. Murray (1938, pp. 305-306) has classified punishment under the following categories: verbal reprimand or censure, striking or spanking, restraints or limitations of action, enforced action, and dispossession. Symonds (1946, pp. 116-118) presented a similar list which included infliction of pain, injury to a loved object, forced labor, physical restraint, deprivation, exclusion from the group, depreciation, threats, and neglect. Thus, the degree of punishment may range from such widely different methods as the deprivation of affection, a slap in the face or a spanking, to even the exploding of the atomic bomb. No matter what type of punishment is used, it will serve to coerce people into behaving in a desired manner. The employer, for example, wants the employee to work in a way which will lead to the accomplishment of specific goals and he insures that the necessary behavior will occur by the threat of potential dismissal. The employee, in turn, expects the employer to behave in certain desirable ways from his standpoint and he enforces this behavior by threatening to strike or actually going out on strike. Similarly, the teacher wishes to see her students study and she threatens them with failing grades in order to achieve this end. The father, in turn, promises to cut off his son's allowance if compliance with his wishes does not follow.

Because the technique of coercion has permeated American culture so widely, many children learn very quickly to submit to those people who have the power to punish them for not doing what is expected. As the children grow older, their power increases and, in turn, they force other people to submit to their desires. Thus, the pattern of coercion is perpetuated and frequently for many persons it is the only way of relating to other people what is ever learned. Suppose, for example, that a wife wants her husband to buy her a fur coat. She suggests the purchase but he reacts with a singular lack of enthusiasm. Whereupon she pouts and refuses to smile and to speak to him. In essence she is saying, "You do what I want you to do or I will punish you by withdrawing my affection and love." Unless she has miscalculated her power over the husband and the punishing value of the withdrawal, her attempt at manipulation may well succeed.

The biggest drawback to the use of coercion, however, is the feeling that the other person develops toward the knowledge that he is being manipulated. Coercion is experienced as the refusal to show respect toward him and the violation of his right to self-determination. Consequently, frustration is nearly always involved. It will be recalled from the chapter on emotions that hostility often results from such frustration. Thus, in the example above, if the husband gives in and buys the coat for his wife, his subsequent feelings toward her are likely to be resentful and unpleasant and the relationship between them a little more strained and tenuous.

On the other hand, the husband may simply refuse to buy the coat and wait for his wife to resume a warmer attitude toward him or he may, in turn, exert coercion by informing her that he does not intend to purchase the coat and what is more if she continues to pout, he knows a secretary at the office who would be only too pleased to provide more congenial company. Thus, coercion has been built upon coercion and the illustration begins to sound uncomfortably like life itself and some of the people who live it.

It is quite possible that many students have come to resist learning and enlightenment because for them the learning situation has been one of coercion in which they had to study or be punished for failure. The result may have been rebellion, withdrawal, or a minimal and unenthusiastic level of performance. In fact, many persons have a sort of instant hostility for authority figures which is foredoomed to interfere with effective performance and happiness throughout their lives. Unfortunately, nearly all people have been coerced too long and too often and, as contact with authority can hardly be avoided, it is difficult for them to resist authority without feeling some degree of anxiety.

COAXING

Coaxing involves the promise of present or future rewards as a result of compliance to another person's wishes. Such activities as promising, pleading, begging, and tempting are variations of coaxing, but if the reward is specific and concrete, the coaxing is more likely to take the form of bribing. English school children, for example, who fulfill their parents' expectations and need for social and academic recognition by passing the "eleven-plus" examination, are rewarded quite frequently with increased spending money, bicycles, trips to the European Continent, etc. On the international scene, the country that complies with the wishes of another nation is provided with perhaps a much needed loan for the improvement of its economy.

One of the unpleasant effects of the continuing use of coaxing is the subsequent development of dependent behavior. Riesman's (1961) description of the other-directed personality and Horney's (1945, pp. 48-62) description of people who tend to move toward others may be viewed as presenting people who have been subjected to the overuse of coaxing. Thus, the youngster who has learned to achieve his goals by pleasing his parents may go through life expecting others to reward him simply for being good and, consequently, he may lose the ability and desire to act upon the environment efficiently in order to satisfy his own individual needs.

Unfortunately, what the person who acquiesces to the request of another does not understand is that, as a general rule, what is offered as a reward is of less value either materially or psychologically than what is expected in return. In actuality, the only defense against this kind of manipulation is the refusal to behave in the manner that is expected.

EVALUATING

Evaluating is really not a separate technique of manipulation but instead is a special instance of coercion and coaxing. It involves assigning a value context to a person's behavior by means of praising, approving, blaming, shaming, and disapproving activities. Consider, for example, a small boy who while playing happily with a doll finds his activity labeled as "sissy" by his outraged father. Most certainly he does not want to be a sissy, which, obviously from the tone of the father's voice, is something pretty bad and so he soon gives up playing with dolls. Later playing ball with some other youngsters is greeted approvingly by the happy father and the boy learns quickly to abhor dolls and value baseball and football. Similarly, the little girl who does not want to be looked upon scornfully as a tomboy retires from the ball game and instead plays at serving tea, thus becoming the object of her mother's affection.

Essentially, then, evaluating consists of manipulation through the use of verbal imagery which identifies the person being manipulated with a class or type, either to be admired or to be scorned. Typical evaluative statements are "act like a big boy," "that's a brave girl," "be your age," "don't be a square," and so forth. When a person is told to stop acting like an idiot, he has two alternatives: either to refuse the evaluation which in actuality means rejecting the person doing the evaluating or to accept the evaluation and comply with the behavior in question. In relating to his parents a child may find that the latter position is the only choice he can take. Similarly, a young person who is subjected to evaluation by his peer group may find the first alternative a difficult one to choose. Few teen-agers wish to be seen as squares, party-poopers, apple-polishers, bookworms, and so forth. Instead, they prefer to be thought of as regular guys, cool, with it, tuned in, etc. Consequently, it is relatively easy for them to accept as their own the behavior leading to positive evaluation but much more difficult to maintain an attitude or position that will be greeted with a negative reaction.

The effectiveness of evaluating is related directly to the prestige or the power of the person making the evaluation. Thus, evaluations by authority figures, leaders, and all representatives of power positions are of greater moment in shaping behavior than are those by non-authority figures, followers, and generally powerless persons. Advertising personnel are particularly aware of the significance of this technique and they use it constantly.

In addition to the danger of over-conformity, loss of selfhood, and repression, one of the cautions to be observed in the use of this technique lies in the fact that a positive evaluation may be rejected as flattery and reacted to with hostility. Usually when this response occurs, the manipulative element shows through too nakedly and the latent hostility toward being manipulated has been aroused. The net effect is that the person who is being manipulated simply does not care what the other person thinks and the relationship may suffer permanent damage.

Perhaps the person who manipulates through evaluation can become more aware of the responsibility he assumes for the behavior he encourages. In fact, Rogers (1961, p. 357) has gone even further and stressed the advisability of providing a climate in which external evaluation is absent in that the individual who finds himself in a social situation in which he is not being evaluated is helped enormously in the fostering and development of his own creativity.

MASKING

Masking includes such behavior as pretending, evading, censuring, distracting, lying, hoaxing, and deceiving. It involves the withholding of correct information. A concrete example may be observed in the attitude of the person who promises a vice-presidency within a few years to a young man whom he has just employed if he will work hard and apply himself diligently above and beyond the call of duty. Since the young man wants the vice-presidency, he drives himself to meet the conditions, working overtime and generally contributing far more energy than is called for in the ordinary interpretation of his responsibilities. What he does not know is that his employer has promised the vice-presidency to a nephew who is to be graduated from college in three more years and no matter how effectively the young man performs he will not receive the promotion.

Another example may be seen in the behavior of a friend of one of the authors who explained recently that he simply had to buy a new car, despite the inconvenience of doing so, because his wife could not operate safely or comfortably the old one which was without power steering and power brakes. The man was convincing in his apprehension over the inconvenience his wife suffered while driving and particularly while parking the car and on occasion he almost approached true nobility in his selfless concern for her welfare. The only problem with his attitude was that subsequent disclosures by his wife, which were not made in his presence, indicated that she was perfectly content with driving the old car and in actuality she preferred buying new furniture over purchasing another automobile.

The usual defense against such masking is unmasking or the confrontation of another person with what has been concealed or disguised. As can be readily imagined, such a situation can be very explosive, and probably more established human relationships have been destroyed as a result of unmasking than for any other single reason.

The intensity of the feelings involved in unmasking was brought home to one of the authors following a particularly unfortunate act on his part.

He suggested quite facetiously to the students in a class while lecturing on unmasking that if any of them were involved in a relationship which they wished to terminate they should confront the person with his pretenses at every opportunity. Two weeks later a co-ed reported quite happily to the author's dismay that, "the unmasking bit really works." It turned out that her husband's mother had been living with her and her husband for some time. After the lecture she had gone home and proceeded to unmask continuously the mother-in-law's actions. In her words, "I let her know what she was really doing every time she turned around." After a little more than a week of such treatment the mother-in-law left for an extended visit with her husband's sister.

The lesson to be learned from the example is that you should unmask only when you are prepared to live with the potential consequences of doing so. If you care about a relationship, it is better to think carefully before going ahead. The person you like may need the particular mask he uses more than you realize and he may be unable to tolerate having it stripped away in too precipitate a manner. The damage to a relationship may be irrevocable and beyond repair, for it is difficult to relate freely to a person who has pointed out aspects of one's life that one himself does not admit. Thus, to care and to love may involve the willingness to let another maintain some of his illusions.

POSTPONING

Postponing involves a delay in making a decision and is based on the awareness that a person's outlook or perception of a situation often changes with the passage of time. Such statements as, "let's sleep on it," and "let's talk about it later" are overt indications that the technique is in operation.

It is relatively useless to appeal to the reason of a person who is emotionally upset or to try to alter his perception of the situation which has caused the difficulty and it is under such conditions that postponement can be utilized most advantageously. Thus, the wise teacher or parent may find it appropriate to delay the discussion of a problem with a rebellious youngster until such time as he is ready to admit that the situation contains some elements of which previously he was not aware.

When used less judiciously the effects of the technique may turn against the person who has the most at stake in the relationship. Postponement of that which must be dealt with inevitably may make a minor problem become a major one and quarrels which would have never occurred at all become arguments that end in the breakdown of communication.

The Effect of Manipulative Techniques

In the ideal sense, manipulative techniques represent quite often a sincere desire to help another person avoid making a mistake. The person who is doing the manipulating may feel, for example, that since he is older, wiser, and more experienced, he is able to help the other person avoid some error or unpleasantness. In short, the intention is to manipulate him legitimately and sincerely for his own good.

The disadvantage to this approach to relationships lies in the fact that simple obedience to another person's instruction is to some extent incompatible with growing and development. As Mumford (1961, pp. 177-178) has pointed out, as long as the effects of disorder, conflict, tension, weakness, and occasional failure are not total or traumatic, they encourage growth and development more than an imposed conformity which avoids these difficulties but sets up its own conflicts concerning over-dependency and failure in accomplishing self-determination.

Perhaps an example may help to clarify the issues involved. One of a young child's goals is that of learning to walk alone and unsupported. On the way to the attainment of this goal, he may learn first of all to crawl and then, as he begins to walk, inevitably he will stumble and fall, sometimes hurting himself. The wise parent, however, does not stop him from attempting to walk, no matter how inefficient his struggles may seem to the adult. He is allowed to fall and to make his mistakes because these experiences are necessary parts of his development. There is no short cut to doing and acting and, consequently, there is no other way to walk.

In such other aspects of living as self-direction and decision making, however, parents do not recognize the necessity for young people to be exposed to the experience of making their own mistakes. Many people feel, for instance, that by making most of the decisions for children and adolescents, they will be able to protect them from the danger of selecting the wrong alternatives.

When a youngster is given freedom to make his own decisions, the emphasis in the control of his behavior changes from meeting the expectations of other people to its effect upon the individual's own life. Thus, the boy of high school age, who is drinking beer, neglecting his studies, and generally sowing his wild oats, instead of being treated with disapproval and constant reminders of how much he is hurting his parents, is better off if he is helped to realize the difficulty of obtaining a job without a high school or college education and the consequences of jeopardizing his future. Although assisting the youngster in appreciating the seriousness of his situation may be difficult, whatever changes that are to be made in behavior will occur only when he feels a need for them and not because his parents perceive them as being necessary. Thus, instead of suggesting to the boy that he discipline his behavior and succeed in his studies in order to make his parents happy, emphasis would be placed upon achieving these goals in order to make himself happy. The basic question, then, for the boy to answer is whether he himself wants to live with the future he is creating or whether he would prefer to reshape his behavior in order to change the consequences of his actions.

Altruistic Relationships

Altruistic relatedness occurs when the attention of one person in the relationship is consciously and deliberately focused upon the goal attainment of the person with whom he is interacting. Whereas in the positive aspect of the manipulative relationship, the person wishes to impose the goals he feels are important for another individual's welfare, in the altruistic relationship the other person is helped and encouraged in the achievement of his own particular goals.

Richardson (1960) has provided an example of responding to the deeper needs of other people with a description of the contrasting behavior of two fathers who have taken their sons to visit an airport. The first father returns home with his son and responds to the boy's request for a model airplane by assembling materials and tools and working with a high degree of skill to construct the airplane. The father and son have a highly satisfying afternoon of companionship and the end result is a remarkably realistic model of which the son is exceedingly proud. The father is pleased with his display of skill and with the feeling he has over being a good father. The boy has his airplane and all is well. What, however, has been the underlying experience of the son? In actuality, he has been placed in a dependent role and he has learned reliance upon a person of superior skill to satisfy his needs. This experience is necessary and valuable in a society where all people turn in part to others to satisfy their needs, but when independent behavior is valued as well, it becomes important for the son to have additional experiences that permit him expression of his own individuality.

The second father whose son expressed also a desire for a model plane responds to his son's interest by asking where they could find some wood for making the airplane. The son remembers some discarded lumber behind the garage and runs to collect the material. When asked what should be done next, the son selects two pieces of wood to be nailed one across the other and with urging he hammers them together awkwardly. When asked if anything else is needed, he says no. He is content, for what he has is an airplane which he built by himself alone.

From an aesthetic point of view it is a pretty sorry model, but the son is both satisfied and proud.

Two weeks later the families visit the airport again. The first boy looks at the airplanes for a few minutes and then expresses a desire to go to a movie. The second boy studies the aircraft and then makes an exciting discovery. He has observed that airplanes have a thing across the back that is called a tail. Engrossed in studying airplanes he has to be dragged away from the airport hours later. His experiences have caused him to become more alert to the environment and he has gained confidence in his ability to change his surroundings through his own efforts. As a result, he is much more likely to rely on his own initiative than the first boy.

A word of caution is necessary, however, against the interpretation that one of these relationships is good and the other bad. Instead, the important point is that people need both types of experience if they are to achieve their maximum potential. The difference lies in the fact that the second father was sensitive to his son's underlying need for self-expression as well as his more obvious desire to possess a model airplane.

In order to behave altruistically it is necessary to develop, insofar as possible, the skill of perceiving the role of another person in a relationship by literally putting oneself in his shoes and viewing the social situation from his standpoint. The ability to see the other person's point of view seems to be related to the extent of the person's democratic outlook on life. Arendt (1963, p. 43) stated that the more decisive flaw in Eichmann's character "was his almost total inability ever to look at anything from the other fellow's point of view." Furthermore, Sarbin's (1954, p. 247) studies of role taking point in the same direction. He found that persons identified as being authoritarian are almost incapable of even temporarily taking the role of another person. Whereas non-authoritarian people could perform on a test the same way as authoritarian persons, authoritarian people, acting under the same instructions, were unable to take the test as if they were not authoritarian.

Unfortunately, many parents relate to their children in an authoritarian and non-altruistic manner. The adult, for example, who tells a child who is rocking a table on which rests an expensive lamp that good children do not act in that way is concerned with his own goal of protecting the lamp. He has failed to appreciate the fact that the child knows nothing of the value of the property and what he is expressing is a need to be active and burn energy. Thus, the parent might provide, instead, firmly if necessary, such alternative outlets for the release of energy as wrestling with the child on the floor, throwing a ball for him to fetch, or he might even go so far as to remove the lamp for a few weeks until the child is able to distinguish between rockable and non-rockable objects in the adult world. In this way, the child may learn boundaries, such as he cannot rock the lamp, but, at the same time, experience a resolution of tension and frustration by being active.

In addition to the expectations of parents and teachers, the youngster continually experiences demands from other sources. The physician wants him to protect his health, the dentist expects him to brush his teeth, and the minister feels he should attend Sunday School. The advertiser wants him to purchase his product and the insurance salesman is already interested in his providing for the future. The banker feels he should start a savings account while both his friends and his parents are interested in his playing baseball so well that his team wins the Little League play-off games. Sometimes it seems that everyone has experience and wisdom to offer him but very few people are willing to let him become what he wants and needs to be. Kant asserted many years ago in his *Critique of Practical Reason* that people must "act so as to treat humanity, whether in your own person or in that of another, always as an end and never as a means only." Perhaps the sentiment is still viable for the truly moral person in today's society.

In conclusion, Rogers (1961, pp. 37-38) has suggested the following general hypothesis which summarizes very well the characteristics of the altruistic relationship and the subsequent effects on human behavior:

If I can create a relationship characterized on my part:
    by a genuineness and transparency, in which I am my
      real feelings;
    by a warm acceptance of and prizing of the other person
      as a separate individual;
    by a sensitive ability to see his world and himself as
      he sees them;
Then the other individual in the relationship:
    will experience and understand aspects of himself which
      previously he has repressed;
    will find himself becoming better integrated, more able
      to function effectively;
    will become more similar to the person he would like to be;
    will be more self-directing and self-confident;
    will become more of a person, more unique and more
      self-expressive;
    will be more understanding, more acceptant of others;
    will be able to cope with the problems of life more
      adequately and more comfortably.

SUMMARY

1. Ideally a person's relationship to society is characterized by a sense of relatedness but with no loss of his own unique individuality.
2. Even in expressive human relationships, experiences are created for other people and, consequently, it becomes important to be aware of the "how" of one's reactions.
3. Generally expressive behavior may be distinguished from manipulative and altruistic behavior by the absence of planning and conscious choice.
4. Despite the fact that it may be used with the best of intentions, the manipulative approach to human relationships still deprives people of the opportunity to make their own decisions.
5. In contrast, the altruistic relationship is characterized by the desire to make sure that the other person has the chance to attain his particular goals.

EXERCISE 13

Creative Problem - Solving

Both groups and individuals must make decisions and most of us can use help with some of those that are difficult to make. Following is a description of one way for creative problem-solving. Begin by getting several of your friends or family together and stating the problem. Make the statement as explicit as possible.

Step 1—*FIND* multiple answers through brainstorming

(a) *F*ree-wheeling participation—try to create an atmosphere where one idea advanced by one individual is followed by another from a second, and so forth in rapid succession. Ideas should be presented in the shortest possible form. At this point, there is to be no discussion of ideas whatsoever. (You may need to be firm in insisting on the latter point.)

(b) *I*maginative solutions—let yourself go. Freely associate ideas and possible solutions to the problem. Do not overlook the new, the innovative, and the creative.

(c) *N*o criticism—no matter how wild or fantastic a solution may sound, share it with the group. At this point, nothing is too wild to be included; no idea too far out. The door to practical solutions is sometimes found in unexpected places.

(d) *D*iverse production—collect as many solutions as possible until the group has exhausted all possibilities. One member should record every idea that is advanced.

Step 2—Exploring the consequences of alternative solutions

(a) Preliminary evaluation—the group is to select the answers which seem to be the most promising from those made available in step 1. Avoid arguing if at all possible. If there is controversy over a particular solution, include it with the preferred solutions.

(b) Taking each solution separately, the group should now brainstorm all the possible outcomes, should this answer be applied. Every possible outcome, "good and bad," should be listed.

(c) Each solution and its outcome should be summarized somewhat as follows so that all the data are available:

Positive Outcomes ....
1. _____
2. _____
3. _____
4. _____

Solution 1 ....

Negative Outcomes ....
1. _____
2. _____
3. _____
4. _____

(d) Rejected solutions should be reviewed. If any of them now looks promising, steps b and c above should be applied to it.

Step 3—Reaching a solution

(a) In discussion of the preferred solutions, be sure every group member has his say. Try to avoid domination of the discussion by one or a few individuals.

(b) Explore compromises that will make it easier for everyone to accept final decisions. Be certain that dissatisfied members have ample opportunity to air their feelings. (If the solution concerns only a single individual, he, of course, would select the solution he prefers after listening to the discussion under Step 3 (a) above.

GENERAL SUGGESTIONS FOR ALL PRECEDING ACTIVITIES

Do not be limited by habit, custom, or tradition.

Look for a new solution to old problems.

Look for modifications of old solutions.

Look for adoptions from other fields. (What else is this like?)

What parallels from the past might be helpful?

Could other processes or ideas be utilized in this situation?

Could the situation be put in new shape or form so that the whole problem changes?

Is the problem related to color, motion, or sound, so that changing these would change the problem?

Is there a new ingredient that could be added to the situation?

Are there additional powers that could be brought to bear?

Is there another way to approach the situation?

Can circumstances be rearranged or reversed to alter the situation?

Is there any way to convert weaknesses to strengths?

Would opposites of expectations help?

Could purposes be combined or reinterpreted?

CHAPTER 15

Helping Human Relationships

Human relationships may be directed either manipulatively or altruistically toward helping other people achieve their own specific goals. Because most people have few problems in providing aid for other persons by means of using manipulative helping relationships, the major emphasis of this chapter will be placed upon the much more difficult to achieve altruistic approach.

Manipulative Helping Relationships

ADVICE GIVING

Of tremendous importance for efficient living in today's world is the process of advice giving which consists of offering suggestions for the solution of problems. Physicians, dentists, lawyers, engineers, athletic coaches, and other professional people are highly educated advice givers. Moreover, a friend or a roommate may be of practical help in offering advice. In fact, nearly all people are capable of providing advice based on a pattern of living that has been proved to them to be beneficial.

Underlying the advice that is given is usually a value judgment that one course of action is preferable to the other choices that are available. While in some cases the advice may be appropriate to the orientation and the value system of the person receiving it, on many other occasions what is perfectly sound thinking in terms of the experiences of the person doing the advising becomes extraneous and unsuitable for satisfying the needs of the person to whom the advice is directed.

INFORMATION GIVING

Without being provided with the appropriate information, all people would face every situation they encountered in life on a trial and error basis. In consequence there can be little question that one of the best and most opportune ways of being helpful is to provide another person with correct and appropriate information.

ENVIRONMENTAL MANIPULATION

In environmental manipulation the helping relationship involves an attempt to reorganize another person's environment. The individual, for example, may help a friend meet new people, look for a place for him to live, obtain another job for him, and generally be of assistance in any one of a countless number of different ways which bring about a change in the person's environment.

Altruistic Helping Relationships

Once a person has been given all the advice and information that he can use advantageously, it is only possible to help him further by turning to altruistic helping relationships. In this way, altruistic relatedness becomes a supplement to manipulative helping and should not be seen simply as a preferred method of relating to other people.

COMMUNICATION

Every human relationship involves communication, the salient features of which are shown in Figure 22, an adaptation of the theory of Schramm (1960, pp. 3-18). Every person formulates and expresses or encodes his ideas in a way which is consistent with his orientation. He may do so verbally or by the written word or he may convey his message through such expressive behavior patterns as trembling, blushing, bodily gestures, voice volume, intonation and inflection, facial expression, and in thousands of other subtle ways. The person who receives the communication, in turn, decodes or interprets it in terms of his own orientation and then encodes his response within the same general framework so that the person who originated the message becomes the decoder. The process is repeated again and again as the communication continues.

Thus each message is created in part by the person who encodes it and partly also by the orientation of the person who decodes it. In this way, not only does the orientation of a person change the meaning of the communication that is sent to him, but it is also possible for a message to influence the orientation of the person receiving it.

Ideally, then, communication represents the efforts of two or more people to establish a commonness concerning some area of experience. No matter whether the people are trying to share ideas, meanings, or feelings, their endeavors are directed always toward creating a "picture in the mind of the receiver" which will resemble as closely as possible the one in the "mind of the sender."

If a university lecturer speaks before forty persons, he encodes in actuality a single observable message. Because of their different orientations,

Observable message
verbal or other behavior

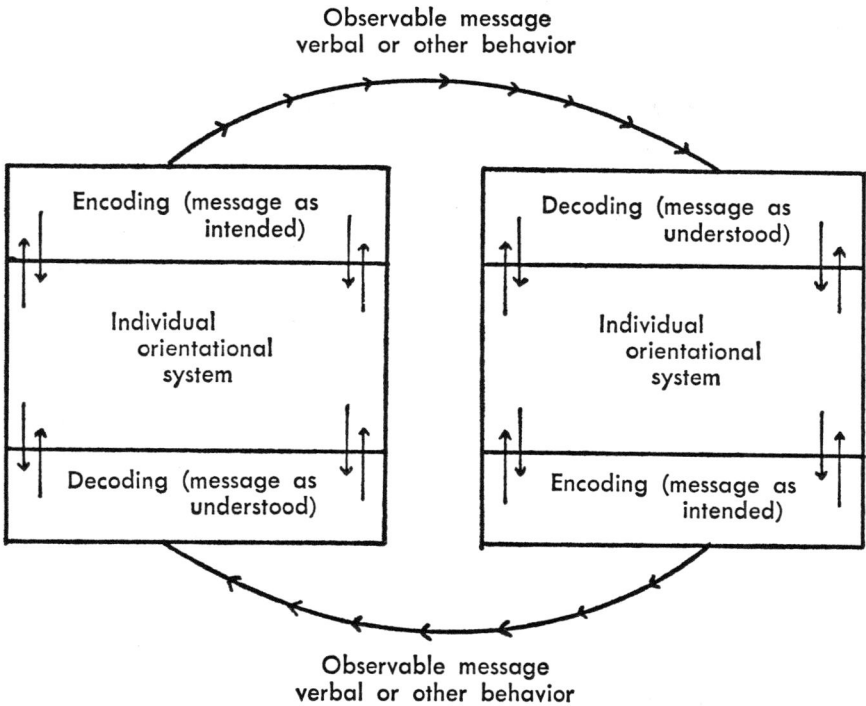

FIGURE 22. The nature of communication.

interests, values, and attitudes, however, the students in the lecture room decode his message in forty completely different ways and consequently forty divergent processes of communication ensue. This situation is especially likely to occur today because the manifold complexity of knowledge makes many meanings possible and because skill in listening is not highly valued in American society. In fact, the art of listening is estimated to be one of the most neglected aspects of the socialization process. A multitude of academic courses are directed toward developing skill in various encoding processes but courses which stress the importance of listening are limited in their number. As a result, in the classroom situation as well as in social situations, instead of listening with full attention, many people are guilty of only giving partial attention to what is being said and of being preoccupied with what they will say once the other person has been silent long enough for them to pick up the conversational ball.

If you are willing to put this hypothesis to the test, you are urged to try the following experiment described by Rogers (1961, p. 332). He suggested that a discussion, or perhaps even better an argument, be carried out according to the following rules: A person is allowed to make an opening statement. Before a second person can respond as he desires, he must restate what the first person has said to the speaker's satisfaction. Only after the restatement has been accepted by the first person may the second person express his own ideas. The same rule remains in effect so that the first person has to restate the remarks of the second person to the latter's satisfaction. It will be seen readily that this exercise is excellent discipline for learning to listen. The difficulty of restating what has been said provides dramatic proof that very little attention is usually given to what is being expressed in either a classroom or social situation.

The first and absolutely necessary step in learning to implement altruistic helping relationships is the development of the ability to listen actively. When such listening occurs, the message dominates the decoding process and there is less likelihood that it will be distorted by the listener's particular orientation.

Even when messages are attended to carefully, there are still many pitfalls to the achievement of accurate communication. The most obvious and concrete example of this difficulty is found in a difference in language. When a message is encoded in French and its recipient can decode it only in English, obviously very little communication can take place. In a similar manner, the English teacher who is decoding the message of a person who "murders the English language," is likely to ignore the person and attend to the mistakes in grammar, thus reducing the communication between the two people. Another person might suggest to his minister that he does not believe in God and subsequently cause the minister to react to his attitude by disregarding him. In short, when the orientation of the encoder tends to match and to be similar and acceptable to that of the decoder, the possibility of accurate communication is enhanced. When the reverse situation is the case, then, of course, there is less likelihood of accurate communication taking place.

Because being accepted and understood is important to man, there is always the temptation for a person to encode his message in terms of the presumed orientation of the decoder. Thus, many feelings which are not likely to be received very well are seldom expressed and, in order to provide an altruistic helping relationship, a person may need to listen and behave in such a way that the other person feels safe enough to bring up those subjects that the average listener would not care to be told.

Figure 23 shows two separate pairs of persons who are in communication with one another. The pair on the left, who have a fairly high degree of congruence in their orientation, would probably find communication quite easy while the pair on the right who have little congruence in their orientations would find it difficult, if not impossible, to communicate

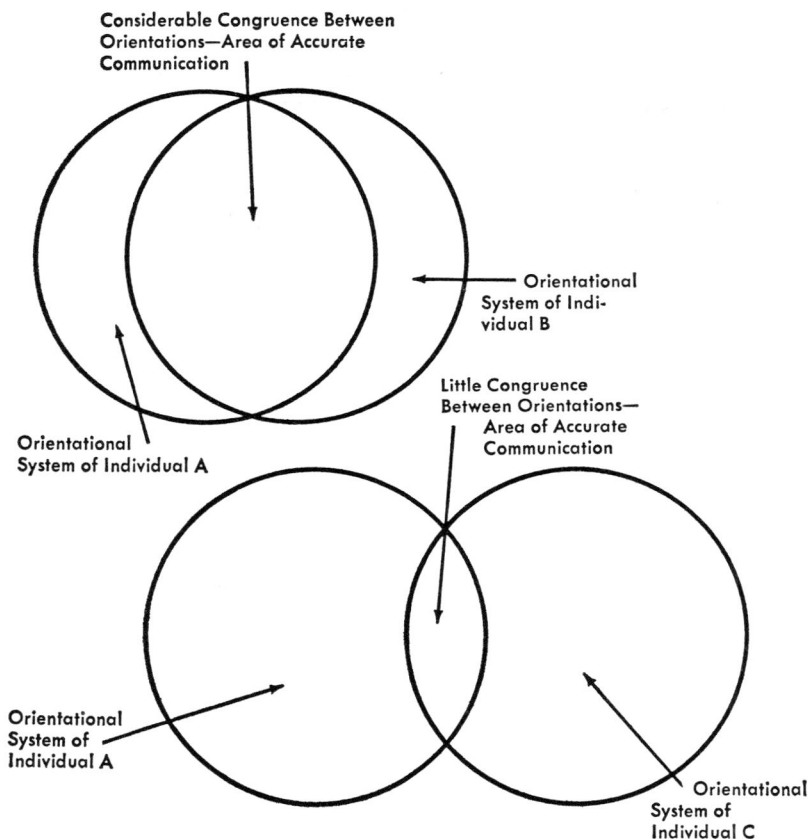

FIGURE 23. The relationship between orientational congruence and the accuracy of communication.

with each other. Many of the tragedies of everyday living may be based on the difficulty of communicating when the initial congruence of orientation is low. Thus, communication is limited sometimes between labor and management, middle class teachers and lower class students, and, in fact, between all diverse groups which exist within the larger cultural totality of American society.

The concept may be illustrated best perhaps in terms of the age old difficulty in communication between the sexes, for to some extent, the worlds of men and the worlds of women are miles apart. It is reasonable to suppose that many marriages founder upon this rock or non-communication. Consistent with his orientation, many a husband feels confident that he is communicating successfully his love for his wife through the sexual attention he pays her and the economic necessities for living which he provides for the family. Perhaps he encodes a message which says, "Would I be true to you and work hard to support you if I didn't love you?" His message is truthful, for he would neither be true nor work so hard if he did not love his wife. As far as he is concerned he is saying, "I love you." However, the key aspect of communication is not what is meant, but what is understood. If his wife does not decode the "I love you" in the message, as far as she is concerned, it has not been said. What she understands, and not what she might be expected to understand, will determine her behavior. Whether due to the influence of Hollywood or to numerous women's magazines, "I love you," in the typical feminine orientation can only be decoded in terms of small gestures and indications of attention that in the male world are more ordinarily associated with courtship. Thus, what seems trivial in the masculine world is vital to the female and what is ignored frequently by the husband, unless he learns to listen accurately to his wife, may make a very real difference to their lives.

Through business activities, the husband's opportunity for goal achievement is augmented considerably. Little signs of respect shown to him by other people may become an accepted part of his relationships in the office. His skills grow as the demands of his job increase and he may have a voice in many decisions which gives him an opportunity to exercise power. Thus, he has feelings of being useful in the on-going excitement of enterprise and of being a vital part of the productive scene. Finally, there is the monthly pay-check which states with some degree of authenticity that his contributions are real and of concrete value.

Conversely, the washing machine, with which his wife works neither respects nor disrespects its operator. The polished floor "speaks for itself" but not very warmly. The "taken for granted" meal must be prepared three times a day. Dishes must be washed and while children are vital parts of her environment, it is open to question whether they augment their mother's ego on a day to day, screaming through the house, basis. Lastly, there is no pay-check at the end of the week or month to indicate in today's world of materialistic recognition of productivity that her contribution is truly appreciated.

Thus, many wives need the communication of love on their own feminine terms, not because they are stubborn or unreasonable, but because the social conditions under which they live force them to rely on the achievement of love and belongingness needs as a means of gaining success. Friedan (1963) has written extensively concerning this predicament of the housewife in modern society.

Communications and messages and, in fact, all stimuli may be thought of as existing along a continuum according to the degree to which they dominate and influence the perception of the person who decodes them. The extremes of the continuum are depicted in Figure 24. They run the gamut from relatively concrete messages like "his office is down this corridor, fourth door on the left" to such abstract and ambiguous messages as John Keats' "beauty is truth, truth beauty—that is all ye know on earth, and all ye need to know."

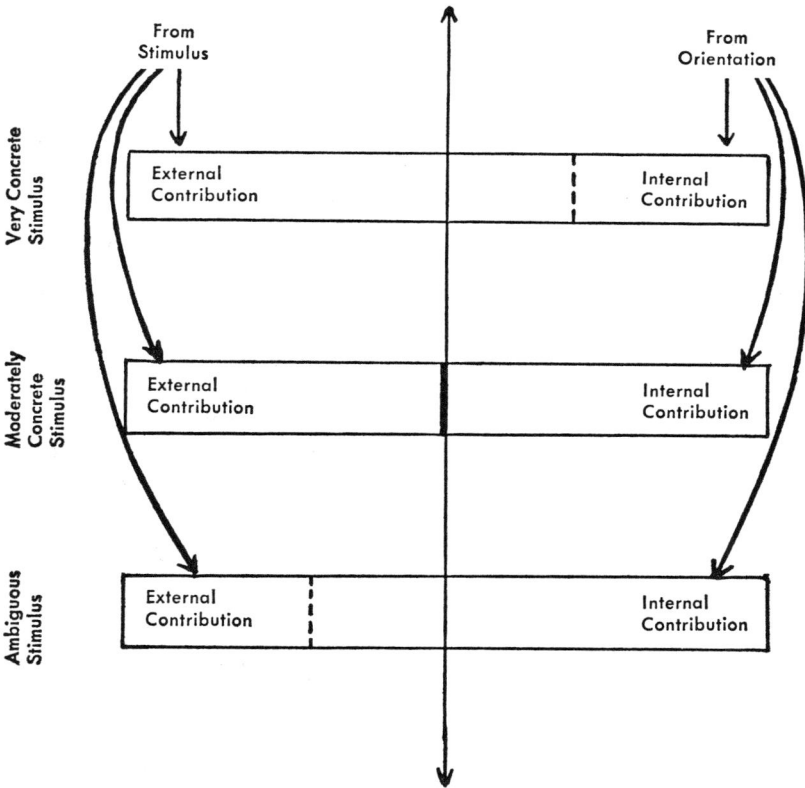

FIGURE 24. Relative domination of perception by concrete and ambiguous stimuli.

COMMUNICATION TECHNIQUES

Underlying the importance of listening is a process known as catharsis which is the discharge of emotional tension through "talking out" or expressing emotions and feelings in an interpersonal situation. It has been found that if a person is allowed to talk about his problems in a permissive atmosphere, he will tend to develop a more realistic appraisal of his situation. Such knowledge has been a part of man's history. As Dunham (1964, p. 83) stated, "The first Christians met in candid, intimate communion. They told one another their hopes, their guilts, their fears. They were encouraged to express rancor if they had it, so that it would no longer fester, as it had done, unseen." Thus, they were "cleansed of negative feeling and in harmony with all."

Probably almost everyone has known the experience of having talked to someone when troubled and, as a result, having felt better. Moreover, with the highly-charged emotional level decreased, additional aspects of the total situation may be perceived and new insights may follow.

In football there is a saying, "when in doubt, punt." Perhaps this statement may be paraphrased in a useful way for altruistic helping relationships. When a person with you is highly emotional and you don't quite know what to do, stay out of the way, do not insert yourself in the conversation more than absolutely necessary, and let the person talk. This approach will probably help and seldom will it harm.

While each person is different and must be related to in terms of his uniqueness, certain general needs exist in most people who are upset and faced with what seems to be an insurmountable problem. First and foremost is the need for unqualified acceptance and understanding, for the feeling that another person cares and is interested is a vital experience of life.

Second is the need to share painful feelings and ideas, which may even be of an immoral or anti-social nature, with another person. Because they are almost certain to be greeted with disapproval, the person is not likely to feel free to discuss them with many of the people he knows and, consequently, these feelings remain bottled up and unexpressed. As a result of sharing what is felt with another person without either condemnation or condonation, however, an attitude of "I am terrible" may change to "This terrible thing has happened, but perhaps I am not so terrible." Moreover, the listener's acceptance may be transformed into self-acceptance and the subsequent decrease in self-hatred will cause the person to be driven less often to destructive behavior directed either inwardly against the self or outwardly upon the environment.

Third is the need for cooperative human relationships with people who are seen as being equal, as opposed to a relationship that has a superior-inferior dimension. For many people the spirit of relatedness gained through working with another person is hard to discover and they never know the experience of cooperative endeavor becoming a source of increased energy and renewed effort. An example of the deleterious effect of continually facing weighty problems alone may be found in the case of the person who must raise children in the absence of the other parent. The necessity of single-handedly making new and sometimes difficult decisions, which may have important ramifications for the child's future, is obviously quite demanding. While the problems may still be onerous, they become more bearable when they are shared with another person. Moreover, the sense of two people doing their best together manages to increase the feelings of self-confidence, both over the decisions that are made and concerning the parents' abilities to handle future problems.

Classification of Verbal Responses

Porter (1950, p. 70) has classified responses to emotional communications into the following categories: probing, evaluating, interpretation, reassurance, and reflection. An example of each category is presented in response to the hypothetical remark, "I became so angry last night when Bill didn't show up that I almost threw something."
Probing—What happened to make you so angry?
Evaluating—You shouldn't lose your temper.
Interpretation—That's because you take yourself too seriously and are too sensitive.
Reassurance—Everybody gets stood up some time or other.
Reflection—You were really burned up.
Probably everyone has heard all of these types of responses at one time or another. It is not suggested that any one of them should be used exclusively but, instead, it is recommended that the person who is interested in becoming sensitive to human relationships become cognizant of the effect of using the different responses. Toward achieving this end, the various types of responses will be discussed in detail.

PROBING

Probing is a response which is directed toward seeking additional information which the listener feels he needs to possess. While probing appears to be the logical thing to do, it is experienced quite often as an intrusion upon the right of privacy. The freedom to tell or not to tell is threatened by a direct question so that the person who is subject to the probing is placed in the awkward position of having to comply with the request for information or to avoid doing so by either evasion or direct refusal. Most frequently he chooses to evade the question and therefore the opportunity to express his real feelings has been lost. In all probability probing parents have forestalled communication with their teenage sons and daughters much more than might be imagined. The "where have you been" response to the hopeful "I'm late" is unlikely to encourage complete frankness or disclosure. Too often such questions as "why did you do that?" are only thinly disguised vehicles for communicating disapproval, no matter what answers may be offered.

People differ greatly in their reaction to probing and, therefore, the person who would become skillful in human relations needs to learn to use such responses differentially, resorting to them on some occasions and avoiding their use at other times. On the occasions when they are used, a general probing response is usually preferable to a specific question. Moreover, a response which is aimed at the feeling involved is more likely to sustain communication than one directed toward eliciting information at a factual level. The following probing responses, adopted from Wolberg (1954), tend to encourage further interchange of thoughts and ideas and leave the person free to reveal as much or as little as he chooses:

> How did you feel about that?
> What would you like to do?
> What do you think might be involved?
> So the conclusion is what?
> What do you think the first step might be?
> You mean that was only the beginning?
> There is no question in your mind about that?
> What are your theories concerning it?
> Can you think why?
> What kind of trouble did you have?

EVALUATING

Evaluating involves, of course, an appraisal or value judgment of another person's ideas or attitudes. In attempting to provide an altruistic helping relationship, it is preferable that such responses be avoided. If the listener cannot accept what he is told and, consequently, evaluates it negatively, probably the speaker will not feel safe enough to pursue the topic any farther. On the other hand, if the listener endorses the statements he is told too enthusiastically, the speaker may have difficulty expressing the negative aspects of any ambivalent feelings that he possesses. In either case, the valuation is liable to threaten either consciously or unconsciously the person who has revealed something of himself and thus he may need to switch from self-exploration to self-justification and even reject the evaluator as well as the evaluation in order to protect his self concept.

As a general rule, all moralistic judgments, over-reactions, expressions of horrified surprise, criticizing, ridiculing, belittling, blaming, rejecting, and flattering will tend to restrict communication. Consequently, in attempting to build altruistic helping relationships it is essential to inhibit these responses as much as possible and to try to avoid such evaluations as the ones included below:

That could get you in a lot of trouble.
What a horrible thing to do.
Well, for heaven's sake.
That's like cutting off your nose to spite your face.
That is boasting.
It doesn't sound as if you behaved very intelligently.
That was pretty irresponsible.
If you won't try, I can't help you.
Every cloud has a silver lining.
I think you are a brilliant person.

INTERPRETATION

In interpretation an attempt is made to point out a cause and effect relationship and to provide insight into a person's behavior. There is always the danger that the interpretation may be wrong, particularly if it is based on sketchy knowledge of all the pertinent circumstances or on the orientation of the interpreter instead of that of the speaker. Even after careful extended study, the highly trained expert approaches an interpretation tentatively and most certainly the relatively inexperienced listener needs to be very sparing with his attempts to explain the causes of human behavior.

A second danger may occur, even when a correct interpretation is made, if some of the defenses of the other person in the relationship are unmasked, as described in the previous chapter. The interpretation is rejected because it is offered before the person is ready to receive it and together with the rejection of the interpretation may come a rejection of the person who is making it.

On a more positive note, non-threatening interpretations, which are close to the person's level of understanding, can be made safely. In Figure 25, for example, it might be possible to move to level B without causing the person too much frustration whereas a direct jump from level A to level C would be too excessive to be accepted.

Long, rambling, and discursive explanations tend to confuse more than clarify and it is better for interpretations to be short, to the point, and presented in simple, non-technical language. It is even more important that they never be presented dogmatically but, instead, be worded so that the other person in the relationship is free to accept or reject whatever state-

C ——————————— Full Interpretation Level

B ——————————— Partial Interpretation Level

A ——————————— Person's Present Level of
                                      Understanding

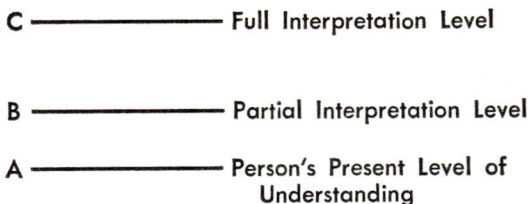

FIGURE 25. The depth of interpretations.

ments are made to him. Such words and phrases as perhaps, it may be that, possibly, suppose you look at it this way, etc., tend to soften the impact of the interpretation and reduce the chances of hostility occurring. Thus, interpretations that are short, easy to understand, and not too threatening are likely to be accepted while such dogmatic statements as "this is the way things are" will result probably in nothing but increased resentment. At best, the average person needs to make fewer interpretations than he is in the habit of doing if he hopes to increase his ability to establish creative, helping relationships.

REASSURANCE

Reassurance is essentially an expression of sympathy for the speaker. Although it is one of the most widely used responses to emotional situations, it is, unfortunately, often nothing more than an unrealistic attempt to make another person's problems appear less disturbing. In actual life, of course, serious problems are not minimized that easily. Imagine, for example, that a person is telling a friend how troubled and despairing he feels and that the listener responds by stating that he, too, has felt that low, but his problems always have passed away and that no doubt the speaker will find himself feeling better in a few days. In actuality, the speaker has lost his job and he fears that his wife is suffering from incurable cancer. Consequently, he is in no mood to accept such easy reassurance that all will be well; in fact, he may go as far as to interpret it as an indication of flatulent stupidity.

Another example of the superficiality of reassurance may be seen in the case of the high school girl with a pimply complexion who is quite convinced that no boy would be interested in dating her. Obviously, the breezy reassurance that she has lots of poise and charm and unquestionably she will become the belle of the ball is not going to meet her needs. Troubled feelings, fears, and anxieties are eased more by airing and talking out than by verbal whitewashing. Although reassurance is not necessarily harmful, it is important that it be relied upon only moderately, preferably in the manner of the examples included below:

But everyone gets upset and acts unreasonably at times.
Those experiences must have been bad to make you feel so unhappy.
You feel like this now, but there may be other aspects to the situation
that will help in time.
Anyone would resent that.
But it is natural to feel that way.
It would bother most people.

REFLECTION

Reflection is a response by the listener which is intended to help the
speaker understand more clearly the meaning behind some of his remarks.
It may consist of a restatement or clarification of what the speaker has
said or it may involve drawing attention to such underlying emotional
expressions as love, anger, jealousy, confusion, ambivalence, etc., which
remain unrecognized by the speaker.

In reflection the listener concentrates on what he has been informed by
the speaker and does not allow his own orientation to influence his
reaction to the same extent that it does with probing, evaluating, interpretation, and reassurance. As a result, not only is the speaker helped in
clarifying the thoughts and feelings that have been bothering him, but also
he is spared the necessity of having to consider new ideas which are
imposed upon him by the listener. In such an atmosphere, he is likely to
feel safe and unthreatened and, consequently, more able to look at
aspects of his own behavior which previously he was unwilling and
unable to consider.

Reflection may help another person express his feelings of inadequacy,
difficulty in personal relationships, uncertainty about his choice of career,
etc., and assist him also in seeing deeper aspects of his personality as expressed through patterns of aggression and submission, dependency and
independency, perfectionism, and so forth.

Often after a person has finished talking the experienced listener will be
aware of a single emotional word that captures the essence of the underlying feeling that has been expressed. It may be joy, love, despondency,
despair, anguish, hatred, or disgust. The speaker may be unaware of the
emotion that prevails throughout everything he says, but by means of an
accurate reflection of his feelings, he can be helped to gain a greater
sensitivity to his physiological experience and what he is aware of socially.

The listener needs also to become sensitive to the many nuances that
are given to the words he is told, to heavy emphasis on particular words,
to omissions, denials, and inconsistencies, to forgetting and unusual
speech errors and distortions, and to stammering and blushing, all of

which provide clues to the emotional meanings that underlie what is said.

Figure 26 may be used to indicate the influence of the listener's orientation upon his responses. With troubled person A, the listener reflects what he hears so that his particular orientation has little impact upon the way he responds. With troubled person B, however, the listener relies upon probing, evaluating, reassuring, and interpreting, all of which are influenced to some extent by the listener's orientation. As a result, the communication with troubled person B tends to be contaminated much more with the listener's own views than is the case in the relationship with troubled person A.

Many persons see the use of reflection as an indirect procedure and find it hard to believe that it is an important influence on human behavior. Greenspoon (1962) has carried out a series of experiments, however, which may help to point up the significance of reflection. The use of plural nouns by the subjects of the experiments was reinforced by

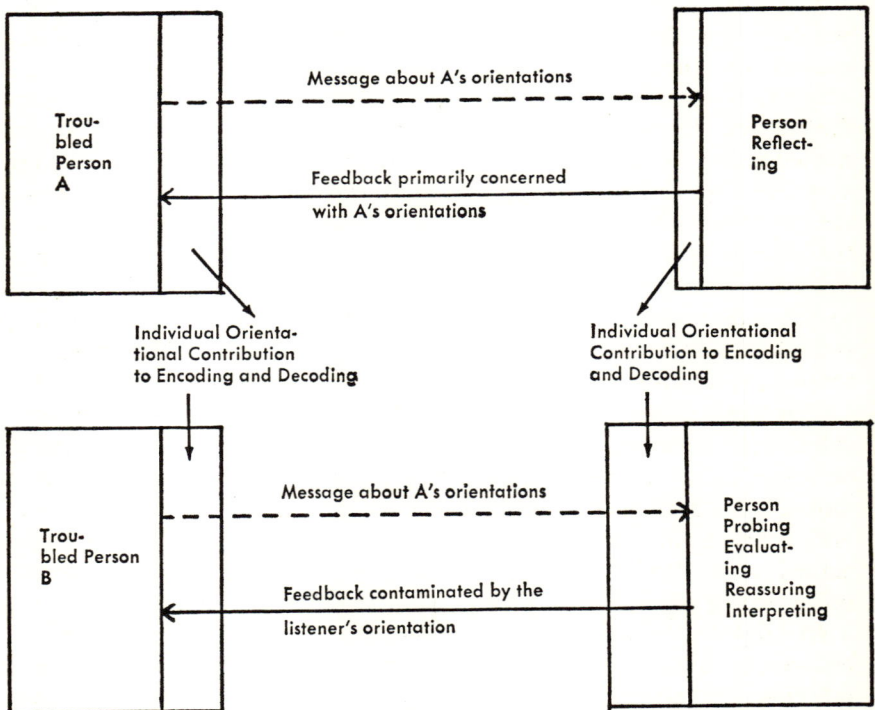

FIGURE 26. Relative degree of influence of the listener's orientation upon reflection and probing, evaluating, reassuring, and interpretative responses.

making mmm hmm sounds. It was found that the usage of plural nouns increased significantly but, after cessation of the response, the usage returned to normal. The subjects were not consciously aware of what they were doing and had no knowledge of the experiment. If verbal behavior is influenced to such a degree by a simple and more or less neutral response, it may be assumed that the more positive aspect of reflection will have at least as much impact upon the other person in a relationship.

Probably a lot more realistic than the concern that reflection may not have any influence on human behavior is the fear that the reflection will be incorrect or shallow and superficial. Very frequently, for example, the inexperienced listener fails to understand with sensitivity what is being communicated to him by the speaker and he responds by either reflecting minor aspects of what he is told or by parroting back the exact words of the speaker. In contrast, the more skilled listener, on hearing a number of feelings that quite conceivably could be reflected, is able to sense what is significant and, through his selection of meaningful feelings and ideas, communicate to the other person that he is being understood.

It is also important to understand that what is said may be reacted to not only according to its surface meaning but also in terms of the implications that underlie the remarks that are made. For example, a mother may say to her son, "I don't want you to play football," in which case the surface meaning is clear and the son perceives that his mother does not want him to participate in that particular game. In addition the son may interpret the mother's statement to contain the underlying meaning that she cares about him a great deal and she does not want him to take the chance of being injured seriously. Conversely, the son may understand her statement to mean that she thinks he is a weakling and unable to take care of himself. From still another orientation, the mother's statement may be construed to mean she does not respect her son and refuses to let him participate in activities with other boys.

The rational and surface content of most messages is easy to understand and, consequently, the impact upon the person receiving them can be controlled with a relative amount of ease. The implications that may be drawn from such messages, however, are a lot more difficult to control, and, consequently, it becomes particularly important for the person concerned with altruistic helping relationships to be sensitive to the way other people receive what he communicates. Suppose, for example, that a friend were to ask you whether or not she should marry the man whom she is dating and that you have a very definite answer to her question. If you give your reaction, you have said literally, "Don't trust your judgment; instead, trust mine, for I know what is good for you." The friend may quite easily interpret your response to be an indication that you do not consider her capable of making a wise decision. If, instead, you choose to reflect her feelings by saying, "It's difficult to know just what to do, isn't it?" You will have accepted her feelings of uncertainty and, as a result, she is likely to feel safe with you. Moreover, since you did not leap in with an easy solution, the process of helping the friend experience himself as a person capable of making decisions has been developed a little more.

Included in the chart below is a series of communications that may be decoded or interpreted differently according to whether or not the person has attained the goal that is involved.

COMMUNICATIONS DECODED DIFFERENTLY

Communication	Goal	Individual A Decoding	Goal	Individual B Decoding
Employee is requested to work overtime	Wealth achieved	I don't need the money and resent giving up the time.	Wealth not achieved	This is a good opportunity to increase my income.
Physician jokes with nurses	Safety achieved	The doctor is a good fellow.	Safety not achieved and consequently threatened.	He can't be too good. He's no better than I am.
Boss requests worker's opinion	Respect achieved	My opinion is important	Respect not achieved	This place is a mess. Even those in charge don't know what to do.
Husband brings home flowers to his wife	Love achieved	He loves me.	Love not achieved	He has been up to something.

A further difficulty lies in the handling of personal prejudices. In the course of living, most people express their particular biases and pet ideas. Leading figures in education, the ministry, politics, etc., all actively proclaim their own specific messages. However, after the various exhortations and presentations of position have been completed, there exists still a need for additional non-persuasive relationships wherein people can sort out from among the differing voices the ideas that are appropriate to them. Perhaps the following example may help clarify the desired meaning. Imagine that a young high school girl of high intelligence from a stable and respected family has fallen in love with a boy who is considered to be the town's ne'er-do-well. The boy is about to drop out of high school and his potential both as a husband and a citizen is minimal. Statistically it may be predicted that a marriage between two such people has little chance of success. Probably the girl's parents, friends, minister, and teachers all have tried to persuade her without success from making what they feel with considerable justification would be a tragic mistake. The question, then, may be raised as to whether another person taking essentially the same position and presenting the same arguments is likely to make any difference. An altruistic helping relationship, using primarily reflection, might, therefore, be attempted instead. As the girl talks, her listener neither argues nor offers advice. She might say, for example, "I'm looking forward so very much to being married to Bill." "It's pretty hard to wait, isn't it?" might be a suitable reflection. As a result of experiencing acceptance of her feelings, she can be expected to continue telling how wonderful she finds life and, as she continues to meet with no resistance, begin to feel safe enough to express, sooner or later, whatever doubts she may have concerning the advisability of the marriage. Thus, she could continue by saying, "That's the way I feel but sometimes I hate the thought of giving up going to college." "You hate to lose the chance of obtaining your education" is a possible response. If the girl's doubts actually outweigh her desire for marriage, she may come to recognize, as the interaction proceeds, that her goals are quite different from the ones she has been defending. Perhaps the desire to be independent and to show her parents and friends that she can do what she wants has led to the decision to marry Bill. Thus, her need for rebellion may cause some distortion in what she really wants for herself. On the other hand, the relationship with the listener may help to remove any doubts and cause the girl to decide even more surely that what she wants is to marry Bill. In either case, the listener's goal has been that of helping the girl decide what is best for her from her own point of view. The situation in real life would be far more complex than hitherto described and many diverse outcomes are possible. For the majority of people such a marriage would be a mistake and most persons, consequently, would tend to bring pressure upon the girl to behave in a way they deem advisable. In the altruistic helping relationship, however, what a person does or does not do in any particular situation must remain a matter of personal choice, for it is within such an atmosphere of freedom that the individual may be able to move toward achieving the goals that are significant in his life.

SUMMARY

1. Communication involves an attempt to create for another person a picture that resembles as closely as possible the one that the sender has in mind.

2. Listening attentively without imposing one's views into the conversation is the most effective way of helping a troubled person.
3. In attempting to establish altruistic relationships, it is important to avoid as much as possible evaluation, probing, interpretation, and reassurance.
4. Reflection is most effective when the listener can capture the underlying feelings that are being expressed.
5. A person who is concerned with establishing altruistic relationships may be recognized by his sensitivity to the way other people are receiving what he is communicating.

EXERCISE 14

Differential Verbal Responses

Included below are a number of different exercises each of which contain six different responses to statements that a troubled person might be expected to make. You are invited to write in the appropriate blanks whether you think the response is primarily a matter of reflection, restatement, support, evaluation, interpretation, or probing. The answers are included at the end of the exercises.

1. Statement: during the entire evening, she didn't speak to me or even look at me.

(a) _____ Lots of times girls go through temporary periods of rejecting boys. Don't worry. There will be plenty more girls in your life.
(b) _____ She just ignored you.
(c) _____ You have been too attentive and now she is taking you for granted.
(d) _____ That really hurt.
(e) _____ It is not good to be so dependent upon someone's attention.
(f) _____ What has happened that would make her so negative toward you?

II. Statement: That teacher doesn't give me a chance no matter how hard I try or how much I recite in class.

(a) _____ You feel cheated.
(b) _____ In that class you just aren't given any opportunity to show what you can really do.
(c) _____ What kind of person is this teacher?
(d) _____ I once had a teacher like that and know just how frustrating this can be.
(e) _____ You mustn't get discouraged.
(f) _____ Maybe that is because you have antagonized him in some way.

III.   Statement: Most of the time my wife is pretty easy going, but sometimes she can be so damned unreasonable.

(a) _____ It probably doesn't help much if you lose your temper when this happens.
(b) _____ Misunderstandings occur between most husbands and wives.
(c) _____ Sometimes she makes you furious.
(d) _____ Maybe there is something about you that upsets her.
(e) _____ What are the kinds of things she is unreasonable about?
(f) _____ Most of the time she is easy to get along with, but at others she can be very difficult.

IV.   Statement: Bill just won't go for his checkup. I think—I'm afraid something is still wrong with him.

(a) _____ Maybe it will turn out to be nothing but your imagination. After all, you don't really know about this.
(b) _____ You're worried and frightened.
(c) _____ What makes you think something is wrong?
(d) _____ It's a feeling something is badly wrong and you want Bill to go back to the doctor. Is that it?
(e) _____ It is because he is afraid of finding out the truth that he doesn't go.
(f) _____ You'd better see to it that he goes, one way or another.

V.   Statement: I think I will quit school. I'm failing two subjects and besides I'm sick of the whole mess.

(a) _____ You are discouraged because you have fallen behind and now your goal seems impossible to attain.
(b) _____ Quitting isn't always the best solution.
(c) _____ I know what you mean. Sometimes everyone feels like giving up.
(d) _____ Have you had trouble with grades before?
(e) _____ You're tired of school and thinking about quitting.
(f) _____ You are just fed-up.

VI.   Statement: I have been doing it for a long time. I'm so ashamed. I don't really understand how it all started.

(a) _____ You're wondering how you became involved in something you can't fully accept.
(b) _____ Don't feel too bad. You're ashamed of what you've been doing and that is a good sign you will whip this thing.
(c) _____ It won't help to worry about yourself.
(d) _____ It all hurts so much.
(e) _____ You are ashamed because your conscience won't really let you accept this aspect of yourself.
(f) _____ When did it first begin?

VII.   Statement: I have the emptiest feeling. Whenever anything
         good happens to me, I just can't believe it.

(a) _____ Good things just don't exist for you.
(b) _____ When your self concept is negative, positive evidence about
            yourself is rejected.
(c) _____ And you are left with just nothing.
(d) _____ I believe in you. Maybe that can be a starting point on which
            to begin.
(e) _____ Tell me about one of these times.
(f) _____ But you've got to stop downgrading yourself.

VIII.   Statement: It's not that I don't want to do something about it—
         I just—well—I know what I ought to do, but for some reason
         I don't do it.

(a) _____ Maybe I can help you figure out what is holding you back.
(b) _____ Let's try to get at what is behind this. Tell me more about it.
(c) _____ You're experiencing conflict. You both want and don't want to
            behave in this way.
(d) _____ You can see what you are supposed to do, but just keep putting
            it off. Is that it?
(e) _____ It's kind of a self disappointment.
(f) _____ Once you are clear in what you want, it is a good idea to put
            it into practice.

IX.   Statement: I don't care what they say, I'm frightened of the
         operation.

(a) _____ Lots of people have gone through this and they are all right.
(b) _____ Come on fellow. You've got to be brave.
(c) _____ Even though you have been told it will be all right, you are
            still frightened.
(d) _____ Your emotional reactions are causing some last minute panic.
(e) _____ When did you first start feeling afraid?
(f) _____ You're so terrified.

Key to exercises in different verbal responses:

I. (a) support
   (b) restatement
   (c) interpretation
   (d) reflection
   (e) evaluation
   (f) probing

II. (a) reflection
    (b) restatement
    (c) probing
    (d) support
    (e) evaluation
    (f) interpretation

III. (a) evaluation
     (b) support
     (c) reflection
     (d) interpretation
     (e) probing
     (f) restatement

IV. (a) support
    (b) reflection
    (c) probing
    (d) restatement
    (e) interpretation
    (f) evaluation

V. (a) interpretation
   (b) evaluation
   (c) support
   (d) probing
   (e) restatement
   (f) reflection

VI. (a) restatement
    (b) support
    (c) evaluation
    (d) reflection
    (e) interpretation
    (f) probing

VII. (a) restatement
     (b) interpretation
     (c) reflection
     (d) support
     (e) probing
     (f) evaluation

VIII. (a) support
      (b) probing
      (c) interpretation
      (d) restatement
      (e) reflection
      (f) evaluation

IX. (a) support
    (b) evaluation
    (c) restatement
    (d) interpretation
    (e) probing
    (f) reflection

Now that you have practiced discriminating between different verbal responses try to distinguish some of them as they occur in conversations among your friends and acquaintances. Which ones encourage further intimacy? Which ones seem to discourage meaningful communication? After having done this, so that the differences between the various responses seem increasingly great, practice using different ones in your own relationships. Do different responses have different results? What are they? Which ones do you prefer in which kinds of situations?

Final Summary

In the context of this book, man is seen as the creator as well as the controller of his own destiny and, for the most part, his behavior is characterized by a capacity for exercising choice in terms of his particular preferences. To the extent that he feels psychologically safe and experiences orientational congruence with the external world, it is easy for him to establish satisfying interpersonal relationships and move toward the successful achievement of his goals. During the course of his life, he experiences a continually expanding contact with the world of reality, causing behavior that was appropriate at one stage of his development to be discarded in order that he may meet the increasingly more challenging expectations of his new environment.

However, when the person's life situation does not provide the emotional climate for such growth, his behavior is geared primarily toward reducing the anxiety that accompanies disappointments and goal failures. As a result, the person may choose to ignore or avoid the source of his difficulty, thus making it even harder for him to move toward experiencing a high level of well-being.

The heart of social existence is to be found, however, through living with an awareness of a responsibility toward helping other people achieve the goals that are important to them without losing sight of one's own desires and needs. You, the reader, are encouraged, therefore, to explore the possibility of participating in a way of life based on such altruistic relationships characterized not only by a sensitive awareness of the needs of other people, but also by the expectation that you will be the person that you want to be.

Primary References

ALLPORT, G. W.: (1961) Pattern and Growth in Personality. New York, Holt, Rinehart and Winston.

ARENDT, H.: (1963) Eichmann in Jerusalem. New York, The Viking Press.

BRINTON, C. (ed.): (1961) The Fate of Man. New York, George Braziller.

BROPHY, B.: (1962) Black Ship to Hell. New York, Harcourt, Brace & World, Inc.

CAMPBELL, J.: (1959) The Masks of God: Primitive Mythology. New York, The Viking Press.

CAMPBELL, J.: (1962) The Masks of God: Oriental Mythology. New York, The Viking Press.

CAMPBELL, J.: (1964) The Masks of God: Occidental Mythology. New York, The Viking Press.

COLEMAN, J. C.: (1964) Abnormal Psychology and Modern Life, ed. 3. Chicago, Scott, Foresman and Company.

DUNHAM, B.: (1964) Heroes and Heretics. New York, Alfred A. Knopf.

EGNER, R. E., AND L. E. DENONN, (eds.): (1961) The Basic Writings of Bertrand Russell. New York, Simon and Schuster.

HAWKES, J., AND SIR L. WOOLLEY: (1963) History of Mankind, Vol. I. New York, Harper & Row.

LASSWELL, H. D.: (1951) The World Revolution of Our Time. Stanford (Calif.), Stanford University Press.

MASLOW, A. H.: (1954) Motivation and Personality. New York, Harper & Brothers.

MATSON, F. W.: (1964) The Broken Image. New York, George Braziller.

MENNINGER, K.: (1963) The Vital Balance. New York, The Viking Press.

MULLER, H. J.: (1958) The Loom of History. New York, Harper & Brothers.

MULLER, H. J.: (1963) Freedom in the Western World. New York, Harper & Row.

MUMFORD, L.: (1961) The City in History. New York, Harcourt, Brace & World, Inc.

PECKHAM, M.: (1962) Beyond the Tragic Vision. New York, George Braziller.

ROGERS, C. R.: (1961) On Becoming a Person. Boston, Houghton Mifflin Company.

Secondary References

ADELSON, J.: (1964) The teacher as a model. In: The American College. N. Sanford (ed.). New York, John Wiley & Sons, Inc. p. 412.

ADLER, A.: (1917) A study of organ inferiority and its psychical compensation. Nerv. Ment. Dis. Monogr. Series, No. 24.

ALLPORT, G. W.: (1937) Personality: A Psychological Interpretation. New York, Holt, Rinehart and Winston, Inc.

ALLPORT, G. W.: (1954) The Nature of Prejudice. Reading (Mass.), Addison-Wesley Publishing Company, Inc.

ANSBACHER, H., AND R. R. ANSBACHER, (eds.): (1956) The Individual Psychology of Alfred Adler. New York, Basic Books, Inc.

ANSBACHER, H. L.: (1948) Attitudes of German prisoners of war: A study of the dynamics of national-socialistic followership. Psychol. Monogr. 62:1.

ASCH, S. E.: (1955) Opinions and social pressure. Sci. Amer. 193:31.

BALDWIN, J.: (1962) Nobody Knows My Name. New York, Dell Publishing Co., Inc.

BARTLETT, S. W.: (1964) A dialogue between cultures. Sat. Rev. 47:44 and 61, No. 29.

BARZUN, J.: (1954) God's Country and Mine. Boston, Little, Brown and Company.

BAZELON, D. T.: (1963) The Paper Economy. New York, Random House.

BECKER, E.: (1962) The Birth and Death of Meaning. Glencoe (Ill.), The Free Press.

BECKER, E.: (1964) The Revolution in Psychiatry. New York, The Crowell-Collier Publishing Co.

BELL, E. H.: (1961) Social Foundations of Human Behavior. New York, Harper & Brothers.

BELLAMY, E.: (1917) Looking Backward, 2000-1887. New York, Random House.

BERLYNE, D. E.: (1960) Conflict, Arousal, and Curiosity. New York, Mc-Graw-Hill Book Company, Inc.

BEXTON, W. H., W. HERON, AND T. H. SCOTT: (1954) Effects of decreased variation in the sensory environment. Canad. J. Psych. 8:70.

BINDRA, D.: (1959) Motivation. New York, The Ronald Press Co.

BION, W. R.: (1952) Group dynamics: A re-view. The Int. J. Psychoanal. 33:235.

BOHR, N.: (1961) Atomic Theory and the Description of Nature. Cambridge (England), The University of Cambridge Press.

BRUNER, J. S.: (1964) The course of cognitive growth. The Amer. Psychol. 19:1.

BRUNER, J. S., AND C. C. GOODMAN: (1947) Value and need as organizing factors in perception. J. Abnorm. Soc. Psychol. 42:33.

BURROW, T.: (1927) The group method of analysis. The Psychoanal. Rev. 14:268.

BURT, C.: (1958) The inheritance of mental ability. Amer. Psychol. 13:9.

CANTRIL, H., AND C. H. BUMSTEAD: (1960) Reflections on the Human Venture. New York, New York University Press.

CATTELL, R. B.: (1957) Personality and Motivation Structure and Measurement. Yonkers-on-Hudson (N. Y.), World Book Co.

CHILD, I. L.: (1954) Socialization. In: Handbook of Social Psychology, Vol. II. G. Lindzey (ed.). Reading (Mass.), Addison-Wesley Publishing Co. Inc., pp. 655-692.

CHURCHILL, SIR W.: Speech at the Lord Mayor's Day Luncheon, London, November 10, 1942.

CIARDI, J.: (1962) Manner of speaking. Sat. Rev. 45:9, No. 22.

COLEMAN, J. C.: (1960) Personality Dynamics and Effective Behavior. Chicago, Scott, Foresman and Company.

COOK, F. J.: (1962) The Warfare State. New York, The Macmillan Company.

COUTU, W.: (1949) Emergent Human Nature. New York, Alfred A. Knopf.

DE BARY, W. T. (ed.): (1960) Introduction to Oriental Civilizations: Sources of Chinese Tradition. New York, Columbia University Press.

DEMENT, W.: (1960) The effect of dream deprivation. Sci. 131:1705.

Du Bois, C.: (1955) The dominant value profile of American culture. Amer. Anthropol. 57:1232.

Durkheim, E.: (1960) On anomie. *In*: Images of Man. C. W. Mills (ed.). New York, George Braziller, Inc., pp. 449-485.

Festinger, L.: (1958) The motivating effect of cognitive dissonance. *In*: Assessment of Human Motives. G. Lindzey (ed.). New York, Rinehart & Company, Inc., pp. 65-86.

15 to 18, A Report of the Central Advisory Council for Education (1959). London, Her Majesty's Stationery Office.

Frankl, V. E.: (1963) Man's Search for Meaning. New York, Washington Square Press, Inc.

French, J. R. P., Jr., and B. Raven: (1959) The bases of social power. *In*: Studies in Social Power. D. Cartwright (ed.). Ann Arbor (Mich.), The University of Michigan Press, pp. 150-167.

Freud, A., and D. T. Burlingham: (1943) War and Children. New York, Foster Parents' Plan for War Children, Inc.

Freud, S.: (1914) Psychopathology of Everyday Life. London, Ernest Benn Ltd.

Freud, S.: (1920) A General Introduction to Psychoanalysis. New York, Horace Liveright.

Friedan, B.: (1963) The Feminine Mystique. New York, W. W. Norton & Company, Inc.

Friedenberg, E. Z.: (1960) The Vanishing Adolescent. Boston, Beacon Press.

Fromm, E.: (1956) The Art of Loving. New York, Harper & Brothers.

Fromm, E.: (1960) Values, psychology, and human existence. *In*: Personality Dynamics and Effective Behavior. J. C. Coleman (ed.). Chicago, Scott, Foresman and Company, pp. 522-527.

Gardner, J. W.: (1961) Excellence: Can We Be Equal and Excellent Too? New York, Harper & Row.

George, P.: (1964) Dr. Strangelove. New York, Bantam Books, Inc.

Gerth, H. H., and C. W. Mills (Trans. and Eds.): (1948) From Max Weber: Essays in Sociology. London, Routledge & Kegan Paul, Ltd.

Green, G. H.: (1922) Psychoanalysis in the Classroom. New York, G. P. Putnam's Sons.

Greenspoon, J.: (1962) Verbal conditioning and clinical psychology. *In*: Experimental Foundations of Clinical Psychology. A. J. Bachrach (ed.). New York, Basic Books, Inc., pp. 510-553.

Griffin, J. H.: (1961) Black Like Me. New York, New American Library of World Literature, Inc.

Gross, N., A. W. McEachern, and W. S. Mason: (1958) Role conflict and its resolution. *In*: Readings in Social Psychology. E. E. Maccoby, T. M. Newcomb, and E. L. Hartley (eds.). New York, Holt, Rinehart and Winston, Inc., pp. 447-459.

Hallowell, A. I.: (1953) Culture, personality, and society. *In*: Anthropology Today. A. L. Kroeber (ed). Chicago, The University of Chicago Press.

Halpin, A. W.: (1960) The unvoiced message. Midway 76, No. 3.

Harlow, H. F., M. K. Harlow, and D. R. Meyer: (1950) Learning motivated by a manipulation drive. J. Exper. Psychol. 40:228.

Harlow, H. F., and R. R. Zimmerman: (1958) The development of affectional responses in infant monkeys. Proc. Amer. Philosoph. Soc. 102:501.

HAVIGHURST, R. J., AND L. J. STILES: (1961) National policy for alienated youth. Phi Delta Kappan 42:286.

HAYAKAWA, S. I.: (1958) Popular songs vs. the facts of life. In: Mass Culture. B. Rosenberg, and D. M. White (eds). Glencoe (Ill.), The Free Press, pp. 393-403.

HEBB, D. O.: (1949) The Organization of Behavior. New York, John Wiley & Sons, Inc.

HEBB, D. O.: (1955) Drives and the C. N. S. (Conceptual Nervous System). Psych. Rev. 62:243.

HEBB, D. O.: (1958) A Textbook of Psychology. Philadelphia, W. B. Saunders Company.

HEILBRONER, R. L.: (1961) The limits of determinism. In: The Fate of Man. C. Brinton (ed.). New York, George Braziller, pp. 352-364.

HENRY, J.: (1963) Culture Against Man. New York, Random House.

HEPNER, H. W.: (1957) Psychology Applied to Life and Work, ed. 3. Englewood Cliffs (N. J.), Prentice-Hall, Inc.

HERNANDEZ-PEON, R., H. SCHERRER, AND M. JOUVET: (1956) Modification of electric activity in cochlear nucleus during "attention" in unanesthetized cats. Sci. 123:331.

HORNEY, K.: (1937) The Neurotic Personality of Our Time. New York, W. W. Norton & Company, Inc.

HORNEY, K.: (1945) Our Inner Conflicts. New York, W. W. Norton & Company, Inc.

HOWE, R. L.: (1961) Herein Is Love. Chicago, The Judson Press.

HOWES, D. H., AND R. L. SOLOMON: (1951) Visual duration threshold as a function of word-probability. J. Exper. Psychol. 41:401.

HUTCHINSON, E. D.: (1949) How to Think Creatively. New York, Abingdon Press.

HUTCHINSON, M., AND C. YOUNG: (1962) Educating the Intelligent. Baltimore, Penguin Books.

ILLING, H. A.: (1963) C. G. Jung on the present trends in group psychotherapy. In: Group Psychotherapy and Group Function. M. Rosenbaum, and M. Berger (eds.). New York, Basic Books, Inc., pp. 180-187.

JACOB, P. E.: (1957) Changing Values in College. New York, Harper & Brothers.

JARRELL, R.: (1962) A Sad Heart at the Supermarket. New York, Atheneum.

JUNG, C. G.: (1956) The Integration of the Personality. S. Dell (trans.). London, Routledge & Kegan Paul, Ltd.

JUNG, C. G.: (1961) The modern spiritual problem. In: The Fate of Man. C. Brinton (ed.). New York, George Braziller, pp. 403-418.

KELLEY, D. M.: (1961) 22 Cells In Nuremberg. New York, MacFadden Publications, Inc.

KELLY, G. A.: (1958) Man's construction of his alternatives. In: Assessment of Human Motives. G. Lindzey (ed.). New York, Rinehart & Company, Inc.

KEYS, A. et al.: (1950) The Biology of Human Starvation, Vol. II. Minneapolis, The University of Minnesota Press.

KING, E. J.: (1958) Other Schools and Ours. New York, Rinehart & Company.

KINSEY, A. C., W. B. POMEROY, AND C. E. MARTIN: (1948) Sexual Behavior in the Human Male. Philadelphia, W. B. Saunders Company.

KINSEY, A. C. et al.: (1953) Sexual Behavior in the Human Female. Philadelphia, W. B. Saunders Company.

KLINEBERG, O.: (1965) The Human Dimension in International Relations. New York, Holt, Rinehart and Winston.

KLUCKHOHN, C., AND D. LEIGHTON: (1958) The Navaho. Cambridge (Mass.), Harvard University Press.

KNEBEL, F., AND C. W. BAILEY, II: (1962) Seven Days in May. New York, Harper & Row.

KRECH, D., AND R. S. CRUTCHFIELD: (1958) Elements of Psychology. New York, Alfred A. Knopf.

LAMPMAN, R. J.: (1962) The Share of Top Wealth-holders in National Wealth, 1922-56. Princeton (N. J.), Princeton University Press.

LECKY, P.: (1951) Self-Consistency. New York, Island Press.

LEHNER, G. F. J., AND E. KUBE: (1955) The Dynamics of Personal Adjustment. Englewood Cliffs (N. J.), Prentice-Hall, Inc.

LEVINE, R., I. CHEIN, AND G. MURPHY: (1942) The relation of the intensity of a need to the amount of perceptual distortion: A preliminary report. J. Psychol. 13:283.

LEWIN, K.: (1935) A Dynamic Theory of Personality. D. K. Adams and K. E. Zener (trans.). New York, McGraw-Hill Book Company.

LIFTON, R. J.: (1960) Methods of forceful indoctrination: Psychiatric aspects of Chinese communist thought reform. In: Identity and Anxiety. M. R. Stein, et al. (eds.). Glencoe (Ill.), The Free Press, pp. 480-492.

MANN, T.: (1958) Joseph and His Brothers. H. T. Lowe-Porter (trans.). New York, Alfred A. Knopf.

MANNHEIM, K.: (1936) Ideology and Utopia. London, Kegan Paul, Trench, Trubner & Co., Ltd.

MASLAND, R. L., S. B. SARASON, AND T. GLADWIN: (1958) Mental Subnormality. New York, Basic Books, Inc.

MASLOW, A. H.: (1962) Toward a Psychology of Being. Princeton (N. J.), D. Van Nostrand Company, Inc.

MAY, R.: (1958) Contributions of existential psychotherapy. In Existence: A New Dimension in Psychiatry and Psychology. R. May, E. Angel, and H. Ellenberger (eds.). New York, Basic Books, Inc., pp. 37-91.

MAY R.: (1961) Existential Psychology. New York, Random House.

McDOUGALL, W.: (1931) An Introduction to Social Psychology, ed. 22. London, Methuen & Co., Ltd.

McKINNEY, J. P.: (1962) A multi-dimensional study of behavior of severely retarded boys. Child Devel. 33:923.

McKINNEY, J. P., AND T. KEELE: (1963) Effects of increased mothering on the behavior of severely retarded boys. Amer. J. Mental Defic. 67:556.

MELZACK, R., AND T. H. SCOTT: (1957) The effects of early experience on the response to pain. J. Comp. Physio. Psychol. 50:155.

MENNINGER, K.: (1959) A Psychiatrist's World. B. H. Hall (ed.). New York, The Viking Press.

MILLER, A.: (1959) The Crucible. New York, Bantam Books.

MORENO, J. L.: (1945) Scientific foundations of group psychotherapy. In: Group Psychotherapy. J. L. Moreno (ed.). New York, Beacon House, Inc.

MULLAHY, P.: (1948) Oedipus: Myth and Complex. New York, Hermitage Press, Inc.

MURRAY, H. A.: (1938) Explorations in Personality. New York, Oxford University Press.

MYRDAL, G.: (1944) An American Dilemma. New York, Harper & Brothers.

NAEGALE, K.: (1949) From De Tocqueville to Myrdal: A Research Memorandum on Selected Studies of American Values. Unpublished: Values Study Project. Cambridge (Mass.), Harvard University.

NICHOLS, R. C., AND J. A. DAVIS: (1964) Characteristics of students of high academic aptitude. Pers. Guid. J. 42:794, No. 8.

NISSEN, H. W.: (1931) A study of exploratory behavior in the white rat by means of the obstruction method. In: Animal Motivation. C. J. Warden (ed.). New York, Columbia University Press, pp. 354-367.

OLDS, J., AND P. MILNER: (1954) Positive reinforcement produced by electrical stimulation of septal area and other regions of rat brain. J. Comp. Physiol. Psychol. 47:419.

OPPENHEIMER, R.: (1956) Analogy in science. Amer. Psychol. 11:127.

ORTEGA Y GASSET, J.: (1964) The dehumanization of art. In: Alienation, Vol. II. G. Sykes (ed.). New York, George Braziller, pp. 724-737.

PECK, R. F.: (1962) Student mental health In: Personality Factors on the College Campus. R. L. Sutherland et al. (eds.). Austin (Texas), The Hogg Foundation for Mental Health, The University of Texas, pp. 161-199.

PIAGET, J.: (1952) The Origins of Intelligence in Children. M. Cook, (trans.). New York, International Universities Press, Inc.

PORTER, E. H., JR.: (1950) An Introduction to Therapeutic Counseling. New York, Houghton Mifflin Company.

POSTMAN, L., J. S. BRUNER, AND E. MCGINNIES: (1948) Personal values as selective factors in perception. J. Abnorm. Soc. Psychol. 43:142.

PRESTHUS, R.: (1965) University bosses: The executive conquest of academe. New Repub. 152:20.

PUSEY, E. B., (trans.): (1953) The Confessions of St. Augustine. London, T. M. Dent & Sons, Ltd.

RANK, O.: (1956) Fate and self-determination. In: The Self. C. E. Moustakas (ed.). New York, Harper & Brothers.

REDL, F., AND D. WINEMAN: (1951) Children Who Hate. Glencoe (Ill.), The Free Press.

RIBBLE, M. A.: (1943) The Rights of Infants. New York, Columbia University Press.

RICHARDSON, J. W.: (1960) The interactive process. Unpublished paper.

RIESMAN, D., N. GLAZER, AND R. DENNEY: (1961) The Lonely Crowd. New Haven (Conn.), Yale University Press.

RIESMAN, D.: (1949) The saving remnant. In: Years of the Modern. J. W. Chase (ed.). New York, Longmans, Green and Company.

ROBINSON, J. A. T.: (1965) The New Reformation. Philadelphia, The Westminster Press.

ROGERS, C. R.: (1951) Client-Centered Therapy. Boston, Houghton Mifflin Company.

ROKEACH, M.: (1960) The Open and Closed Mind. New York, Basic Books, Inc.

ROLO, C. J.: (1958) Simenon and Spillane: The metaphysics of murder for the millions. *In*: Mass Culture. B. Rosenberg and D. M. White (eds.). Glencoe (Ill.), The Free Press, pp. 165-175.

RUCH, F. L.: (1958) Psychology and Life, ed. 5. Chicago, Scott, Foresman and Company.

SALISBURY, H. E.: (1958) The Shook-up Generation. New York, Harper and Row.

SANFORD, F. H.: (1964) Letter to a Freshman Daughter. Austin (Texas), The Hogg Foundation for Mental Health.

SANFORD, N.: (1962) Developing status of the entering freshman. *In*: The American College. N. Sanford (ed.). New York, John Wiley & Sons, Inc, pp. 253-282.

SAPPENFIELD, B. R.: (1954) Personality Dynamics. New York, Alfred A. Knopf.

SARBIN, T. R.: (1954) Role theory. *In*: Handbook of Social Psychology, Vol. I. G. Lindzey (ed.). Reading (Mass.), Addison-Wesley Publishing Company, Inc., pp. 223-258.

SCHERICH, M.: (1960) Unpublished Lecture. Stillwater (Okla.), Oklahoma State University.

SCHILLER, C. H.: (1957) Innate motor action as a basis of learning. *In*: Instinctive Behavior. C. H. Schiller, (trans. and ed.). New York, International Universities Press, Inc., pp. 264-287.

SCHRAMM, W.: (1960) The process of communication. *In*: The Process and Effects of Mass Communication. W. Schramm (ed.). Urbana (Ill.), University of Illinois Press, pp. 3-18.

SCHULZINGER, M. S.: (1956) The Accident Syndrome. Springfield (Ill.), Charles C Thomas.

SEARS, R. R., E. E. MACCOBY, AND H. LEVIN: (1957) Patterns of Child Rearing. Evanston (Ill.), Row, Peterson and Company.

SEELEY, J. R., R. A. SIM, AND E. W. LOOSLEY: (1956) Crestwood Heights. New York, Basic Books, Inc.

SERLING, R.: (1962) Requiem for a Heavyweight. New York, Bantam Books.

SHERIF, M.: (1935) A study of some social factors in perception. Arch. Psychol., pp. 5-60, No. 187.

SHOBEN, E. J., JR.: (1957) Toward a concept of the normal personality. Amer. Psychol. 12:183.

SHRIVER, S.: (1965) How goes the war on poverty. Look 29:30, No. 15.

SIIPOLA, E. M.: (1935) A group study of some effects of preparatory set. Psychol. Monogr. 46:27.

SIMEONS, A. T. W.: (1961) Man's Presumptuous Brain. New York, E. P. Dutton & Co., Inc.

SKINNER, B. F.: (1953) Science and Human Behavior. New York, The Macmillan Company.

SKINNER, B. F.: (1958) Reinforcement today. Amer. Psychol. 13:96.

SLICHTER, S. H.: (1956) The growth of moderation. Atlantic Monthly 198:61.

SMITH, G. J. W., D. P. SPENCE, AND G. S. KLEIN: (1959) Subliminal effects of verbal stimuli. J. Abnorm. Soc. Psychol. 59:167.

SNYGG, D., AND A. W. COMBS: (1949) Individual Behavior. New York, Harper and Brothers.

SPIEGEL, J. P.: (1960) The resolution of role conflict. *In*: A Modern Introduction to the Family. N. W. Bell and E. F. Vogel (eds.). Glencoe (Ill.), The Free Press, pp. 361-381.

SPITZ, R. A., AND K. M. WOLF: (1955) Autoerotism during the first year of life. *In*: Studies in Motivation. D. C. McClelland, (ed.). New York, Appleton-Century-Crofts, Inc.

STRATTON, G. M.: (1897) Vision without inversion of the retinal image. Psychol. Rev. 4:341 and 463.

SULLIVAN, H. S.: (1947) Conceptions of Modern Psychiatry. Washington (D. C.), The William Alanson White Psychiatric Foundation.

SYMONDS, P.: (1946) The Dynamics of Human Adjustment. New York, D. Appleton-Century Company.

SZCZESNY, G.: (1961) The Future of Unbelief. New York, George Braziller, Inc.

TALESE, G.: (1963) The over-reachers. Esquire 60: 152.

TALESE, G.: (1964) The loser. Esquire 61:65 and 139.

TERMAN, L. M.: (1954) The discovery and encouragment of exceptional talent. Amer. Psychol. 9:221.

THOMAS, W. I., AND F. ZNANIECKI: (1960) Three types of personality. *In*: Images of Man. C. W. Mills, (ed.). New York, George Braziller, Inc.

THOMETZ, C. E.: (1963) The decision makers: The power structure of Dallas. J. Grad. Res. Cen. Southern Methodist University, Dallas (Texas), p. 32, Nos. 1 and 2.

THORNDIKE, E. L.: (1932) Reward and punishment in animal learning. Comp. Psychol. Monogr. No. 39, pp. 1-65.

TINBERGEN, N.: (1951) The Study of Instinct. London, Oxford University Press.

TÖNNIES, F.: (1957) Community and Society. C. P. Loomis, (trans. and ed.). East Lansing (Mich.), The Michigan State University Press.

TOWNSEND, J. C.: (1953) Introduction to Experimental Method. New York, McGraw-Hill Book Company, Inc.

VEBLEN, T.: (1919) The Place of Science in Modern Civilisation. New York, B. W. Huebsch.

WATSON, J. B.: (1926) Experimental studies on the growth of the emotions. *In*: Psychologies of 1925. C. Murchison (ed.). Worcester (Mass.), Clark University, pp. 37-57.

WHITE, T. H.: (1961) The Making of the President 1960. New York, Pocket Books, Inc.

WHITEHEAD, A. N.: (1929) Process and Reality. New York, Macmillan Company.

WOLBERG, L. R.: (1947) Hypnotic experiments in psychosomatic medicine. Psychosom. Med. 9:337.

WOLBERG, L. R.: (1954) The Technique of Psychotherapy. New York, Grune & Stratton, Inc.

WOLFF, K. H., (trans. and ed.): (1950) The Sociology of Georg Simmel. Glencoe (Ill.), The Free Press.

WRENN, C. G.: (1962) The Counselor in a Changing World. Washington (D. C.), American Personnel and Guidance Association.

WRIGHT, R.: (1963) Black Boy. New York, The New American Library of World Literature, Inc.

Author Index

Subject Index